ADVANCES IN WRITING RESEARCH VOLUME TWO

Writing in Academic Disciplines

Writing Research

Multidisciplinary Inquiries into the Nature of Writing

edited by Marcia Farr, University of Illinois at Chicago

Advances in Writing Research, Volume Two:

Writing in Academic Disciplines

David A. Jolliffe, Editor
University of Illinois at Chicago

ABLEX PUBLISHING CORPORATION
NORWOOD, NEW JERSEY

LIBRARY OF CONGRESS
Library of Congress Cataloging-in-Publication Data

Writing in academic disciplines / David A. Jolliffe, editor.
    p.   cm.—(Advances in writing research)
  Bibliography: p.
  Includes index.
  ISBN 0-89391-434-7
  1. English language—Rhetoric—Study and teaching.
2. Interdisciplinary approach in education. I. Jolliffe, David A.
II. Series: Writing research (Norwood, N.J.)
PE1404.W724 1988
808'.042—dc19   87-35062
                                            CIP

Ablex Publishing Corporation
355 Chestnut Street
Norwood, New Jersey 07648

Contents

Introduction

David A. Jolliffe

University of Illinois at Chicago

In the late 1970s and early 1980s, Lee Odell was one of the leaders of a cadre of researchers who began to examine, for very good reasons, the nature and uses of writing that take place outside of academia. If we hope to provide useful writing instruction in schools, these researchers argued, we must see what kinds of demands writing places on people after they leave school. This field of research came to be labeled in conference programs and journal articles as *real-world writing*, and many of its diligent practitioners were represented in the volume Odell and Dixie Goswami edited, *Writing in Nonacademic Settings* (1986). Yet Odell would not himself use the "real-world" label. At a session of the 1985 Pennsylvania State University Conference on Rhetoric and Composition, Odell took issue with a participant who contrasted writing in academia with "real-world" writing. Odell pointed out clearly—and I wish I could quote him directly—that the contrast suggested that academic writing was, in some way, "unreal." He urged the questioner to consider writing inside and outside of academia as equally real "worlds of writing," both deserving serious scholarly attention.

This volume is a testimony to that perspective, acknowledging, as it does, that every year millions of students are socialized into the intellectual conventions of academic fields, and thousands of faculty and researchers make their livelihoods, largely by the writing they must do. The chapters in this volume implicitly argue, not only that writing in academia is as important and "real" as writing outside the academy, but also that writing situated in academic contexts has not been examined fully enough in the last two decades of writing research. To be sure, abundant research has examined writing that takes place in schools. By far, most of the studies that have come to be known collectively as *composing process research* have investigated the behaviors, attitudes, and texts of basic writers or students in entry-level, *general* composition classes in high schools, colleges, and universities. These studies, of course, have provided the teaching and research communities with valuable insights about the nature of writing as an amalgam of complex, recursive processes, and have led to some important reforms in the way written composition is taught.

But the research largely ignored two important facts. First, it did not consider fully enough that *all* writing, even writing produced for composition classes or empirical studies, is constrained by a myriad of contextual variables which influence the ways even beginning writers evaluate and interpret reality in order to write about it. As Bizzell (1982) points out, "Writing is always writing for some purpose that can only be understood in its community context" (p. 227). Second, it did not take fully into account that students *do* write in other academic settings besides general composition classes, and that successful writing requires students, as they take courses in different fields, to be sensitive to the demands of shifting academic contexts (Bartholomae, 1985). By concentrating on the be- haviors of young, beginning writers and slighting the importance of context, the research largely ignored that writers' processes, attitudes, and texts *do* change as people become engaged in the writing demanded by upper-division courses, advanced studies in a major field, graduate school, postdoctoral studies, faculty employment, and so on.

We hope in this volume to redress this lack of attention to writers struggling, and succeeding, with the demands of work as students and professionals in academia. The overviews, methodologies, and reports of research in this volume represent the convergence of two movements, one primarily pedagogical and the other primarily research-oriented. The first is the movement known generally as "writing across the curriculum" and represents the efforts of teachers and admin- istrators to promote the role of writing as an aid to learning in all content areas. As Chris Anson's chapter in this volume points out, the writing-across-the- curriculum movement has its roots in early twentieth-century progressive educa- tion, gained impetus from the works of British educational researchers (e.g., Martin, D'Arcy, Newton, & Parker, 1976), and has burgeoned in colleges and universities in the United States. The second is the movement to study writing as it functions within academic disciplines, especially the ways writing is used to establish and advance knowledge in a field. This movement grew from roots in the sociology of science, found its clearest early examplar, I believe, in the work of Charles Bazerman (1981), and has flourished, among other places, in such impressive interdisciplinary activities as the Rhetoric of Inquiry project at the University of Iowa (Gronbeck, McCloskey, McGee, Megill, & Nelson, 1985) and the Prism Project of the Society for Critical Exchange (Harkin & Jarratt, 1986).

Because we are interested in both the nature and function of writing within academic disciplines and the ways writing is taught, both purposely and acciden- tally, in academic fields, the contibutors to this volume feel no qualms about conflating what would normally be considered "basic research" and "dissemina- tion." Indeed, this dual focus gives some sense of the kind of readership to whom we hope this volume appeals. We hope the chapters will be of interest to other researchers who are interested in the ways writers' processes, products, attitudes, and knowledge are influenced by studying or working in an academic field. We also hope, though, that our work will be interesting and useful to teachers, students, and administrators who are trying to establish courses, curricula, methods, and materials that will enable writing to be taught and used more effectively in academic fields.

One explanatory note on an important term in the title of this volume is necessary: we realize that the word *discipline* carries special meanings, especially to scholars in the philosophy and sociology of science who have debated for decades what exactly a discipline is and does. The contributors to this volume have largely avoided this controversy. Being aided by the compartmentalization of colleges and universities into academic units and departments, the contributors have focused on student and faculty writers in well defined major areas. Our use of the term discipline, therefore, should be taken to denote a group of students, teachers, and/or researchers, usually affiliated with a common department, who collectively study and try to give explanations of similar subject matters.

The volume is divided into three parts. Part I is a single chapter, by Chris M. Anson, setting out the current state of knowledge about writing in academic disciplines. Acknowledging that a bulk of the literature about the writing-across-the-curriculum movement has been testimonial and discursive, rather than research-oriented, Anson describes writing-in-the-diciplines research from three perspectives: the professional, which examines how writing functions to argue claims and disseminate knowledge with fields; the curricular, which shows how writing is incorporated within curricula in different academic departments; and the developmental, which investigates how writing is used to foster learning in academic disciplines. Anson fleshes out the research problems and issues inherent in each perspective and builds a model for future research on writing in the disciplines.

Part II consists of two chapters describing and demonstrating methodologies for conducting research on writing in academic fields. In the chapter which Ellen M. Brier and I have coauthored, we emphasize the importance of writers' knowledge, the manifestation of education and experience that writers bring to any writing task in their discipline. We explain and demonstrate a methodology that can be used with large numbers of writers to assess the relation between writers' knowledge and actual writing tasks in different disciplines. In the second chapter in Part II, Michael M. Williamson describes a qualitative methodology for examining the relation between the social contexts of academic disciplines and the processes of learning to write within them. Relying on extensive, observational field research, Williamson explains how he studied the nature, functions, and uses of writing in departments of sociology, biology, and English.

Part III contains three reports of research on writing in different disciplines. Anne J. Herrington shows the connection between writing and learning in an undergraduate English literature class, examining in the particular the ways an instructor influences the use of specific interpretive approaches in student papers. Herrington exemplifies the use of the discourse-based interview and explains

how to generate case studies of writers in the disciplines. Kristine Hansen con-
dusts rhetorical text analyses of texts from two disciplines in the social sciences,
demonstrating how the texts from the fields give evidence of the different epistemologies that underlie their research efforts. Finally, Jone Rymer studies the
writing processes of eminent academic scientists. Using protocol analysis to
dispel some myths about the ways scientists are thought to compose written
texts, Rymer shows successful, faculty-level writers employing both general and
discipline-specific processes and strategies.

All of the contributors share the idea, explained in Anson's chapter, that
research in academic disciplines is relatively young and offers fertile territory for
future work. We hope our work helps steer this research in a productive
direction.

REFERENCES

Bartholomae, D. (1985). Inventing the university. In M. Rose (Ed.), *When a writer can't
write: Studies in writer's block and other writing process problems*. New York:
Guilford.

Bazerman, C. (1981). What written knowledge does: Three examples of academic discourse. *Philosophy of the Social Sciences, 11,* 361–387.

Bizzell, P. (1982). Cognition, convention, and certainty: What we need to know about
writing. *Pre/Text, 3,* 213–243.

Gronbeck, B.E., McCloskey, D.N., McGee, M.C., Megill, A., & Nelson, J.S. (1985).
The rhetoric of inquiry project at the University of Iowa. Unpublished manuscript.

Harkin, P., & Jarratt, S. (1986). *The Prism Project for the Society for Critical Exchange*.
Unpublished manuscript, University of Akron.

Martin, N., D'Arcy, P., Newton, B., & Parker, R. (1976). *Writing and learning across
the curriculum, 11–16*. London: Ward-Lock.

Odell, L., & Goswami, D. (1986). *Writing in nonacademic settings*. New York:
Guilford.

1 Toward a Multidimensional Model of Writing in the Academic Disciplines

Chris M. Anson

The University of Minnesota

INTRODUCTION

Until recently, research on writing has been preoccupied with understanding the writing processes of students in generalized academic settings. That research has resulted in valuable knowledge about how students compose and revise, how they develop writing abilities over time, and how they read and evaluate their own and each others' writing. Yet, as Hillocks' (1986) review of experimental treatment studies in composition over the past 20 years clearly shows, the bulk of our new knowledge about composing processes has come from research whose context is a typical language arts or English composition class, or whose subjects are students enrolled in such classes. Consequently, there has been limited opportunity to probe the *multiple frames of reference*—personal, educational, or contextual—in which a writer may be operating when responding to a task (Bloom, 1985). For purposes of understanding the moment-by-moment features of composing, or the quantity and quality of a subject's prewriting, or the kinds of changes made to a text during revision, it did not seem very important what sort of instructional context the writer was in or what purposes for writing were embodied in the task.

Increasingly, however, composition theorists are pointing out the need to consider the role of context in writing. Beach and Bridwell (1984), for example, suggest that studying writing without taking into account the many dimensions of context is a little like "studying animal life by visiting zoo cages" (p. 6). In our zeal to understand the complexities of the writing process itself, we've neglected to consider how specific discourse communities might influence the formulation and expression of ideas in writing (Odell, 1985, p. 249). We have, in other words, avoided looking at writing from a social and contextual point of view (Brandt, 1986; Faigley, 1985, pp. 234 ff.; cf. Bizzell, 1982a; Mishler, 1979; Purves & Purves, 1986; Scribner & Cole, 1981).

1

Central to this view is the recognition that institutions of higher education are themselves groups of heterogeneous intellectual communities brought together under the rubric of learning. Educational contexts have long been perceived as relatively unified and stable, somehow independent of the larger society, and thus impervious to the ravages of social and political change (Lindquist, 1978). Without their archives of texts, without their embodiment of the history of ideas, without the common motives of their scholars, there could be no foundation on which to build new knowledge. Diversity within the academy—particularly of goals, methods, or characteristics— seems inimical to the perpetuation of cultural and intellectual traditions.

But while, historically, the academy may well have been of one body and mind, it was bound to see an eventual division of parts. Toward the latter years of the nineteenth century, fueled by faculty psychology and the view that each discipline has its own inherent logic, the academic curriculum soon found itself split into discrete, seemingly self-contained fields of interest (Applebee, 1974, p. 253; Berlin, 1984, p. 9). Of course, with the increasing proliferation of new knowledge, the natural separation of specialized disciplines, each with its own assumptions, methods, and linguistic characteristics, was not only inevitable but irreversible (see Merton, 1957). Consequently, intellectual processes once thought to be global became associated with individual academic disciplines, many of which now themselves consist of several specific domains of research or practice.

Because writing was strongly tied to a literary tradition, it was housed in the department of English, where it took on a belletristic and, later, a skills orientation, eventually moving to the periphery of the curriculum (Rose, 1985). Simultaneously, the use of writing in many academic contexts decreased in favor of direct learning of facts, which could be measured by tests which did not require extended written responses. Because writing was thought to occupy its own intellectual domain, educators in many disciplines, particularly scientific and technical ones, were not particularly worried about seeing it fade from an already overloaded curriculum.

Many theorists have justifiably criticized this extraordinary separation of subject areas and the resulting isolation of writing from the rest of the academic curriculum (e.g., Marland, 1980). In direct response to this problem, the educational movement toward "writing across the curriculum" has burgeoned, and with it attention to writing in diverse subject areas has increased dramatically. Dozens of new, interdisciplinary composition texts have flooded the market (see Bizzell & Herzberg, 1985, for a critique). National networks on writing across the curriculum have formed. Over 100 American colleges and universities now report having developed whole programs in cross-disciplinary writing (Griffin, 1985; Haring-Smith & Stern, 1985). And scores of articles on the subject have appeared in scholarly and educational journals and in edited collections (Anson, 1985).

Yet the majority of this new work has been discursive and testimonial, lacking the sort of carefully designed research which might lend support to the movement and provide it with coherence. In spite of the overwhelming consensus—at least among composition teachers and specialists—that writing should be an important component of all academic subjects, questions central to such integration have not been very fully explored in the research. It is clear, for example, that while separate disciplines may inhabit the same educational context and work toward similar generalized goals, they often embody quite different assumptions about the nature of written discourse—assumptions of audience, purpose, and the conventions of style and format. Unfortunately, we know very little about how these assumptions are operationalized in disciplines with which we may have only general familiarity. Nor do we understand much about the relationships between the professional practice of writing within academic disciplines and the way this practice translates, if at all, into instructional methods and expectations. Clearly, we must begin to consider more fully the role of disciplinary context on the writing process and on learning to write.

The paucity of this research is exacerbated by the lack of operational definitions for the concept of a *discipline*. While few would deny that epistemological demarcations separate broad areas of study such as medicine, the law, and the humanities, there is considerable disagreement as to how those demarcations should be characterized or further specified. Research has shown, however, that the typical organization of academic departments by subject matter (music, philosophy, economics, history, management, English literature, etc.) reflects differences in the structures of various knowledge systems—for example, in their methods of inquiry, their criteria for evaluation, and their ways of reporting knowledge. The reality of these differences is suggested in correlations between individuals' learning styles and their educational experiences, choices, and expectations (Biglan, 1973a,b; Bereiter & Freedman, 1962; Kolb, 1981). Because the typical components of the post-secondary curriculum would seem to reify our social and epistemological constructs of different knowledge systems, they will provide a useful (if rough) definition for *disciplines* in the context of this chapter. As I shall argue later, however, this is exactly the sort of definitional problem which research on writing must address.

Given the commonly defined areas of inquiry embedded in our educational system, what does it mean to write in a particular academic discipline? How do the criteria for good writing differ among diverse disciplines? What sorts of instructional beliefs about writing do scholars in different academic disciplines hold, and to what extent are those beliefs influenced by the conventions of the writing produced in their disciplines at a professional—rather than a pedagogical—level?

The purpose of this chapter is to address these and similar questions by considering three areas of scholarship on writing in the academic disciplines: (a) studies of variations in the characteristics or processes of writing relative to its disciplinary context; (b) studies of the instructional uses or functions of writing across different academic disciplines; and (c) studies of the relationship between writing and learning, particularly the distinction between acquiring the conventions specific to the writing of a discipline vs. using writing as a means of learning the subject matter through which the discipline is defined.

These clusters of research may be said to derive, respectively, from three more general perspectives for the study of writing in the academic disciplines: the *professional*, which refers to the nature of academic discourse used to mediate among experts in a given field and advance the field's base of knowledge; the *curricular*, which refers to how writing is used in and across discipline-specific school settings; and the *developmental*, which refers to the nature of the intellectual transitions that take place when members of one culture or discourse community (e.g., students) must acquire the normative social conventions, processes, and assumptions of another (e.g., academics; see Bizzell, 1982b). Clearly, there is considerable overlap among the three perspectives—and, as I shall argue, it is precisely these areas of overlap that hold much potential for our further explorations of this new and largely uncharted territory.

Some of the gaps and discrepancies to be noted in the existing research are based on a review of over 300 published books, articles, research reports and dissertations focused on writing across the curriculum or on writing within specific academic disciplines (Anson, 1985). At various junctures in this exploration, I will consider some important dimensions which we have yet to integrate fully into an epistemology of academic writing. In this way, I will construct in several stages a tentative but multidimensional model of writing in the academic disciplines—a model designed to show some of the issues that might guide our future research and lead to a richer, more principled basis for our practice.

CONTEXTUAL RELATIVITY AND THE NATURE OF ACADEMIC DISCOURSE

Writing and Context

Belief in the importance of context for the study of writing has led scholars recently to urge continued research on correlations between the social structures of organizational settings where people write and the functional and semantic features of their discourse (Brandt, 1986; cf. Halliday & Hasan, 1980; Kinneavy, 1983).

We have gleaned most of our knowledge of these correlations, however, from analyses of particular texts or groups of texts said to represent the discourse of the communities in which or for which they were written. Typically, text analyses simply describe the formal features of discourse, often explicitly avoiding speculations about authorial intentions and their antecedents in communicative contexts (see Kinneavy, 1971, p. 49). Most such analyses focus on the language of scientific discourse, including its syntax and organization (for discussions of differerent text-analytic methods, see Colomb & Williams, 1985; Cooper, 1983).

Some studies, however, attempt to move beyond the linguistic characteristics of the texts themselves by extending the analysis to include speculations about the character of the discipline's endeavors. To demonstrate this method, Bazerman (1981) analyzes three discipline-specific articles, one in molecular biology, one in sociology, and one in literary criticism. By looking "through the texts to the realms represented in [them]," Bazerman argues convincingly for the existence of fundamental differences in the noetic characteristics of each discipline—the way the authors construe the object under study, the literature of the field, their anticipated audience, and their persona and role. Similar findings have been reported in studies of writing in economics (McCloskey, 1983), literary criticism (Secor & Fahnestock, 1982), science (Fahnestock, 1986), engineering (Miller & Selzer, 1985), and business writing (Johns, 1980; Laroche & Pearson, 1985).

However, while even context-sensitive textual analyses may help to reveal important defining characteristic of different disciplines' genres, they allow little more than a surface understanding of the cultures in which the texts are produced, failing to demystify these cultures' deeper qualities (Bizzell, 1982b, p. 193; Faigley, 1985). Following from this assumption, recent research has begun to explore the relationship between context and writing in nonacademic settings, through surveys of writing across various professions or job categories (e.g., Anderson, 1985b; Barnum & Fischer, 1984), through studies of individual writers on the job (e.g., Brown & Herndl, 1986; Gould, 1980; Odell, 1985; Odell & Goswami, 1982; Odell, Goswami, & Herrington, 1983), and through studies of writing within entire organizations (e.g., Doheny-Farina, 1986; Knoblauch, 1980; Paradis, Dobrin, & Miller, 1985).

The conclusions of this and related research confirm, first, the assumption that the characteristics of writing vary considerably from context to context, from one intellectual domain to another. Beyond this simple observation, however, the research also hints at some of the ways that context influences both the texts and the composing processes of writers in specific professions (see Bazerman, 1983, for a review). Invention for many business writers, for example, typically involves telephone conversations, meetings, work sessions, and other social and collaborative activities (Selzer, 1983). Individual texts are often seen as means to ends, not ends in themselves, and frequently become part of the larger managerial process through *document cycling*—a collaborative pattern of drafting, reading, responding, and revising in which supervisers and managers try to make the text reflect their work objectives and organizational priorities and establish leverage over the timing and substance of the staff's labor (Paradis et al., 1985, p. 294). As business writers create texts, in other words, they are simultaneously interpreting and negotiating the activities of their work within the organization. Together with their prior knowledge of these contexts, this *social invention* usually translates into specific textual decisions (see Odell & Goswami, 1982).

But by itself, the observation that the composing process varies across different social and organizational contexts assumes that any one of these contexts influences its writers in roughly the same way, and its writing will show roughly the same normative features. On the surface, this may seem like a valid conclusion. But until and unless we explore the more personal dimensions of each writer's role and attitudes within the professional setting, we may be glossing over other equally important influences.

Brown and Herndl (1986), for example, initially found that certain formal features in the writing of management personnel at a large corporation (e.g., nominalization and narrative structures) were powerful signs of group affiliation. However, when they explored why some of the writers resisted changing their habits after being given advice about their writing by experts, the researchers also discovered a relationship between the writers' use of the features and their perceptions of job status or security. Similarly, in an ethnographic study of writing in an emerging organization, Doheny-Farina (1986) found that executives' views of their rhetorical situation were actually manifestations of different *interpretations* of their organizational context ("promotion/entrepreneurial" vs. "production/committee management"; pp. 169 ff.). The results suggest that context is not translated directly through the writer to the text, but that writers make operational decisions on the basis of their conception of the task environment (see Flower & Hayes, 1981)—and it is these conceptions, rather than the environment per se, which explain both the text's features and the thinking processes through which they are created.

Academic Writing: Definitions and Discrepancies

Many researchers of writing in professional settings have found it convenient to separate *academic writing*—the writing produced within educational institutions—from *nonacademic writing*—writing in the world of industry and corporate management, the government, and public service agencies. Academic and nonacademic writers become members of separate groups involved in completely different enterprises.

From the perspective of the academic discipline's professional discourse—the discourse of experts whose goal is to increase the field's base of knowledge—the research has been focused mainly on the sciences (see Faigley, 1985, for a brief review). Ironically, the growing importance of context in this research has led to a situation in which discourse communities are seen to be cut off from each other, existing as microcosms of intellectual activity. Several studies, however, indicate that the kinds of writing found even within specific organizations cannot be clearly categorized (see Tebeaux, 1985).

For purposes of conducting research, distinctions such as academic and non-academic may be desirable and necessary. We must be careful, however, not to assume that the domains we define for research also clearly define the boundaries of the intellectual activities we are observing. If the distinction between non-academic and academic disciplines is not integrated into a broader theory of professional writing, it may become limiting and unrealistic. Colomb and Williams (1985), for example, define the term *professional discourse* as discourse "created to bring about, by means of informing some person, some end beyond the experience of the discourse—a category most readily exemplified in the kinds of discourse generated within such professions as business, the law, medicine, and academics" (p. 127). Under this definition, differences between academic, nonacademic, and professional writing blur together, and it is difficult to imagine just where a discipline begins and ends.

Part of the problem, as Faigley (1985) has suggested, stems from confusion over what we mean by a discourse community or a context for writing:

> In examining nonacademic writing, we find many overlapping communities. For example, the biologist writing an environmental-impact statement abides not only by certain disciplinary conventions in biology, certain legal forms determined by the Environmental Protection Agency, and certain unstated and stated conventions particular to her company, but also by a complex set of conventions of political language (consider the use of the term *endangered species*). If the notion of discourse communities is to be illuminating, it must not be used without attending to how such communities might be identified and defined and how such communities shape the form and content of specific texts. (pp. 239–240)

Given their interdependence, therefore, the academic and nonacademic contexts of a discipline cannot be bifurcated without some loss of explanatory power. A field of study such as microbiology, firmly seated in the school of medicine, will often share the discourse conventions of the field of medicine as a whole, including its lexicon and its structural, stylistic, and rhetorical features. In turn, the medical research conducted (and reported on) in the academic institution adds to and influences the field's professional discourse. Microbiologists reporting on research under the auspices of profit-making private laboratories will share with academic microbiologists some assumptions about and knowledge of the conventions of writing within the field.

Because the activities and goals of nonacademic and academic writers who are thought to occupy the same discipline may differ, each must also contribute to or borrow from communities of discourse not shared by the other. The non-academic microbiologist's research report, written with shareholders and clients in mind, may contain features of business discourse which the academic microbiologist's would not. And, as research on the cognitive precedents of such features shows (e.g., Odell & Goswami, 1985), such situational factors cannot be ignored in understanding how a text is created.

The precise nature of independent vs. overlapping or shared assumptions, however, is not at all understood in writing research. Some of the mixed results of case studies focusing on writing as a professional activity might be explained, as Faigley (1985) suggests, by taking a wider perspective on the concept of discourse community. Citing the work of Willard (1983), Faigley suggests adding to the study of academic communities (or *normative fields*) some dimensions of shared or communal knowledge, such as schools of thought that cross disciplinary boundaries (*issue fields*). Thus it is possible that a microbiologist and a molecular physicist might share knowledge of a group of texts and by default share knowledge of the conventions exhibited in that group of texts, even though the texts themselves may be conventionally "located" in only one person's immediate field of study.

In addition to whatever differences might exist in prior knowledge, the most important distinction between the academic and nonacademic writer appears to be that the former is immersed in a world of teaching and learning and the latter in a world of entrepreneurialship, production, marketing, and distribution of goods and services. As Knoblauch (1980) has shown, writers act on both global and operational purposes defined by the purposes of their institutional context and by the personal goals associated with their career choices—what Schank and Abelson (1977) call their *life-themes*. Clearly, we need to look more closely at the concept of purpose as it relates to organizational context and the features and processes of writing.

Research might also begin to distinguish more completely between two kinds of knowledge writers must possess in any discourse community: composing *processes* influenced by procedural knowledge within the context, and mutual knowledge of organizational *content*—or the distinction between "knowing how" and "knowing that" (Ryle, 1949; cf. Steinmann, 1982). In drawing this distinction, Hirsch (1983) has argued recently that the ease of comprehending or producing discourse is directly related to shared cultural knowledge: a writer will write more fluently about common topics in our culture of he or she has read Shakespeare and the Declaration of Independence, and knows something about DNA. The importance of mutual knowledge in academic writing is, of course, beyond question; but, as Bazerman (1981) clearly shows in his text analysis, it is not nearly as simple as Hirsch's claim makes it seem, partly because mutual knowledge is, like the features of discourse, always relative to particular contexts.

Writing in the Disciplines: Professional

Recognizing the findings of research on the conventions and processes of writing across diverse communities, we might begin to construct a model of writing in the academic disciplines by simply showing this relationship. As we have seen, however, not only do separate communities often share conventions, but the conventions are translated into composing processes as a function of each writer's individual position—and disposition—within the context itself.

In Figure 1 below, disciplines are described, at a very general level, by their academic and nonacademic goals (e.g., those of a private research laboratory vs. biology department in a large state university with a strong research orientation). While such goals may appear to be purely epistemological, they resound through all of the endeavors and activities—right down to the purposes of phone calls and meetings—of the professionals working in the context of the discipline. Differences in behaviors motivated by higher-level goals will become important later

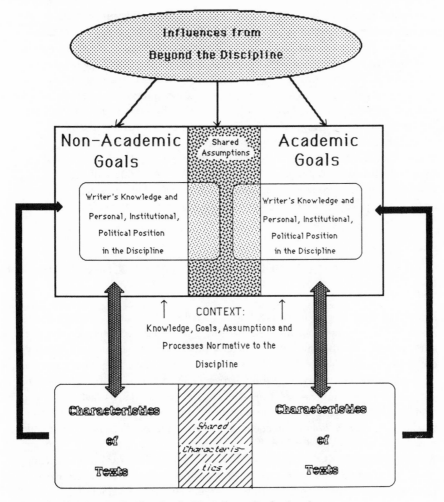

Fig. 1.   Writing in the Academic Disciplines: Professional

when we consider the surrounding pedagogical values reflected in the academic side of the model.

Professionals in either type of context create a construct of their environment based partly on their institutional or political position, their personal and occupational goals, and their attitudes toward their roles, their work, their colleagues, and readers of their writing. To the extent that the academic and nonacademic variations of disciplines overlap significantly in goals, methods, and prior knowledge, then so must some of the intellectual processes of their writers. These processes translate into characteristics of texts within the disciplines which reveal, in observable ways, some of these shared features.

If this were the end of the model, then it would not show how texts and/or composing processes become normative to each discipline. In particular, we must recognize the cyclic, mutually influencing nature of social and organizational contexts, on the one hand, and their individual or cumulative writing, on the other (Doheny-Farina, 1986). Figure 1 therefore delineates each academic discipline as both creating and being created by the discourse it produces. The possiblity of influences from contexts beyond the disciplines explains how, in the midst of what might otherwise seem to be a mutually reinforcing (and changeless) process, the language of various communities evolves and grows.

As this model suggests, further research on writing in the academic disciplines from the professional perspective must explore the "fluid and multiple nature of discourse communities" (Faigley, 1985). And this will mean seeing writers not as mediators between static contexts and relatively stable groups of texts, but as people who themselves interpret and embody the characteristics of many contexts.

STUDYING THE CURRICULAR FUNCTIONS OF WRITING IN THE DISCIPLINES

In addition to the largely unexplored professional functions of writing in academic settings are the functions for which writing is used in the academic curriculum. Early research on this subject is generally limited to studies of the frequency, use, and forms of writing in various subject-area courses. The publication of Britton's influential study of writing across the curriculum in British secondary schools (Britton, Burgess, Martin, McLeod, & Rosen, 1975) had brought to many educators' attention the tendency for school-sponsored writing to be overwhelmingly *transactional*—intended to convey information in a pragmatic way—and directed predominantly to the teacher in the role of an examiner. Britton's team also discovered that, as students moved upward in their school years, the range of functions their writing served became increasingly narrow, lessening their chances to use writing expressively or as a vehicle for learning unfamiliar material.

The results of survey studies on the uses of writing in American secondary schools generally corroborate the findings reported in Britton et al.: that students are not encouraged to use writing in ways that foster both their intellectual development and their overall writing abilities. Donlan's (1974) survey of schools (K-graduate) in Riverside, California, revealed that while writing became more extended with increasing grade level, the frequency of assigned writing tended to decrease: students were asked to write less often, and their texts were expected to be longer, perhaps in keeping with the loss of functional diversity.

The predominance of these intellectually limited uses of writing is also supported by Clemmons (1980), whose survey of 133 high-school science and social studies teachers revealed that the most frequently used writing tasks are those that require simple, mechanical procedures: answering study questions and reporting or restating information. More recently, Applebee's thorough national study of writing in several high school subject areas (Applebee, 1981, 1982, 1984a) showed a general lack of attention to writing (3% of students' school time) and an impoverishment of functional diversity (writing was used most often as a vehicle for testing knowledge of specific content, with the teacher playing the role of an examiner). As Bader and Pearce (1983) suggest from a survey of junior high school teachers, such mechanical uses may be related to the tendency to see writing as a convenient method for classroom management and control.

At the college level, however, the results of survey studies on the uses of writing seem less conclusive. Some, such as Donlan's (1980) survey of science and math teachers at American University, generally show the same patterns as those documented in the secondary schools: that teachers use writing more often for reporting information and rehearsing facts and details than for exploring ideas. In a survey of 266 faculty members in education, humanities, fine arts, natural sciences, social sciences, and business at a mid-sized midwestern university, Eblen (1983) also found that writing was used more often as a mode of testing than as a mode of learning. However, there seemed to be general support for the frequent use of writing, with 85% reporting that writing was used in the first class of each week. While the essay test dominated the survey as the most often used form of writing, the results nevertheless showed considerable diversity in types; also used (in decreasing order of frequency) were analytical papers, documented papers, abstracts of readings, laboratory reports, case reports, technical reports, book reports, essays or themes, teaching materials, personal writing and journals, and specialized forms of writing such as computer documentation, memos, and fiction.

More recently, Bernhardt (1985) surveyed faculty in 14 departments across Southern Illinois University about writing in the disciplines, finding that both students and faculty members valued writing ability highly and that a great deal more writing, of all sorts, was being required across the curriculum than they had imagined (p. 55). Types of writing considered important by the faculty responding (n = 193) included (with number of times mentioned) expository writing (153), problem descriptions (77), procedural-instructional pieces (60), creative pieces (54), letters (52), case studies (46), lab reports (35), and legal briefs (8). Also mentioned were research reports, essays, mathematical arguments, and translations.

In a survey of the entire faculty at Illinois State University at Normal, Scharton (1983) drew similar conclusions, claiming that faculty "make assignments at all levels, for diverse purposes, and with confidence that they are using a powerful instrument for teaching and learning" (pp. 12–13). Similarly, in a survey of faculty in 190 academic deparments at 34 universities in the United States and Canada, Bridgeman and Carlson (1984) found general diversity among different disciplines as to preferred mode of discourse for evaluating student ability, with no single type universally approved or disapproved.

Findings like these suggest that immersion in a range of academic disciplines results in exposure to and practice of a variety of both general and specific forms of written discourse, albeit more often transactional than expressive, and more often directed to a teacher-examiner than other audiences. Thus, while there appears to be some evidence that, at the college level, writing is not used as often to foster thinking and learning (or, for that matter, to improve writing abilities) as it is to measure the retention of facts and details, the research is too inconclusive to afford any generalizations that might inform current practice.

Questions from Mixed Results

While the survey research may seem problematic, it is especially useful as a heuristic for further conjecture and study. Several weaknesses in survey methodology, for example, suggest some interesting possibilities for further research on the functions of writing in the academic disciplines from a curricular perspective.

Methodology and the perceived purpose of research. It is widely acknowledged that those who habitually fill out and return surveys are often predisposed to thinking and behaving differently than those who are habitually unwilling to cooperate in such research unless forced to do so (Anderson, 1985a). Because most surveys are responded to by choice, even a relatively good return may still represent a skewed sample. Zemelman's (1977) interviews with 17 faculty members at Livingston College-Rutgers, for example, suggests a relationship between the enthusiasm and dedication of a faculty member and the likelihood that writing will be frequent and of diverse types. Similarly, Rose's (1979) study of 96 faculty members at UCLA found a connection between positive attitudes toward writing and the tendency to see a shared responsibility for the instructional use of writing.

More problematic, the assumed goal of the research, and the nature of its designers and their institutional affiliation, often influence those who are responding to survey instruments. Anticipating that the survey results may fuel a desired or undesired effort, many survey responders are variously inaccurate in the information they provide. Others may simply believe in certain principles of teaching or learning, responding to a questionnaire under the assumption that their choices accurately reflect what they do in practice.

Recognizing the limitations of surveys and questionnaires as data-gathering tools, some researchers have used several methodologies simultaneously to gather parallel data. In his study of writing in American secondary schools, for example, Applebee and his team (Applebee, 1984a) conducted case studies of all subjects areas at two grade levels in two high schools. Methodologically, these case studies included interviews with the 68 participating teachers and their students, and observations of some 13,293 minutes of classroom instruction. To place the results of these case studies in a more generalized context, however, Applebee also conducted a national survey of writing instruction based on a stratified sample of 200 American high schools. And, under the auspices of the same project, he also analyzed the writing activities suggested in popular textbooks. Thus, conclusions from one phase of the study could be interpreted in terms of conclusions from another.

In contrast, there has been very little use of parallel research methodologies in the college-level studies of writing functions. Suspicious of self-report data from faculty who might "attempt to make themselves look good," Bernhardt (1985) added to his survey of 14 departments at Southern Illinois University a second questionnaire for students, to test agreement on frequency and types of writing tasks assigned at different curricular levels. Although students were "slightly more sanguine" about their skills than were the faculty, both faculty and students agreed on the frequency and types of tasks assigned as well as the importance of writing to intellectual development. In a similar dovetailed survey conducted at Ball State University, however, Trimmer (1985) found notable differences in faculty and student reports about and attitudes toward writing in different disciplines.

The reflection of institutional role.   The dangers of deriving research conclusions from mixed and sometimes unreliable survey results are even greater when we consider that the uses of writing in academic contexts are very often a function of larger institutional goals or educational levels. The size or type of a particular institution—2-year vs. 4-year, community vs. national, private vs. public, large vs. small, etc.—and its members' tacitly understood "mission" often greatly influence specific practices (Wilson & Gaff, 1975; Witte & Faigley, 1983).   Given the diversity of institutions in which surveys have been conducted, it would not be surprising to find less expressive writing in college courses than in secondary or elementary schools. In particular, college-level writing in a given discipline may be the product of implicit assumptions about the discipline's normal practices: if one common activity of the discipline is to report the results of original experimental research, then that function may well influence the use of writing instructionally—e.g., to provide opportunities to learn the discipline's typical forms of discourse. Furthermore, we might expect such functions to become increasingly narrow and specific even within the college setting, reaching, at the graduate level, a nearly perfect match with the professional writing of the discipline itself.

Such changes in educational assumptions at different curricular levels raise questions about the way we define *growth* in writing ability. The tendency has been to criticize transactional functions if and when they are superordinate to writing as a mode of discovery and self-expression. As we will see in the developmental perspective, however, there is an important distinction between transactional functions used in the service of building new discourse knowledge, and other transactional functions (e.g., note-taking and regurgitating memorized information) which do not encourage much intellectual growth.

The problem of functional taxonomies.   The extent to which the results of surveys differ may also depend heavily on the rubric used to classify *uses* or *functions* of writing in particular institutions. Although we have made great strides in understanding the functions of writing since the days of the *modes* of discourse (see Connors, 1981), we have yet to build an adequate theory of writing which would account for the functional range of writing across the disciplines, or suggest something of its varying textual characteristics.

Beneath every survey or questionnaire lies a classification system reflecting one or another theory of discourse. Britton et al. (1975), for example, is perhaps more fully a work describing and attempting to validate a functional theory than it is a report of how teachers use writing in the public schools. But where Britton's team had documented a division of discourse into *poetic*, *expressive*, and *transactional*, Applebee (1982, 1984a) assigns more processual terms based on an earlier scheme developed by Britton (1971): *mechanical uses*, *informational uses*, *personal uses*, and *imaginative uses*, each of which is subdivided into several further categories. Where Donlan's survey (1974) relied on a scheme resembling the traditional modes of discourse (*narration, exposition, argumentation*, and *reporting*), Eblen's (1983) results are based on categories such as *essay tests*, *abstracts of readings*, *lab reports*, and *personal/journals* (p. 346), some of which are generic, common to most educational contexts, while others are specific to certain disciplines or groups of disciplines. Aware of this problem, Bridgeman and Carlson (1984) developed for their questionnaire 10 topic types which would provide concrete examples of actual tasks that might be required of students (p. 254). This list, however, arbitrarily combines *kinds* or genres of discourse (e.g., *personal essay*) with processes common to many different kinds of discourse (*compare and contrast, summarize a passage*, etc.).

This range of classification systems raises important questions about the use of writing in academic disciplines. Two different disciplines may differ significantly in their definition of the type of discourse beneath any of the labels. An *informational* use of writing may be construed in a number of ways—a test of knowledge in which the reader already possesses the information conveyed; a report of original findings, perhaps from an experiment or a study; or a discursive essay in which the writer presents a new perspective on some social condition. Similarly, one teacher's use of a lab report may allow for expressive or exploratory functions typical of a scientist's journal of observations, while another's may adhere closely to the dicta and formulas of the discipline's scientific publications. Unfortunately, most discourse taxonomies have failed to correlate the textual characteristics of writing—its mode, genre, or conventions—with the pragmatic characteristics of its use, such as its purpose and the discourse community that surrounds it (see Fulkerson, 1984).

Ideologies and the Functions of Writing in the Disciplines

A second line of research relevant to the functions of writing in the academic disciplines is suggested by studies relating teacher ideology to instructional practice. Typically, ideologies are defined as systems of beliefs, expectations, and attitudes concerning some domain of knowledge or practice; they constitute a "world view of what should be the goal of a particular enterprise" (Mosenthal, 1983). As defined by Bernier and Williams (1973), an ideology is

> an integrated pattern of ideas, system of beliefs, or a "group consciousness" which characterizes a social group. Such a pattern or system may include doctrines, ideals, slogans, symbols, and directions for social and political action. Ideologies also include objectives, demands, judgments, norms, and justifications, and in this sense they are value-impregnated systems of thought which may be perceived as sacred. (p. 27)

Academically, the use of writing is often, if not always, partly defined by the ideology of the authority figure who designs, administers, and evaluates the tasks. Thus, writing in academic disciplines must be viewed as a function of the sociopsychological realities embedded in ideological constructs (Bernier, 1981)—whether these are specific to an individual teacher within the discipline or common to the discipline as a whole.

Several theories of teacher attitudes and ideologies and their relationship to the functions of writing have been developed within the field of composition (Fulkerson, 1978; Kroll, 1980; Mosenthal, 1983). Taken together, these theories suggest that the predominant focus of writing in an academic context—its stated or implied purposes, its task design, its evaluation, etc.—develops from generalized beliefs or constructs about the nature of writing as a social or academic activity. Kroll (1980), for example, has identified two general ideological dispositions among writing teachers—the *interventionist* and the *maturationist*. The first emphasizes the external conventions of written texts—standard usage, sentence and paragraph structure, etc. The second is aimed at fostering personal growth, and therefore centers on context, intention, past performance, and effort.

In a scheme based on the writing context, Mosenthal (1983) suggests five partial specifications by ideological type: the academic, the utilitarian, the romantic, the cognitive-developmental, and the emancipatory. Each ideology defines its goals in terms of "an optimal configuration of variables within or between contexts" such as the writer, setting, materials, task, and situation organizer (p. 39). In a partial specification from an academic ideology, for example, the goal is to pass on the knowledge, skills, and values which previous generations have deemed important for succeeding generations to acquire. Thus, the instruction will focus on conforming to an established set of norms, and is preoccupied with the output (written text) rather than the context, the writer, or the task.

Research exploring the reality of such ideological constructs and their effects on writing instruction is limited and scattered, but tends to support the relationship between belief and practice. Based on a study of 93 writing teachers, Diamond (1979a,b) has identified 20 separate constructs of writing which group into two competing ideologies—one which is skills-based, structured, detailed, and behavior-analytic, and one which is oriented toward inquiry and learning. This finding is further supported by research suggesting a relationship between the functions of writing in academic contexts and faculty belief that writing is either a means of transmission or a means of interpretation (Barnes & Shemilt, 1974). And, in a recent study of 311 Washington state teachers' attitudes toward writing, Gere, Schuessler, and Abbott (1984) found evidence supporting the two ideological dispositions suggested by Kroll (1980): faculty placed functional priority either on students' language development, focusing on meaning, or on their adherence to the proper conventions of discourse, focusing on text. Thus, it appears that composition teachers define writing differently on the basis of their belief systems, whose sources are both the private realms of personal constructs and the more objective realm of the social and institutional contexts they participate in.

There has been little empirical research, however, exploring the way these systems function across different academic disciplines. A few studies (Freedman, 1979; Weaver, 1982) suggest that faculty in different disciplines express the same values about writing, implying that, to the extent that writing differs among different discourse communities, it is not reflected in the beliefs of academics identified with such communities. However, these findings seem to contradict those of Bridgeman and Carlson (1984), Tighe and Koziol (1982), Schwartz (1984), Trimmer (1985), and Williamson (1984), who discovered a range of values or emphases across faculty in different disciplines.

While not designed as empirical research, the many workshops and seminars conducted under the auspices of "writing across the curriculum" have yielded some important and interesting information about teachers' beliefs and attitudes in different academic disciplines (Connelly & Irving, 1976; Freisinger, 1980; Fulwiler, 1981, 1984; Herrington, 1981; Maimon, 1979; Notchimson, 1980; Raimes, 1980). Because they do not suffer from the effects of experimental intrusion on normal behavior, these faculty workshops might be thought of as natural research whose data, albeit reported testimonially, can provide some needed direction for more formal studies.

The most important observations of these workshops is that scholars from a range of academic disciplines hold different beliefs about writing. Some of these beliefs, as might be predicted from existing research on ideology, are formed from scholars' misconceptions about the nature of writing in disciplines other than their own (Dick & Esch, 1985). Other beliefs may be explained in terms of teachers' *centers of interest*, as Swanson-Owens (1986) reports in a case study of two teachers' responses to a particular set of writing-to-learn assignments for students. The new methods were accepted more readily to the extent that they met each teacher's instructional conditions—conditions related, ultimately, to their instructional ideologies.

In creating a forum for discussing shared interests in writing, faculty workshops eventually allow the participants to strip away their ideological misconceptions, either about writing in general or about writing in disciplines other than their own, revealing the more important differences in the way each discipline defines its writing: differences in nomenclature, purpose, audience, stylistic features, and contexts for writing.

As these workshops reveal, much of what people in different academic disciplines think about writing is partly tacit (at least until they engage in the kind of critical introspections encouraged by the workshops); and while they appear to have more conscious knowledge of writing than writers in nonacademic settings (perhaps because teaching requires it), they frequently hold monolithic conceptions of writing and even express insecurity about their own abilities, alluding to stereotypes of quality largely associated with departments of English (Walvoord & Smith, 1982; Zinsser, 1986). Their beliefs about writing and writing instruction, then, must consist of both ideological and highly subjective elements as well as more objective, shared characteristics that define their field.

Writing in the Disciplines: Curricular

As suggested in Figure 2 below, the use of writing in specific academic settings is usually (but not always) a function of a teacher and the construct this teacher has of the writing purpose and context. Typically, the teacher's task designs are influenced by his or her curricular agenda. In parallel with this agenda are certain influences from personal ideologies of writing—for example, whether expressive forms are more conducive to learning than transactional forms; beliefs about student writing abilities; or attitudes toward writing as an intellectual activity.

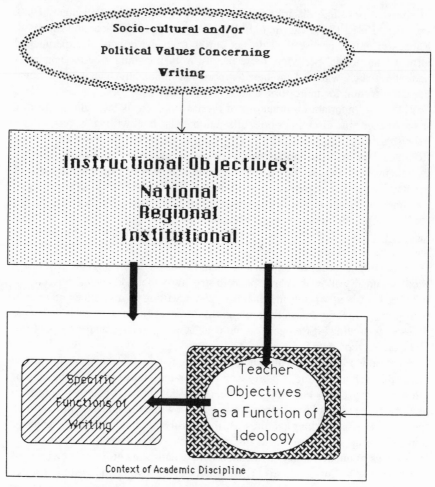

Fig. 2.   Writing in the Academic Disciplines: Curricular

The teacher may also be influenced by other aspects of the discipline's context—for example, if an administrator, committee, or other controlling body mandates certain uses or types of writing, frequency of tasks, etc. Even faculty free to use writing in any way they please often follow the lead of higher-level administrative goals or even beliefs about the "mission" of the institution in which the writing is being used. In turn, generalized socio-political movements may bring certain pressures to bear both on an entire institution or on individual teachers or administrators within the institution. As Piché (1977) has pointed out, for example, neither schools nor curricula exist in social isolation, but are "socially constituted relevance systems, reflecting and amplifying larger sets of social and cultural values in the emphases they give to kinds or ways of know-ing" (p. 17).

Reflecting on this partial model of writing across academic disciplines, we can begin to understand why research on the uses of writing in academic contexts appears mixed and inconclusive. The responses of any faculty member to a questionnaire or even to an interview may reflect an institutional mission, a personal belief, an expectation of the uses to which the responses will be put, an interpretation of actual practice, or an accurate reflection of that practice. If such diversity in practice is common within the field of composition or language arts, then simply creating a rough functional index for other academic disciplines may be seriously misleading if conclusions about the nature of writing are inferred from such an index. Depending upon the ideologies surrounding a particular academic discipline, curriculum, or individual classroom, a little writing used well may foster more productive learning and attitudes on the part of the student than a lot of writing used in unproductive or intellectually limiting ways.

With these dimensions of personal ideology included in the model, we can begin to see a more complicated network of relationships between the way that writing is used in a specific disciplinary context, on the one hand, and the personal belief system of the individual teacher, on the other. When we add to this the teacher's knowledge and contructs of writing as a practicing member of the discipline on a professional level, as shown earlier in Figure 1, the question of curricular function becomes even more challenging. In particular, we know nothing of the curricular balance between specific professional knowledge and generalized pedagogical practices in the uses of writing within or across various academic disciplines. One problem we face, for example, is sorting out the differences between *instructional ideology* and *disciplinary ideology*, and the way these influence the use of writing in the educational setting.

WRITING AND LEARNING IN THE ACADEMIC DISCIPLINES

Contributions of Writing to Learning

Much of the impetus for the writing-across-the-curriculum movement has come from a growing body of theory linking writing to learning (see Emig, 1977; Beach & Bridwell, 1983; Herrington, 1981; and Yates, 1983, for representative discussions and reviews). This theory argues that writing is ideally suited for the discovery, formulation, and expression of ideas, particularly in personal and exploratory modes rather than merely mechanical or communicative ones (Freisinger, 1982).

Academic disciplines, whose instructional goals are to teach students a body of knowledge while also helping them to acquire the thinking processes of professionals in the field, would seem suited to an emphasis on writing as a mode of learning. From the developmental perspective, however, we have only limited knowledge of how writing contributes to learning in academic disciplines. Applebee (1984b) has provided a thorough review of existing research on writing and reasoning, including studies of the contributions of note-taking and other "simple" forms of writing activities. Most of this research, however, is limited in scope or contextually unfocused, ignoring cognitive or processual variations that might occur in certain activities used across different disciplines rather than a single course chosen for experimental treatment or control.

The results of more extensive research are mixed. In a study examining the effects of different writing tasks on students' understanding of informational texts, Newell (1984) found that extended writing enabled the students to learn significantly more from the texts than taking notes or completing short-answer exercises. In a controlled study of expressive writing in high school biology courses, Tierney (1981) found no significant evidence that students who wrote about their subject matter performed better on tests of their knowledge, although they showed significantly better recall and their writing abilities seemed to improve compared to the nonwriting group. In contrast, Weiss' (1979) study of 178 college students and five teachers in the areas of history, psychology, physical sciences, reading theory and practice, and statistics found that more subject-area writing did not produce better writing but did increase learning of the subject matter.

The effects on learning of different *types* of writing is also ill understood. In a study of writing about literature, Marshall (1984) found that essay writing in either personal or formal modes led to better understanding of literary texts compared with no writing or with answering study questions. Differences between the two modes of essay writing were indistinguishable. However, Newell, Suszynski, and Wiengart (1986) report that expressive writing used as a means of learning literature was judged to be of higher quality than formal writing used for the same purpose.

Writing, Learning, and the Educational Forum of a Discipline

The general lack of research on intellectual development or the acquisition of writing abilities in particular academic disciplines may owe to some fundamental discrepancies in how writing and learning are connected.

At one level, all academic discourse is "a form of language use that unites a particular community," an academic culture, which is often different from the culture in which students are immersed (Bizzell, 1982b, p. 193). To write academically, students have to "invent the university," and "learn to speak our language, to speak as we do, to try on the peculiar ways of knowing, selecting, evaluating, reporting, concluding, and arguing that define the discourse of our community" (Bartholomae, 1985, p. 134).

At a more particular level, students must also differentiate the languages of separate academic communities (Perelman, 1986), not only learning the conventions of thinking and writing like people in each defined field, but understanding "the kinds of issues the discipline tries to address, and shared assumptions about the audience's role, the writer's *ethos*, and the social purposes for communicating" (Herrington, 1985b, p. 332).

Finally, to write successfully in individual classrooms, students must also understand their teacher's way of *interpreting* the language of the entire academic community as well as the language of the discipline in which the course is located. As suggested in the model depicted earlier in Figure 2, what is produced as writing in that part of the academic setting devoted to instruction is closely tied to a specific teacher's curricular goals and personal or instructional ideologies—factors which, as research on children's writing in elementary school has shown, are powerful determinants of how students think when they respond to tasks (see Mosenthal, Davidson-Mosenthal, & Krieger, 1981; Mosenthal, Conley, Colella, & Davidson-Mosenthal, 1985). We must be cautious, then, not to assume that simply documenting what students do within an academic setting is sufficient to understand all that falls under "learning" to write in a particular discipline. What students do is in part a reflection of how they interpret their teacher's instructional agendas.

As students learn to write in a discipline, in other words, they are learning about and becoming indoctrinated into the entire world of academic discourse; they are acquiring tacit knowledge about writing in the field; and they are interpreting (and acting on) a much more specific representation of both of these through their teacher's classroom organization, expressed beliefs, writing tasks, and responses to the students' writing. Whether these simultaneous demands foster or inhibit the development of writing abilities is yet to be understood; but, clearly, they pose special intellectual problems for the developing writer (see McCarthy, 1985).

The power of teachers to determine what students learn about writing has been demonstrated in recent research on students' writing across different disciplines. In a study of two college chemical engineering courses, Herrington (1983, 1985a,b) found that each teacher held different conceptions of writing and learning; the courses represented different forums for writing: "different issues were addressed, different writer and reader roles assumed, and different social purposes served by writing" (1985b, p. 340). Faigley and Hansen (1985) report similar conclusions from a study of students' writing in the social sciences. Interviews with the students and analyses of their writing show how in one course (Psychology), writing a successful text meant quite rigidly adhering to the basic format and conventions of articles in the field. In Sociology, the professor seemed to value the student's adherence to the conventions of the field, yet he based his evaluation on his greater interest in "what knowledge the student had acquired than in how well the report was written" (p. 147). An English teacher grading the same paper for simultaneous credit in a course on writing in the social sciences had written in his course syllabus that his criteria would be based on whether a professional in the field would consider the paper worth reading. Yet this teacher judged the student's paper mainly on the basis of surface correctness, and rated it lower than did the professional, the professor of sociology.

These differences of emphasis within academic disciplines—even in otherwise coherent school contexts—seem to contradict the findings of research suggesting that faculty generally recognize and agree on the normative criteria for discourse in their fields (see Williamson, 1984). Herrington (1985a), however, sheds some light on this discrepancy in her analysis of classroom contexts as forums for learning. Faculty who are aware of efforts to integrate writing into discipline-specific courses generally fall into two groups: those who explain academic writing from the perspective of a school community, and those who explain it from the perspective of a disciplinary community. The first group centers on the benefits of writing as a means of learning, particularly through the sorts of intellectual and epistemological explorations afforded by expressive writing. In contrast, the second group's definition focuses on the benefits of acquiring the intellectual and social conventions of particular discourse communities.

Just as we lack an adequate definition of professional discourse communities, we also need to define what it means for a student to learn and use writing in an academic discipline. If the situation were simply a matter of matching each discipline with a clear set of conventions and processes for writing, students would have far less difficulty growing as writers than they now do. But the circumstances of schooling belie such coherence and lead to mixed practices, both within and across courses and disciplines. As Powell (1985) observed during an analysis of writing in his organic chemistry course, his students were specializing in a *gallery* of disciplines: chemistry, biology, pre-medicine, pre-dentisty, medical technology and allied health, mathematics, and chemical engineering. Faced with this mix, Powell included both reflective writing and writing to teach the conventions of writing in chemistry and to "introduce students to the stylistic requirements of recording technical information and data and of generating and writing laboratory reports from this information base" (p. 417).

Also reflected earlier in Figure 2 are the influences of specific institutional contexts on the way that teachers and students interpret the generalized discipline they are working in. Two-year and vocational schools, for example, act on different assumptions about what it means to write in a discipline than do small, private 4-year liberal arts colleges or large, research-oriented state universities. This tendency was shown in the model as influencing teachers' tacit assumptions about the instructional functions of writing; however, it must also influence students' behaviors as well. As Odell (1985) has put it, the dominant "ethos"— the shared beliefs and patterns of behavior—defined by a particular school may influence students' writing and reading (p. 274).

Of course, students are themselves members of a culture which does not always share the same beliefs or attitudes as teachers—a point not to be taken lightly in our understanding of how students accommodate those new beliefs and attitudes as they learn. Herrington's study of engineering courses, for example, showed that students and teachers could hold different assumptions about what it meant to write in a discipline (p. 342)—a finding mirrored in Schwartz' (1984) multidisciplinary study of faculty and students' attitudes toward writing. In exploring this tendency in detail, Newkirk (1984) found that students often judge the quality of writing on the basis of their own dispositions and interests, rather than on extrinsic criteria that might match those of their teachers.

Writing in the Academic Disciplines: Developmental

Figure 3 below shows some of the assumptions and processes related to writing and learning within academic disciplines. Students' knowledge of the conven-

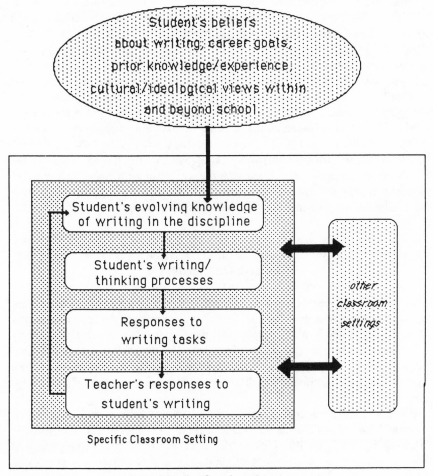

Fig. 3.   Writing in the Academic Disciplines: Developmental

tions and processes of discipline-specific writing is constantly growing and evolving as they create texts from teachers' assignments and receive responses to those texts. The academic setting, as Perelman (1986) has suggested, is extremely powerful in directing students' attention toward specific instructional expectations and goals which are often, as we saw in Figure 2, influenced by national, regional, institutional (or even departmental) objectives.

But students' knowledge is not limited only to their immediate instructional context. Their interpretations of the cultural and political values concerning writing also influence the way they think and act. These might be interpretations of general social and economic trends toward or away from certain intellectual areas and the careers associated with them (e.g., science and technology vs. the humanities), or they might be values associated with the students' own culture, as Bizzell (1982b) suggests. As they learn about and practice the writing specific to a discipline, their generalized values change and evolve as well. In addition, their movement toward committed beliefs about certain intellectual perspectives and activities (often associated with their career goals) will certainly include changes in their attitudes toward writing in their fields (see Perry, 1970).

Finally, it might be pointed out that "evolving knowledge of writing in the disciplines" can be circumvented if the students use writing predominantly as a mode of learning the content of the discipline or exploring their interpretations of it. Students who practice nothing but expressive writing in the only course they take in art history, for example, will probably not gain much specific knowledge or composing strategies associated with the writing of art historians. If the goal of such a course is to enculturate students into the field of art history, then their knowledge of its discourse may suffer (see Jolliffe, 1985).

CONCLUSION: TOWARD AN UNDERSTANDING OF WRITING IN THE DISCIPLINES

From the point of view of research, it is clear that we must begin to explore more deeply the interconnections between and among the various dimensions depicted in Figures 1, 2, and 3. Methodologically, these interconnections are particularly difficult to understand without careful qualitative study in addition to larger-scale measures of belief and practice, or the manifestation of these in written texts (see Lutz, 1981, for a discussion of ethnographic approaches to research on schooling).

Clearly, further research on the processes, characteristics, and functions of writing in the academic disciplines must begin to take the perspective of triangulated inquiry (Sevigny, 1981), using multiple comparisons of a single phenomenon or gathering and analyzing multiple data from several phenomena (p. 73). Focused research—even ethnographic studies of individual colleges, departments, or groups of teachers, for example (see Doheny-Farina & Odell, 1985)—

must be accompanied by broader data from a variety of populations, and vice versa. The fact that writing varies among many curricular, functional, and social dimensions suggests that conclusions derived from data elicited even by a carefully designed instrument used in a closed context may not be generalizable to a wider population.

In this chapter I have suggested some questions for further research by taking three perspectives on writing in the academic disciplines: the professional, the curricular, and the developmental. From each perspective, I have created a tentative model, based on existing research and speculation, designed to show some of the influences—personal, social, institutional, textual—which might

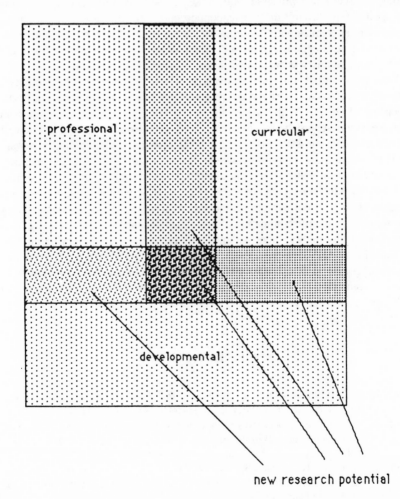

new research potential

Fig. 4.   Research Perspectives for Studying Writing in the Academic Disciplines

begin to explain the phenomenon of writing as it is produced and used within and across academic disciplines. As the rest of the studies in this volume thoroughly demonstrate, we are well on the way toward such explanations, but there is still a long way to travel.

The distance becomes more real if the three models are brought together into a single group of perspectives for research on academic writing, as illustrated in Figure 4. All of the dimensions described in each model interact, however greatly or slightly, with those in the other models. To study the writing of newly employed legislative analysts, for example, as did Odell, Goswami, and Quick (1983), is not only to see the influence of the nonacademic context on their writing behaviors and processes, but to see as well the influence of academia both as it filters through the nonacademic context (to the extent that it shares some common characteristics with the academic study of government and legislation) and as it filters through the individual writer, in the remnants of his or her development as this was facilitated through a specific curriculum.

There is one final dimension, however, which for purposes of simplicity I have left out of each model and the research that has helped to construct it: the dimension of change. While we usually study writing at a particular moment in time, we cannot ignore the fact that everything included in the model in Figure 4 is itself in a constant state of flux and development. Academic disciplines are evolving, sometimes undergoing whole Kuhnian paradigm shifts, sometimes losing power or influence, sometimes splitting into several subareas or becoming consolidated into larger areas of study. The field of writing studies is a good example of such recent evolution, and the great variety of its discourse shows something of its interdisciplinary qualities. To understand writing in the academic disciplines thoroughly, then, we must also see what we are observing through the lens of historical development—and that will require more than studying just the writing, or its immediate surrounding context; it will require that we know, in addition, something about *the discipline* itself, as a forum for the production and exchange of knowledge.

REFERENCES

Anderson, P. V. (1985a). Survey methodology. In L. Odell & D. Goswami (Eds.), *Writing in nonacademic settings* (pp. 453–502). New York: Guilford.

Anderson, P. V. (1985b). What survey research tells us about writing at work. In L. Odell & D. Goswami (Eds.), *Writing in nonacademic settings* (pp. 3–83). New York: Guilford.

Anson, C. M. (1985, November). *Writing across the curriculum: The current state of research*. Paper presented at the National Council of Teachers of English Assembly on Research, Philadelphia.

Applebee, A. N. (1974). *Tradition and reform in the teaching of English: A history*. Urbana, IL: NCTE.

Applebee, A. N. (1981). *Writing in the secondary school: English and the content areas.* NCTE Research Report No. 21. Urbana, IL: NCTE.

Applebee, A. N. (1982). Writing and learning in school settings. In M. Nystrand (Ed.), *What writers know: The language, process, and structure of written discourse* (pp. 365–381). New York: Academic Press.

Applebee, A. N. (1984a). *Contexts for learning to write: Studies of secondary school instruction.* Norwood, NJ: Ablex Publishing Corp.

Applebee, A. N. (1984b). Writing and reasoning. *Review of Educational Research, 54,* 577–596.

Bader, L. A., & Pearce, D. L. (1983). Writing across the curriculum, 7–12. *English Education, 15,* 97–106.

Barnes, D., & Shemilt, D. (1974). Transmission and interpretation. *Educational Review, 26,* 213–228.

Bartholomae, D. (1985). Inventing the university. In M. Rose (Ed.), *When a writer can't write* (pp. 134–165). New York: Guilford.

Barnum, C. M., & Fischer, R. (1984). Engineering technologists as writers: Results of a survey. *Technical Communication, 31,* 9–11.

Bazerman, C. (1981). What written knowledge does: Three examples of academic discourse. *Philosophy of the Social Sciences, 11,* 361–387.

Bazerman, C. (1983). Scientific writing as a social act: A review of the literature of the sociology of science. In P. V. Anderson, R. J. Brockmann, & C. Miller (Eds.), *New essays in technical writing and communication: Research, theory and practice.* Farmingdale, NY: Baywood.

Beach, R., & Bridwell, L. S. (1983). Learning through writing: A rationale for writing across the curriculum. In A. Pellegrini & T. Yawkey (Eds.), *The development of oral and written language in social contexts* (pp. 183–198). Norwood, NJ: Ablex Publishing Corp.

Beach, R., & Bridwell, L. S. (Eds.) (1984). Introduction. *New directions in composition research* (pp. 1–14). New York: Guilford.

Behrens, L. (1978). Writing, reading, and the rest of the faculty: A survey. *English Journal, 67*(6), 54–60.

Bereiter, C., & Freedman, M. (1962). Fields of study and the people in them. In N. Sanford (Ed.), *The American college.* New York: Wiley.

Berlin, J. A. (1984). *Writing instruction in nineteenth-century American colleges.* Carbondale, IL: Southern Illinois University Press.

Bernhardt, S. A. (1985). Writing across the curriculum at one university: A survey of faculty members and students. *ADE Bulletin, 82,* 55–59.

Bernier, N. R. (1981). Beyond instructional context identification—Some thoughts for extending the analysis of deliberate education. In J. L. Green & C. Wallat (Eds.), *Ethnography and language in educational settings* (pp. 291–302). Norwood, NJ: Ablex Publishing Corp.

Bernier, N. R., & Williams, J. E. (1973). *Beyond beliefs: Ideological foundations of American education.* Englewood Cliffs, NJ: Prentice-Hall.

Biglan, A. (1973a). The characteristics of subject matter in different academic areas. *Journal of Applied Psychology, 57,* 195–203.

Biglan, A. (1973b). Relationships between subject matter characteristics and the structure and output of university departments. *Journal of Applied Psychology, 57,* 204–213.

Bizzell, P. (1982a). Cognition, convention, and certainty: What we need to know about writing. *Pre/Text, 3*, 213–143.

Bizzell, P. (1982b). College composition: Initiation into the academic discourse community. *Curriculum Inquiry, 12*, 191–207.

Bizzell, P., & Herzberg, B. (1985). Writing-across-the-curriculum textbooks: A bibliographic essay. *Rhetoric Review, 3*(2), 202–216.

Bloom, L. S. (1985). Anxious writers in context: Graduate school and beyond. In M. Rose (Ed.), *When a writer can't write* (pp. 119–133). New York: Guilford.

Brandt, D. (1986). Toward an understanding of context in composition. *Written Communication, 3*, 139–157.

Bridgeman, B., & Carlson, S. B. (1984). Survey of academic writing tasks. *Written Communication, 1*, 247–280.

Britton, J. (1971). What's the use? A schematic account of language functions. *Educational Review, 23*, 205–219.

Britton, J., Burgess, T., Martin, N., McLeod, A., & Rosen, H. (1975). *The development of writing abilities (11–18)*. London: Macmillan Education.

Brown, R. L., Jr., & Herndl, C. (1986). An ethnographic study of corporate writing: Job status as reflected in written text. In B. Couture (Ed.), *Functional approaches to writing: Research implications*. Norwood, NJ: Ablex Publishing Corp.

Clemmons, S. (1980). *Identification of writing competencies needed by secondary students to perform assignments in science and social studies classes*. Unpublished doctoral dissertation, Florida State University.

Colomb, G. C., & Williams, J. M. (1985). Perceiving structure in professional prose: A multiply determined experience. In L. Odell & D. Goswami (Eds.), *Writing in nonacademic settings* (pp. 87–128). New York: Guilford.

Connelly, P. J., & Irving, D. C. (1976). Composition in the liberal arts: A shared responsibility. *College English, 37*, 668–670.

Connors, R. J. (1981). The rise and fall of the modes of discourse. *College Composition and Communication, 32*, 444–455.

Cooper, C. R. (1983). Procedures for describing written texts. In P. Mosenthal, C. Tamor, & S. A. Walmsley (Eds.), *Research on writing: Principles and methods* (pp. 287–313). New York: Longman.

Diamond, C. T. P. (1979a). *The constructs, classroom practices, and effectiveness of grade ten teachers of written expression*. Unpublished doctoral dissertation, University of Queensland.

Diamond, C. T. P. (1979b). *The headwaters: English teachers' constructs of teaching writing*. (ERIC Document Reproduction Service No. ED 198 519)

Dick, J. A. R., & Esch, R. M. (1985). Dialogues among disciplines: A plan for faculty discussions of writing across the curriculum. *College Composition and Communication, 36*, 178–182.

Doheny-Farina, S. (1986). Writing in an emerging organization: An ethnographic study. *Written Communication, 3*, 158–185.

Doheny-Farina, S., & Odell, L. (1985). Ethnographic research on writing: Assumptions and methodology. In L. Odell & D. Goswami (Eds.), *Writing in nonacademic settings* (pp. 503–535). New York: Guilford.

Donlan, D. (1974). Teaching writing in the content areas: Eleven hypotheses from a teacher survey. *Research in the Teaching of English, 8*, 250–262.

Donlan, D. (1980). Teaching models, experience, and locus of control: Analysis of a summer inservice program for composition teachers. *Research in the Teaching of English, 14*, 319–330.

Eblen, C. (1983). Writing across-the-curriculum: A survey of a university faculty's views and classroom practices. *Research in the Teaching of English, 17*, 343–348.

Emig, J. (1977). Writing as a mode of learning. *College Composition and Communication, 28*, 122–128.

Fahnestock, J. (1986). Accommodating science: The rhetorical life of scientific facts. *Written Communication, 3*, 275–296.

Faigley, L. (1985). Nonacademic writing: The social perspective. In L. Odell & D. Goswami (Eds.), *Writing in nonacademic settings* (pp. 231–280). New York: Guilford.

Faigley, L., & Hansen, K. (1985). Learning to write in the social sciences. *College Composition and Communication, 36*, 140–149.

Fillion, B. (1979). Language across the curriculum. *McGill Journal of Education, 14*, 47–60.

Flower, L., & Hayes, J. (1981). A cognitive process theory of writing. *College Composition and Communication, 32*, 365–387.

Freedman, S. W. (1979). How characteristics of student essays influence teachers' evaluations. *Journal of Educational Psychology, 71*, 328–338.

Freisinger, R. (1980). Cross-disciplinary writing workshops: Theory and practice. *College English, 42*, 154–166.

Freisinger, R. (1982). Cross-disciplinary writing programs: Beginnings. In T. Fulwiler & A. Young (Eds.), *Language connections: Writing and reading across the curriculum* (pp. 3–14). Urbana, IL: National Council of Teachers of English.

Fulkerson, R. P. (1979). Four philosophies of composition. *College Composition and Communication, 30*, 343–348.

Fulkerson, R. P. (1984). Kinneavy on referential and persuasive discourse: A critique. *College Composition and Communication, 35*, 43–56.

Fulwiler, T. (1981). Showing, not telling, at a writing workshop. *College English, 43*, 55–63.

Fulwiler, T. (1984). How well does writing across the curriculum work? *College English, 46*, 113–125.

Gere, A. R., Schuessler, B., & Abbott, R. (1984). Measuring teachers' attitudes toward instruction in writing. In R. Beach & L. S. Bridwell (Eds.), *New directions in composition research* (pp. 348–361). New York: Guilford.

Gould, J. D. (1980). Experiments on composing letters: Some facts, some myths, and some observations. In L. W. Gregg & E. R. Steinberg (Eds.), *Cognitive processes in writing* (pp. 97–127). Hillsdale, NJ: Erlbaum.

Griffin, C. W. (1985). Programs for writing across the curriculum: A report. *College Composition and Communication, 36*, 398–403.

Halliday, M. A. K., & Hasan, R. (1980). *Text and context: Aspects of language in a social-semiotic perspective*. Tokyo: Sophia University Press.

Haring-Smith, T., & Stern, L. (1985). Beyond the English department: Writing across the curriculum. In T. Haring-Smith, N. Hawkins, E. Morrison, L. Stern, & R. Tatu, *A guide to writing programs: Writing centers, peer tutoring programs, and writing-across-the-curriculum* (pp. 19–27). Glenview, IL: Scott Foresman.

Herrington, A. J. (1981). Writing to learn: Writing across the disciplines. *College English*, *43*, 379–387.

Herrington, A. (1983). *Writing in academic settings: A study of the rhetorical contexts for writing in two college chemical engineering courses.* Doctoral dissertation, Rensselaer Polytechnic Institute, Troy, NY.

Herrington, A. (1985a). Classrooms as forums for reasoning and writing. *College Composition and Communication*, *36*, 404–413.

Herrington, A. (1985b). Writing in academic settings: A study of the contexts for writing in two college chemical engineering courses. *Research in the Teaching of English*, *19*, 331–361.

Hillocks, G., Jr. (1986). *Research on written composition: New directions for teaching.* Urbana, IL: ERIC/NCRE.

Hirsch, E. D., Jr. (1983). Cultural literacy. *The American Scholar*, Spring, 159–169.

Johns, A. M. (1980). Cohesion in written business discourse. *The ESP Journal*, *1*, n.p.

Jolliffe, D. A. (1985). *Audience, subject, form, and ways of speaking: Writers' knowledge in the disciplines.* (Doctoral dissertation, Univ. of Texas-Austin, 1984). *Dissertation Abstracts International*, *46*, 367A.

Kolb, D. A. (1981). Learning styles and disciplinary differences. In A. W. Chickering (Ed.), *The modern American college* (pp. 232–255). San Francisco: Jossey-Bass.

Kinneavy, J. L. (1971). *A theory of discourse.* New York: Norton.

Kinneavy, J. L. (1983). Writing across the curriculum. *ADE Bulletin*, *76*, 14–22.

Klinger, G. C. (1977). A campus view of college writing. *College Composition and Communication*, *28*, 343–347.

Knoblauch, C. (1980). Intentionality in the writing process: A case study. *College Composition and Communication*, *31*, 153–158.

Kroll, B. M. (1980). Developmental perspectives and the teaching of composition. *College English*, *41*, 741–752.

LaRoche, M. G., & Pearson, S. S. (1985). Rhetoric and rational enterprises: Reassessing discourse in organizations. *Written Communication*, *2*, 246–268.

Lindquist, J. (1978). *Strategies for change.* Berkeley, CA: Pacific Soundings Press.

Lutz, F. W. (1981). Ethnography—The holistic approach to understanding schooling. In J. L. Green & C. Wallat (Eds.), *Ethnography and language in educational settings* (pp. 51–63). Norwood, NJ: Ablex Publishing Corp.

Maimon, E. P. (1979). Writing in the total curriculum at Beaver College. *CEA Forum*, *9*, 7–16.

Marland, M. (1980). *Language across the curriculum.* London: Heinemann.

Marshall, J. D. (1984). Process and product: Case studies of writing in two content areas. In A. N. Applebee, *Contexts for learning to write: Studies of secondary school instruction* (pp. 149–168). Norwood, NJ: Ablex Publishing Corp.

McCarthy, L. P. (1985). A stranger in a strange land: A college student writing across the curriculum. *Dissertation Abstracts International*, *46*, 05A.

McCloskey, D. N. (1983). The rhetoric of economics. *Journal of Economics Literature*, *21*, 481–517.

Merton, R. K. (1957). *Social theory and social structure.* New York: Free Press.

Miller, C. R., & Selzer, J. (1985). Special topics of argument in engineering reports. In L. Odell & D. Goswami (Eds.), *Writing in nonacademic settings* (pp. 309–342). New York: Guilford.

Mishler, E. G. (1979). Meaning in context: Is there any other kind? *Harvard Educational Review*, *49*, 1–19.

Mosenthal, P. M. (1983). On defining writing and classroom writing competence. In P. Mosenthal, L. Tamor, & S. A. Walmsley (Eds.), *Research on writing: Principles and methods* (pp. 26–71). New York: Longman.

Mosenthal, P. M., Davidson-Mosenthal, R., & Krieger, V. (1981). How fourth graders develop points of view in classroom writing. *Research in the Teaching of English*, *15*, 197–214.

Mosenthal, P. M., Conley, M. N., Colella, A., & Davidson-Mosenthal, R. (1985). The influence of prior knowledge and teacher lesson structure on children's production of narratives. *Elementary School Journal*, *85*, 621–639.

Newell, G. E. (1984). Learning from writing in two content areas: A case study/protocol analysis. *Research in the Teaching of English*, *18*, 265–287.

Newell, G. E., Suszynski, K., & Weingart, R. (1986, March). *The effects of writing in a reader-based and text-based mode on students' understanding of two short stories.* Paper presented at the annual meeting of the American Educational Research Association, San Francisco.

Newkirk, T. (1984). How students read student papers: An exploratory study. *Written Communication*, *1*, 283–306.

Notchimson, M. (1980). Writing instruction across the curriculum: Two programs. *Journal of Basic Writing*, *2*, 22–35.

Odell, L. (1985). Beyond the text: Relations between writing and social context. In L. Odell & D. Goswami (Eds.), *Writing in nonacademic settings* (pp. 249–280). New York: Guilford.

Odell, L., & Goswami, D. (1982). Writing in a non-academic setting. *Research in the Teaching of English*, *16*, 201–223.

Odell, L., & Goswami, D. (Eds.). (1985). *Writing in nonacademic settings.* New York: Guilford.

Odell, L., Goswami, D., & Herrington, A. (1983). The discourse-based interview: A procedure for exploring the tacit knowledge of writers in non-academic settings. In P. Mosenthal, L. Tamor, & S. A. Walmsley (Eds.), *Research on writing: Principles and methods* (pp. 221–236). New York: Longman.

Odell, L., Goswami, D., & Quick, D. (1983). Writing outside the English composition class: Implications for teaching and learning. In R. W. Bailey & R. M. Fosheim (Eds.), *Literacy for Life: The demand for reading and writing* (pp. 175–194). New York: Modern Language Association.

Paradis, J., Dobrin, D., & Miller, R. (1985). Writing at Exxon ITD: Notes on the writing environment of an R&D organization. In L. Odell & D. Goswami (Eds.), *Writing in nonacademic settings* (pp. 281–308). New York: Guilford.

Perelman, L. (1986). The context of classroom writing. *College English*, *48*, 471–479.

Perry, W. G., Jr. (1970). *Forms of intellectual development in the college years: A scheme.* New York: Holt, Rinehart & Winston.

Piché, G. L. (1977). Class and culture in the development of the high school English curriculum, 1880–1900. *Research in the Teaching of English*, *11*, 17–27.

Powell, A. (1985). A chemist's view of writing, reading, and thinking across the curriculum. *College Composition and Communication*, *36*, 414–418.

Purves, A. C., & Purves, W. C. (1986). Viewpoints: Cultures, text models, and the activity of writing. *Research in the Teaching of English, 20,* 174–197.

Raimes, A. (1980). Writing and learning across the curriculum: The experience of a faculty seminar. *College English, 41,* 797–801.

Ryle, G. (1949). *The concept of mind.* New York: Barnes & Noble.

Rose, M. (1979). When faculty talk about writing. *College English, 41,* 272–279.

Rose, M. (1985). The language of exclusion: Writing instruction at the university. *College English, 47,* 341–359.

Schank, R. C., & Abelson, R. P. (1977). *Scripts, plans, goals, and understanding.* Hillsdale, NJ: Erlbaum.

Scharton, M. (1983). Composition at Illinois State University: A preliminary assessment. *Illinois English Bulletin, 71,* 11–22.

Schwartz, M. (1984). Response to writing: A college-wide perspective. *College English, 46,* 55–62.

Scribner, S., & Cole, M. (1981). Unpackaging literacy. In M. F. Whiteman (Ed.), *Writing: The nature, development, and teaching of written communication* (vol. 1) (pp. 71–87). Hillsdale, NJ: Erlbaum.

Secor, M., & Fahnestock, J. (1982, July). *The rhetoric of literary argument.* Paper presented at the Penn State Conference on Rhetoric and Composition, University Park, PA.

Selzer, J. (1983). The composing processes of an engineer. *College Composition and Communication, 34,* 178–187.

Sevigny, M. J. (1981). Triangulated inquiry—A methodology for the analysis of classroom interaction. In J. L. Green & C. Wallat (Eds.), *Ethnography and language in educational settings* (pp. 65–85). Norwood, NJ: Ablex Publishing Corp.

Steinmann, M., Jr. (1982). Speech-act theory and writing. In M. Nystrand (Ed.), *What writers know: The language, process, and structure of written discourse* (pp. 291–323). New York: Academic.

Swanson-Owens, D. (1986). Identifying natural sources of resistance: A case study of implementing writing across the curriculum. *Research in the Teaching of English, 20,* 69–97.

Tebeaux, E. (1985). Redesigning professional writing courses to meet the communication needs of writers in business and industry. *College Composition and Communication, 36,* 419–428.

Tierney, R. (1981). Using expressive writing to teach biology. In A. Wotring & R. Tierney (Eds.), *Two studies of writing in high school science.* San Francisco: Bay Area Writing Project. Reprinted in M. Myers (1985), *The teacher-researcher: How to study writing in the classroom* (pp. 149–166). Urbana, IL: NCTE.

Tighe, M. A., & Koziol, S. M., Jr. (1982). Practices in the teaching of writing by teachers of English, social studies, and science. *English Education, 14,* 76–85.

Trimmer, J. F. (1985). Faculty development and the teaching of writing. *WPA: Writing Program Administration, 9,* 11–30.

Walvoord, B. F., & Smith, H. L. (1982). Coaching the process of writing. In C. W. Griffin (Ed.), *Teaching writing in all disciplines* (pp. 3–14). (*New Directions for Teaching and Learning,* No. 12). San Francisco: Jossey-Bass.

Weaver, B. T. (1982). Competency testing and writing program development. In K. L. Greenberg, H. S. Weiner, & R. A. Donovan (Eds.), *Notes from the National*

Testing Network in Writing, October. New York: Instructional Resource Centers, City University of New York.

Weiss, R. H. (1979, November). *Research on writing and learning: Some effects of learning-centered writing in five subject areas.* Paper presented at the annual meeting of the NCTE, San Francisco. (ERIC Document Reproduction Service No. ED 191 073)

West, G. K., & Byrd, P. (1982). Technical writing required of graduate engineering students. *Journal of Technical Writing and Communication, 12*, 1–6.

Willard, C. A. (1983). *Argumentation and the social grounds of knowledge.* University, AL: University of Alabama Press.

Williamson, M. M. (1984). The functions of writing in three college undergraduate curricula. *Dissertation Abstracts International, 45*, 755A.

Wilson, R. C., & Gaff, J. G. (1975). *College professors and their impact on students.* New York: Wiley.

Witte, S. P., & Faigley, L. (1983). *Evaluating college writing programs.* Carbondale, IL: Southern Illinois University Press.

Yates, J. M. (1983). *Research implications for writing in the content areas.* Washington, DC: National Education Association.

Zemelman, S. (1977). How college teachers encourage students' writing. *Research in the Teaching of English, 11*, 227–234.

Zinsser, W. (1986, April 13). A bolder way to teach writing. *New York Times* (Education Life), pp. 58–61.

2 Studying Writers' Knowledge in Academic Disciplines

David A. Jolliffe
Ellen M. Brier

University of Illinois at Chicago

Nearly every researcher who examines writing in schools or colleges at some point must concede that academic settings are far more complex than they initially seem. Witte and Faigley (1983), for example, explain that a researcher can only investigate the effects of a college writing program by taking into account the cultural and social context that influences all writing instruction; the context of the institution housing the actual program; the program's structure, administration, and curriculum; and the actual classroom teaching. Because school contexts are so complex, a researcher who chooses to study writing in academic disciplines, whether the disciplines have programs of actual writing instruction or not, must determine which facets of the context he wants to examine. Faigley, Cherry, Jolliffe, and Skinner (1985) suggest one avenue for research on writing in academic disciplines when they urge scholars to extend their examinations "beyond the relative 'goodness' of [writers'] texts to focus on their knowledge and strategies" (p. xiv).

The purpose of this chapter is to describe, justify, and demonstrate one research method potentially useful, we believe, for examining the nature and development of writers' knowledge in academic disciplines.[1] Our interest lies in the kinds of knowledge that enable a writer in academia to execute processes and to produce written texts that experienced practitioners in an academic discipline deem successful and perhaps even distinctive. We argue in this chapter that a person's participation in the intellectual activities of an academic discipline directly affects his or her acquisition, use, and awareness of these kinds of knowledge. Before demonstrating our research method, we discuss briefly the

---

[1] We would like to acknowledge gratefully the assistance of Roger Chesswas, Cheeling Chan, and Marjorie Powers, and thank Ann Matsuhashi, Victoria Chou Hare, and Mitchell Rabinowitz for helpful readings of drafts.

35

nature of writers' knowledge, set out several dimensions of writers' knowledge on which our research concentrates, and speculate about different kinds of academic disciplines and the ways writers come to know and use a discipline's writing conventions.

WRITERS' KNOWLEDGE: GENERAL AND DISCIPLINE-SPECIFIC

When investigating writers' knowledge, a person takes a different perspective than someone studying writers' processes of composing texts. A person who examines processes usually gives attention either to behaviors writers demonstrate as they write or to writers' self-reports of their writing processes. A person studying writers' knowledge tries to discover, using both observational and text-analytic methods, what writers know that enables them to execute such behaviors (Faigley et al., 1985). Inevitably, studying writers' knowledge requires a researcher to separate and characterize its dimensions, to define the whole by analyzing the parts. One way to analyze writers' knowledge is to characterize it along two general dimensions: competent versus strategic writing, and conscious versus unconscious use of writers' knowledge. Let us examine these two dimensions before we set out the specific components of competent writers' knowledge which our study examines.

Since we designed our research to investigate people learning to write in academic and professional settings, it is appropriate to explain these two dimensions of writers' knowledge as they are manifest in relatively advanced, fluent writers, people who are not struggling to master basic composing skills, but are instead writing or learning to write for their study or work in a particular field. When confronted with writing tasks, such writers draw on several elemental kinds of knowledge just to get a readable, coherent text on the page or the screen. Such knowledge components as, for example, how to abide by the cultural conventions of the written language and how to make logical inferences from texts can be included within a broad interpretation of Chomsky's (1964) definition of basic linguistic competence: "what one knows about language" (p. 915). On the other hand, certain components of a writer's knowledge lead not only to the production of readable and coherent texts, but also to the production of texts that are minimally competent in specific academic or professional situations. To write even minimally competent texts, a writer must draw upon his or her knowledge of a discipline's subject matters, knowledge of the functions written texts serve, knowledge of audience characteristics, knowledge of formatting and stylistic conventions, and so on. Scardamalia and Bereiter (1986) would include such components under the rubric of *expert competence*: the ability to generate more content than one actually needs, the ability to set goals and subgoals for texts, the ability to make and clarify meaning as one writes, and so on. Finally, such knowledge components as how to generate a special kind of insight on a subject, how to add distinctive characteristics to textual formats, how to use a specific kind of rhetorical device in order to impress readers, and so on, seem to lie in a separate realm of expert competence. Let us call these components *writers' strategies*, activities that writers often consciously engage in to achieve not just adequate but, in their minds, distinctive texts for a situation. Suppose, for example, that an experienced writer in the biological sciences wanted to suggest that traditional ways of explaining similarities in tRNA and dRNA molecules were inadequate. He might point out his own special insight into the possible causes of similarities by using rhetorical questions, rather than noun phrases, as subheadings in the discussion section his research report (see Jolliffe, 1984, pp. 201–202). He would be using a writer's strategy to make the text distinctive from conventionally arranged articles on the subject.

The question of whether writers consciously use components of writers' knowledge is particularly difficult. Consciousness appears to be affected both by the writing situation at hand and by the individual writer's experience. First, as Scardamalia and Bereiter (1986) point out, even adult, expert writers seem to exhibit different degrees of awareness from one writing experience to the next in their knowledge of such whole-discourse matters as how to argue a position and how to create a certain text type, as well as in their knowledge of word- or sentence-level linguistic alternatives. Scardamalia and Bereiter echo a similar idea proposed by Chafe (1980), that a writer's consciousness focuses in "spurts of language" as he or she produces a narrative. Second, whether a person consciously activates a certain kind of writers' knowledge seems to depend on his or her experience in a given context. Writers beginning graduate school in one of the natural sciences, for example, even to write a minimally competent paper might need to think consciously about organizing their research reports in the introduction-methods-results-discussion format since they may have had little experience writing entire articles on their own. They may, however, unconsciously use the passive voice throughout their writing, having been socialized in undergraduate school into valuing prose that emphasizes the action accomplished rather than the agent of the action. Foreign students coming to study in an American university might find that knowing how to use the definite article, which most native American speakers seem to do intuitively, is for them a conscious act. The conscious use of writers' knowledge is also affected by anything in the context that calls attention to a knowledge component. Highly experienced journalists might have in their repertoire a store of stylistic devices that they use unconsciously. What for most people would be writers' strategies are for these experienced journalists components of expert competence which they use unconsciously. If an editor calls attention to one of these stylistic devices, the journalists may be aware that they used it, but usually they do not consciously consider them as they write.

The kinds of writers' knowledge we examine would be included within expert competence. Our study is not intended to investigate novice writers just learning how to produce a coherent, readable text. Our research methodology is designed to examine the operations and influences of four interrelated components of competent writers' knowledge that appear to be affected by writing, or learning to write, in an academic discipline. These components are:

- Knowledge of the discipline as a discourse community;
- Knowledge of the subject matters writers in a discipline may write about, the methods writers in the discipline use to investigate subject matters in order to write about them, and the lines of argument or explanation writers employ in their texts;
- Knowledge of the ways writers in a discipline organize, arrange, and format their texts; and,
- Knowledge of the acceptable styles—in general terms, the syntax and diction—that writers in a discipline employ.

Because we consider writing for an academic discipline essentially rhetorical behavior, in which writers are crafting texts to achieve specific effects with readers, we must acknowledge the connection of these four kinds of writers' knowledge to traditional rhetorical tenets. The knowledge of the discipline as discourse community corresponds roughly to the rhetorical concept of *audience*. The knowledge of subject matters and methods of investigation corresponds roughly to *invention*, the knowledge of organization and formats to *arrangement*, and the knowledge of syntax and diction to *style*. As we review the four kinds of knowledge, however, we will point out ways in which our conceptions of them differ from their treatment in rhetorical theory.

These four kinds of knowledge are certainly interrelated. Indeed, the first component, knowledge of the discipline as a discourse community, may be seen as a superordinate category of knowledge under which the other three components fall. For purposes of clarity and explication, let us consider them as separate components of writers' knowledge. In each of the following sections, however, we will point out some specific interrelationships among the four components.

An Academic Discipline as a Discourse Community

To write or learn to write successfully in an academic discipline, we believe the most important kind of knowledge a person must have is knowledge of the intellectual community who will read and pass judgment on his or her work. A writer's knowledge of auditors or readers is surely one of the oldest concerns of communication theory. Rhetorical theorists refer to this concern simply as audience. Yet explanations of audience analysis and accommodation provided by traditional rhetoricians do not match exactly our understanding of how a writer in an academic or professional discipline interacts with other readers in the field. To understand more fully how a writer in a specific field comes to know and interact with readers' knowledge and expectations, we must turn to a body of scholarship that embraces what has been called a social view of writing. A central concept in this scholarship is the idea of a writer's audience as a discourse community.

The traditional rhetorical view of audience is grounded in the notion that a text must change the readers or listeners in some way. This view suggests that a speaker or writer, for each discourse, must determine his or her audience; analyze it by ascertaining its members' knowledge, emotions, beliefs, and so on; and then shape the discourse so that the audience will know, feel, and believe what the speaker or writer wants them to. Aristotle develops this view in the second book of the *Rhetoric*, devoting 10 chapters to the emotions a speaker can arouse in an audience and six chapters to the types of social groups audience members might fall into. Aristotle's treatment emphasizes that the *pathe*, the fundamental components of an audience member's moral constitution, lie dormant until they are activated by the *dynamis* of a speech (see Cope, 1867, pp. 113–116). This Aristotelian view has had strong adherents. Bryant, for example, asserts that "modern enlightenment has produced no method of analyzing an audience which can replace Aristotle's" (1972, p. 18). The determine–analyze–change model has been incorporated into instruction in both technical writing (e.g., Mathes & Stevenson, 1976) and general composition (e.g., Hairston, 1978; Pfister & Petrick, 1980).

A group of researchers influenced by cognitive-developmental psychology has tried to examine and validate the notion of audience embodied in the traditional rhetorical view. Building on the theoretical foundation laid by Piaget (1955), Vygotsky (1962), and Flavell (1968), such researchers as Kroll (1978), Crowhurst and Piché (1979), and Rubin and Piché (1979) have studied children's abilities to assume the existence of another's perspective, analyze the perspective, and adapt communicative strategies to meet it. While some cognitive-developmental researchers (e.g., Rubin, 1984) have tried to expand their field's concept of audience, they still have adhered to the concept's central tenet— namely, that the audience is some general or determinate other in whom the speaker or writer must effect change.

The knowledge of how to determine, analyze, and change an audience does not seem to correspond exactly to the kind of knowledge writers in academic disciplines must possess about their readers. Academic professionals learn about their discourse community as an audience by sharing drafts of their writing and interacting with their peers about the community's knowledge work. For such profesionals who regularly write for a readership of other professionals in a discipline, and for students who are learning to do so, the audience is not solely some other whom the writers have to analyze and change. A writer in an academic discipline often conceives of an audience that is generally in solidarity with him or her, even though it may not immediately deem acceptable everything he or she puts forward. The audience is a community of readers who create and share conventional behaviors: standards of thought, purpose, organization, and style to which writers must adhere. The audience comprises the discipline's *discourse community*, an entity Nystrand (1982), borrowing terminology from sociolinguistics, defines as those people who "may very well *never* speak or write to each other" but who "*could effectively so interact if required* since they know the ways-of-speaking of the group" (p. 15; emphasis in original).

Depending largely on his or her purpose and subject matter, a writer's discourse community can be conceptualized as a series of concentric circles. The largest circle represents all people with whom the writer could conceivably achieve his or her purpose in writing about this subject. The successively smaller circles represent groups or individuals with greater and greater levels of interest and expertise with texts that accomplish similar purposes about similar subject matters. A writer operating within a discipline's discourse community must consider the opportunities and responsibilities for constituting and interpreting experience that each circle embodies.

What kinds of knowledge does the writer use as he or she constitutes and interprets experience? Since knowledge of the discourse community is a superordinate category, the following sections will address that question in detail, but we can generally assert here that, as writers come to understand the audience as a discourse community, they acquire discipline-specific kinds of discourse competence. According to Faigley et al. (1985), when writers understand the nature of a discourse community, they "know what is worth communicating, how it can be communicated, what other members of the community are likely to know about that topic, how members of the community can be persuaded, and so on" (p. 20). Bartholomae (1985) argues that novice writers in universities must come to know "the peculiar ways of knowing, selecting, evaluating, reporting, concluding, and arguing that define the discourse of our community" (p. 134). As they gain experience within a discourse community, writers also learn that successful writing within a discourse community does not involve boldly reporting information or asserting claims and then hoping the audience accepts the data or assertions. As studies by Knorr-Cetina (1981), Gilbert and Mulkay (1980), and Myers (1985) show, successful writers in a discipline negotiate their claims with the discourse community, trying out data and assertions and then revising and reconstructing texts based on the quality of their readers' responses.

Specific groups of writers within discourse communities have drawn a great deal of critical attention in the last two decades. Examining scholars in sociology and mathematics, for example, Crane (1972) refers to networks of "invisible colleges" in which members "were not so much linked to each other directly, but were linked to each other indirectly through . . . highly influential members" (p. 49). In his studies of both literary criticism and jurisprudence, Fish (1980, 1982) consistently invokes the image of *interpretive communities*," groups of scholars who are constrained by their audience to accept certain methods of reading texts and responding to literature.

The process of coming to know one's audience as a discourse community is often difficult, in part because experienced writers in the discipline often do not consciously think about their use of the community-specific kinds of discourse competence and teach them to their students. Bartholomae (1985) describes the difficulties a novice writer in an academic discipline experiences as he or she is required "to appropriate . . . a specialized discourse . . . as though he were comfortably one with his audience, as though he were a member of the academy or an historian or an anthropologist or an economist" (p. 135). One implication of our research, which we discuss in this chapter's conclusion, is that experienced writers in any discipline can help novice writers by consciously initiating them into the use these specialized kinds of discourse competence.

Knowledge of Subject Matters

When students begin to take advanced courses in academic disciplines, ideally they acquire very quickly one specialized kind of writers' knowledge: an awareness of what kinds of subject matters the discourse community allows them to investigate and what kinds of investigations and arguments the community permits them to pursue. English majors/would-be literary critics studying contemporary American fiction in a traditional Department of English, for example, would probably be encouraged to write a paper about the novels of Thomas Pynchon but not about the works of Sidney Sheldon. Students would be taught to examine critically some thematic or formal aspect of the fiction; they would not be expected, though, to evaluate their personal reactions to reading the works.

Every discipline seems to have some level of conventional wisdom about its subject matters and their treatments that writers must come to know. But despite its obvious importance to successful writing in any field, subject knowledge has been largely neglected in writing research. Until recently, this research has largely neglected the influence of context in writing. When writing researchers begin to reintegrate writing and context, it becomes necessary to examine knowledge of subject matters. Scholarship in other fields—particularly rhetoric, psychology, and sociology—has historically been concerned with the ways writers come to know and treat their discipline's subject matters in acceptable ways.

A concern for subject matter treatment was important for rhetorical theorists in antiquity and has returned to prominence in modern rhetorical theory. In ancient Greece and Rome, speakers could be expected to adhere to certain communal conventions of selecting and developing subject matters. A speaker's subject matters were the ones that concerned the life of the *polis*: the topics that would be argued in the legislative assemblies, the cases that were argued in the courts, the subjects that were expounded in speeches on ceremonial occasions. By the time Aristotle wrote the *Rhetoric*, there existed a set of stock arguments and examples that could be inserted anyplace in a speech. Aristotle defined these *topoi* as the "places" or "heads" of arguments, and identified four of them—the possible and impossible, past fact, future fact, and the greater and the less--as universal *topoi*, common to all fields of inquiry. He also listed 28 miscellaneous *topoi*—for example, arguing from definition, or arguing about the whole based on an examination of the parts—from which speakers might form enthymemes, or rhetorical syllogisms. These 28 special lines of argument could also be used to develop subject matters for any political, judicial, or ceremonial speech.

Aristotle makes it clear as well that there are specific *topoi* which are not universal but which are, instead, applicable only in discourses about specialized subject matters. He writes, thus, that "there are propositions in physics from which it is impossible to form an enthymeme or syllogism for ethics, and propositions in ethics from which it is impossible to do so for physics, and so on through all the special subjects" (1932, 1358a).

Aristotle's system of *topoi* was not the only doctrine in classical rhetoric concerned with subject matter treatment. Roman rhetoricians, particularly Cicero and Quintilian, taught a doctrine called *stasis theory*, which directed speakers to examine four questions in any case: Did an act take place? What was the exact nature or definition of the act? What were the component parts or qualities of the act? What court or body should have jurisdiction over this act? Although it was most useful in developing subjects in forensic speeches, rhetoricians attempted to extend stasis theory for use in political and ceremonial discourse as well.

The systems of *topoi* and stasis theory were collected and taught in the Middle Ages and Renaissance, but later rhetoricians began to question their utility as tools for invention. In the sixteenth century, Peter Ramus (1983) turned rhetorical scholars' attention away from systematic attention to subject matter treatment by arguing that rhetoric does not comprise an art of invention but is, instead, merely concerned with style and delivery. A generation later Francis Bacon (1974) saw the *topoi* as useful for calling forth the knowledge a speaker already has, but not for generating new insights. Especially after the rise of associationist psychology and empiricist thought, such British rhetoricians as Adam Smith, George Campbell, and Hugh Blair saw the *topoi* as inimical to originality in rhetorical invention (Howell, 1971). Throughout most of the eighteenth and nineteenth centuries, rhetoricians were not concerned with the systematic and common knowledge a speaker and an audience might have about a subject matter as much as they were fascinated by the "genius" that allowed the speaker to generate idiosyncratic insights about it.

Modern rhetoric has seen a revived interest in the ways speakers or writers come to know and use their community's ways of selecting and developing subject matters. Examining the pragmatics of argumentation, Toulmin (1958) establishes a distinction between the *force* of an argument, which remains invariant no matter what field uses it, and the *criteria* of an argument, which are based on what Toulmin calls "field-dependent" standards of judgment (p. 15). A group of scholars who study what they call *field theory* have extended Toulmin's work. For example, Willard (1983) explains how participants in an "argument field . . . objectify their thinking by testing it against others' views through the most explicit means available to them. Their arguments reveal the judgmental and veridical standards they trust—their trust stemming from, inter alia, the pragmatic results of arguments" (pp. 12–13).

Other modern scholars have been interested in the structure of community-specific methods of developing subject matters. Kinneavy (1971) suggests the existence of a modern set of field-specific topoi, asserting that "in each discipline of the academic world there are particular techniques and methodologies of proof," and adding that "a practitioner of discourse in any given area must be initiated into his unique scientific methods and employ them in discourse in that area" (p. 106). Fahnestock (1986) demonstrates a similar assertion, showing how writers who produce scientific reports for the popular press use different *topoi* than writers who report scientific discoveries in academic journals. Perelman and Olbrechts-Tyteca (1969) maintain that all arguments, even claims about empirical data, begin with shared assumptions about the nature of the world. Perelman and Olbrechts-Tyteca's six *loci*—quantity, quality, order, existence, essence, and person—constitute kinds of *topoi* that guide speakers' or writers' treatments of subject matters. Secor's (1984) analysis of articles published in *PMLA* show how Perelman's loci structure arguments produced in the discourse community of literary scholars.

A body of research in cognitive psychology can also help us understand how writers come to choose and develop their subject matters. A few researchers (e.g., Bereiter & Scardamalia, 1983; Caccamise, 1981; Quinn, 1987) have examined the knowledge structures novice writers display as they generate ideas, and other scholars (e.g., Langer, 1984; Newell, 1984) have investigated the organization of knowledge certain school activities require from students.

More important for our purposes in this chapter, however, are the theoretical statements and studies produced by schema theorists. Although primarily designed to study reading comprehension, investigations of schema theory have shown that writers' mental representations of knowledge can affect both the quality and quantity of their texts. In general, schema theory suggests that writers bring different levels of knowledge to any task. The most general levels, or schemata, represent the writers' general world view based on previous experience. Other schemata, however, are organized into hierarchical subschemata and represent more specific levels of knowledge (Anderson, 1978; Rumelhart & Ortony, 1977). Schallert (1982) demonstrates that schemata develop, becoming more elaborate and specific, with experience. McCutchen (1986) characterizes content schemata as "specific conceptual nodes in a network with labeled links connecting the nodes, links specifying such things as similarity or contrastive relations, or part-to-whole relations" (p. 433).

The application of schema theory to understanding writers' knowledge of subject matters seems clear. A student in social work studying early childhood development, for example, might have only the most general schemata about children and their behavior available to guide his or her writing of case studies. As he or she became more familiar with the kinds of "objective" evidence and conclusions he or she is expected to gather and produce, however, he or she would develop more specific subschemata about the relation between children's behaviors and their physical, social, and emotional development (see Jolliffe, 1984, pp 220–223).

Certain types of schemata are believed to be most important for producing and comprehending writing. Van Dijk (1977) refers to a *frame* as the "set of propositions characterizing our conventional knowledge of some more or less autonomous situation" (p. 99). Schank and Abelson (1977) describe four more specific kinds of schemata: *scripts*, which contain a person's knowledge of the sequence of events in a common experience, such as going to a restaurant; *plans*, which contain a person's knowledge of general actions associated with achieving specific goals; *goals*, which indicate when actual scripts and plans are appropriate; and *themes*, which contain "background information on which we base our predictions that an individual will have a certain goal" (Black, Wilkes-Gibbs, & Gibbs, 1982, p. 334).

Only a few studies have actually demonstrated the way schema theory explains writers' manipulations of their subject matters. Two such studies are noteworthy. Voss, Vesonder, and Spilich (1980) tested 20 people about their knowledge of baseball and divided them into high- and low-knowledge groups. All 20 then were asked to write a narrative about a half-inning of a fictional baseball game. Basing their analyses on the writers' abilities to fill slots in a problem-solving model, the investigators found that the high-knowledge writers produced significantly more specific propositions about causal actions in the game itself, while low-knowledge writers produced significantly more information about activities irrelevant to the game itself, such as fan reaction and crowd size. The researchers concluded that the high-knowledge writers had a larger *problem space* (see Newell & Simon, 1972) and a greater ability to monitor their selected paths through the problem-solving model. In other words, the high-knowledge writers apparently demonstrated their more specific subschemata guiding their treatments of the subject matter they were writing about. They had internalized scripts, plans, and goals about understanding and writing about baseball, and their themes indicated that activating these schemata was appropriate. McCutchen (1986) tested 30 boys in grades 4, 6, and 8 on their knowledge of football and asked them to write a series of narratives and essays about football and about a common-knowledge topic. She found that the students with a high knowledge of football produced more coherent and elaborated texts about football than did the low-knowledge subjects.

Perhaps the area of inquiry that has contributed most strongly to our understanding of the ways writers select and develop subject matters is the sociology of science. Certainly the best known theoretical statements in this area are found in Kuhn's explanations of *normal science* and *paradigms*. Kuhn's early (1962;

revised 1971) definition of paradigms— configurations of "law, theory, application, and instrumentation together" which "provide models from which spring
particular coherent traditions of scientific research" (p. 10)—made clear the
connection between learning a discipline's methods of treating subjects and
participating in the normal science, including writing, of the field:

> The study of paradigms . . . is what mainly prepares the student for membership in
> the particular scientific community with which he will later practice. Because he
> there joins men [sic] who learned the bases of their field from the same concrete
> models, his subsequent practice will seldom evoke overt disagreement over funda-
> mentals. Men whose research is based on shared paradigms are committed to the
> same rules and standards for scientific practice. That commitment and the apparent
> consensus it produces are prerequisites for normal science, i.e., for the genesis and
> continuation of a particular research tradition. (pp. 10–11)

Kuhn's idea that paradigms guide the knowledge work of disciplines has been
widely accepted (for its application to writing research and instruction, see
Young, 1978, and Hairston, 1982), but many scholars faulted Kuhn for using the
term *paradigm* imprecisely. Thus, Kuhn (1977) later clarified two senses of the
term. The first he called the *disciplinary matrix*, intending it to encompass "all
the shared commitments of a scientific group" (p. 294) that come from its
members' common education and apprenticeship. Among the components composing the disciplinary matrix are *symbolic generalizations*, or "those expressions, deployed without question by the group, which can readily be cast in some
logical form"; and *models*, which "provide the group with preferred analogies
or, when deeply held, with an ontology" (pp. 297–298). The second sense of
paradigm Kuhn calls *exemplars*, or "concrete problem solutions accepted by the
group as, in the quite usual sense, paradigmatic" (p. 298).

Other scholars in the sociology of science have suggested knowledge components that might supplement Kuhn's concept of the disciplinary matrix. Both
Price (1965) and Crane (1972), for example, argue that citation patterns in
scientific papers show that writers must know and cite works from a basic corpus
of the literature of their fields. Holton (1965) describes how scientists' data
collection and analyses are influenced by *themata*, or "fundamental presupposi-
tions that are neither objectively observed nor quantified but are remarkably
persistent in scientific thought" (Crane, 1972, p. 30). Gilbert (1976) shows how
a research model suggests which problems are open for investigation, indicates
which theories may be appropriate for the selected problem, points to the techniques and apparatus to be used in the research, and "has an important role in
writing up the research," by suggesting "which kinds of experimental error are
likely to arise, which procedures should be carried out to minimalize error, and
what what eventual margin of error seems acceptable" (p. 285).

Scholars in the humanities and social sciences as well have explained how members of discourse communities share and validate methods of selecting and developing subject matters. Concentrating first on literary criticism and then on law, Fish (1980, 1982) has described how communities of thinkers share strategies that lead them to read and interpret their disciplines' subject matters in similar ways. White (1983) outlines the *cultural syntax* that governs legal writing, the community of writers' "expectations (that) are constantly at work, directing argument, shaping responses, determining the next move, and so on" (p. 139). McCloskey (1983) discounts the idea that economists' investigations are guided solely by the tenets of logical positivism. Instead, he points out that economists base their arguments on "the aptness of economic metaphors, the relevance of historical precedents, the persuasiveness of introspections, the power of authority, the charm of symmetry, [and] the claims of morality" (p. 482). These studies highlight an important point about writers' knowledge of subjects and subject-matter treatment. The tenets that underlie this kind of knowledge may by explicitly stated in the discipline's exemplary texts, or they may be tacitly embedded in the everyday work of the field. Whichever the case, they can be made available for writers' inspection and instruction.

Knowledge of Organization, Arrangement, Form, and Genre

As novice writers are learning to participate in a discipline's discourse community and to select and develop subject matters in its conventionally accepted ways, they are also learning the kinds of organizational patterns, arrangements, forms and genres writing in the discipline must exhibit. Indeed, the two components of writers' knowledge, knowledge of subjects and knowledge of forms and genres, are intimately related. As both Fort (1971) and Coe (1987) point out, the methods writers are able to use to develop their subjects are sharply constrained by the form that their texts must take. Knowledge of organization, arrangement, form, and genre, therefore, has a heuristic function: writers are systematically led to know their subject matters by systematically considering textual form.

For purposes of simplicity, let us reduce our terms in describing this kind of writers' knowledge to two: form and genre. Let us also acknowledge from the outset that writers' knowledge of form and genre is difficult to describe. The source of the difficulty lies in the elusive definitions of the two terms. As Winterowd (1975) points out, "'genre' and 'form' overlap and obscure one another's boundaries" (p. 164). To solve this problem, Winterowd accepts that genre is a textual manifestation of form, which he defines as "the internal set of consistent relationships perceived in any stretch of discourse, whether poem, play, essay, oration, or whatever" (p. 165). Winterowd's emphasis on relationships within the discourse differs from Burke's (1931) reader-oriented emphasis in his famous definition of form. Form, Burke writes, "is an arousing and fulfillment of desires. A work has form in so far as one part of it leads a reader to anticipate another part, to be gratified by the sequence" (p. 124).

Actually, writers' knowledge of form and genre is more than merely the knowledge that superficial text structures both manifest internal relationships and fulfill readers' desires. Writers' knowledge of form and genre grows out of the idea that certain types of texts accomplish specific actions in recurrent situations. Recent research in rhetoric, linguistics, and literary theory demonstrates this point. Rhetorical theorists Campbell and Jamieson (1978) point out that "a genre is a complex, an amalgam, a constellation of substantive, situational, and stylistic elements" (p. 18). They note further that "in the discourses that form a genre, similar substantive and stylistic strategies are used to encompass situations perceived as similar by the responding rhetors" (p. 20). Thus, knowledge of form and genre is closely related both to knowledge of subject matters and to knowledge of ways of speaking, the subject of the following section of this chapter. Miller (1984) takes a similar perspective. According to Miller, the essence of a genre is the social action that a text accomplishes. In typical, recurrent situations, Miller proposes, text types emerge that have a social motive, a specifiable audience, and typical constraints of purpose, content, arrangement, and style. These text types become signficant genres by their nature as action, not as form. Genres thus are essentially pragmatic, not syntactic or formal, entities. In simple terms, then, writers' knowledge of form comprises an understanding that participation in a discourse community puts writers in situations where they must accomplish some action with a written text. These situational calls to action prompt writers to use characteristic, conventional substantive and textual strategies that lead to the action desired. In other words, they lead writers to produce their discourse community's genres.

Text linguistic theory and literary theory offer compatible characterizations of the relation between situation and writers' knowledge of form and genre. Beaugrande (1980), for example, defines a text type as "a distinctive configuration of relational dominances obtaining between or among elements of: (1) the surface text; (2) the textual world; (3) stored knowledge patterns; and (4) a situation of occurrence" (p. 197). Jauss (1982) proposes that literary genres are constituted as readers form "horizons of expectations" against which they can judge the degree of originality or novelty of a text in a "specific situation of understanding" (p. 79).

Because writers' knowledge of form and genre depends so strongly on situational constraints, many concepts about form that students learn in writing classes—where situational context is often ignored—are not germane to learning to write in academic disciplines. Classical rhetoricians were often wont to be prescriptive about the forms and genres of discourse. Isocrates, for example, taught that a speech consisted of four divisions—introduction, narration, proofs, and epilogue—and Cicero urged that an oration ought to incorporate an entrance, a narration, a proposition, a division, a confirmation, a refutation, and a conclusion (see Kinneavy, 1971, p. 264; Cope, 1867). Traditional composition instruction continues to adapt these classical precepts about form. Instructors who teach the methods of development originally codified in the nineteenth century, for example, are teaching classical principles of confirmation, and those who teach students to create such fixed forms as the five-paragraph theme are expanding on the classical concepts of proposition and division (Coe, 1987). The five-paragraph theme is perhaps most prevalent in composition instruction. The influence of this form is so widespread that Emig (1971) refers to it as the "50-Star Theme" (p. 97). There are three problems in teaching students to write using these fixed forms. First, as Hartwell (1979) points out, they represent "mechanical . . . inversions—even perversions—of natural writing processes" (p. 550). Writers rarely choose a subject matter, narrow it to a specific thesis, and find three points to support it. Second, the forms probably have no real use beyond the composition classroom: there is little evidence that writers in any academic discipline ever have to compose five-paragraph themes using established methods of development. Third, and most damning, they are situationally rigid—they do not teach students to produce genres, texts that display the unique configurations of substance and organization that actual, recurrent situations call for.

We should point out instruction in fixed forms, without any consideration of situational demands, is not limited to composition texts and classes. In his extremely popular book on writing a scientific paper, Day (1983) claims that producing a scientific research report "is a question of organization. . . . if the ingredients are properly organized, the paper will virtually write itself" (p. 5).

Even though much writing instruction does not help students see that specific situations call forth accepted genres, there is substantial evidence that novice writers learn some genres and forms from their general reading and writing experiences. The research on story grammars, for example, suggests that young children develop schemata containing their knowledge of the structural properties of stories. Early work on story grammars grew out of both structural anthropology, where scholars found similarly structured stories in different cultures (see Hawkes, 1977) and schema theory. Later research found that these schemata helped readers both to encode and retrieve information from memory (Mandler & Johnson, 1977) and that the schemata were indeed organized around story structure rather than specific content (Thorndyke, 1977; see Black & Wilensky, 1979, for a dissenting view). Rumelhart (1980) claims that nearly all story grammars have the same structure in which "something happens to a protagonist which sets up a goal that must be satisfied. Then the remainder of the story is a description of the protagonist's problem solving behavior in seeking the goal coupled with the results of that behavior" (p. 313).

Researchers in cognitive psychology in recent years have extended theories of story grammars to describe schemata for other kinds of text types. For example, McCutchen (1986) characterizes discourse knowledge as "schemata for various discourse forms, procedures and strategies involved in instantiation of those schemata, and local sentence-generation procedures (including grammatical knowledge)" (p. 432). McCutchen makes it clear, however—as do researchers in other fields, such as Fort (1971) and Coe (1987)—that what she calls discourse knowledge and content knowledge are closely interrelated: "The Content component (determining what will be discussed) interacts with the Discourse component (determining how that discussion will be expressed. . . . The Content component is activated, retrieved, and restructured for use in a given text by procedural or schema knowledge from the Discourse component" (p. 433).

Just as novice writers learn about discourse forms from their general reading and writing experiences, writers or would-be writers in academic disciplines learn principles of genre and form through their experiences reading and writing the valued texts of the discipline. Indeed, scholars in the sociology of science have argued that writers come to know the forms which their discourse communities use as they learn the prevailing ideologies that guide research within these communities.

For example, consider the research article writers in the natural and social sciences often create. Despite some criticism that the scientific article does not faithfully represent the processes that produced it (e.g., Medawar, 1964), many scholars assert that the research article's form is a function of the social and rhetorical structures of scientific disciplines. Gusfield (1976), for example, contends that the structure of social science research articles on drinking and driving consists largely of rhetorical devices demanded by the disciplinary ideology that guides such research. Using the terminology of Burke's (1945) dramatistic pentad, Gusfield concludes that drinking-and-driving research articles keep the agent—that is, the author—largely invisible and instead emphasize the agency of investigation and transformation of scene from the site of the investigation—the laboratory or the highway—to policy-making bodies such as legislatures and social service agencies. Gusfield's analysis shows that the social science research report keeps author-audience and author-subject contact to a minimum, but that frequently the impressive "scenic surrounding"—a learned journal which puts authors' names and university affiliations at the top of the article—and the "neatness" of the agency—the appearance that everything in the investigation went exactly according to plan—lead to a strong rhetorical effect. Moreover, Gusfield contends that the research establishes the drinking driver as a stock villain, while the social drinker is seen as an Everyman character.

Woolgar (1980) argues that the ideology of impersonal and objective research leads successful writers in physics to structure an article so it not only argues a proposition about a physical phenomenon, but also creates the phenomenon for the reader. He explains that "the practical expression of, or reference to, a phenomenon both recreates and establishes anew the existence of the phenomenon. In describing a phenomenon, participants [that is, writers and readers] simultaneously render its out-there-ness" (p. 246). Woolgar analyzes the ways four text structure features work together to effect this necessary negotiation of reality: *preliminary instructions*, such as the title, author, and first paragraph, which establish credibility and set up a tension to be resolved; *externalizing devices*, such as "quasi-passive instructions" and allusions to community membership (e.g., "surely we all know that X is true"), which establish that the unfolding events were both coincidental and unavoidable; *pathing devices*, such as explicit citations and informal allusions, which lead the reader from previous research to the inevitable conclusion; and *sequencing devices*, which keep the reader from considering possible alternative argument paths and explanations. With these kinds of text features as evidence, Woolgar asserts that the logic of scientific discovery is only implicitly conveyed by the text, not explicitly stated. What gives explicit shape to the genre of the physics research article is the discipline's accepted beliefs about impersonal and objective research.

Bazerman (1984) has also shown how the form of scientific discourse emerges from the dominant ideologies of disciplines. In an examination of articles in *Physical Review* from 1893 to 1980, Bazerman charts changes in article length, number and age of citations, word choice, graphic features, and organizational headings, noting developments that show the emergence of authors who want to be "theory-makers" rather than mere reporters of research. Similarly, Gross (1985) argues that the experimental paper is organized in those four sections because it is "an instantiation of a myth that induction is philosophically unproblematic, that it can lead unproblematically to reliable knowledge about natural world" (p. 15).

Knowledge of Ways of Speaking

Strictly from an analytic perspective, perhaps the most salient component of writers' knowledge is style. It is a relatively simple matter to examine texts from any discipline for such features as, say, activity versus passivity of verbs, pronoun reference patterns, sentence structures, or average length of words, phrases, and clauses. As conspicuous as style usually is, however, writers in academic disciplines rarely receive any instruction in the kinds of diction and syntax that members of their discourse community use and value. Instead, writers usually learn to execute the preferred styles of the field unconsciously, through socialization into the community's speaking and writing practices.

To a limited degree—perhaps it was greater in the past than now—writers in academic disciplines have had to know something about the doctrine of fixed styles which has occupied a central place in rhetorical history. According to this doctrine, as set out in the anonymous *Rhetorica ad Herennium*, there are three styles of language: the grand, the middle, and the simple. A speaker should vary his or her style depending upon the purpose, the subject, and the occasion of the discourse. Milic (1975) criticizes the fixed-style doctrine for being "based on a belief in ideas unrelated to their form, on a hierarchy of occasions, . . . on teachability of style from models to the virtual exclusion of individuality, and on the dominance of diction as an expressive feature of style" (p. 30).

Writers in academic disciplines, however, have relatively few opportunities to vary their style to suit their purpose and the occasion. Most writing is done to contribute to the intellectual "conversation," to the knowledge work (Bazerman, 1980; Herzberg, 1986) of the discipline. Moreover, scholars who study writing in the disciplines generally do not accept that style is merely content dressed up. As with form and genre, the syntax and diction of writing in the disciplines directly reflect the ideologies that underlie research in the field.

Writers come to know the preferred styles of their discourse communities, thus, by learning to participate in their *ways of speaking*, a phrase developed as a key concept in sociolinguistics during the past two centuries. Hymes (1972) established the groundwork for the concept by setting out seven components of *communicative events*: (a) a code or codes, intelligible to (b) participants in (c) an event, characterized by (d) a channel or channels, (e) a setting or context, (f) a definite form or shape of the message, and (g) a topic or comment that says something about something (p. 26). Communicative events, thus, can be described in terms of the relationships among, and the capacity and state of, these components. Following Hymes' work, Gumperz (1972) defined a *speech community* as "any human aggregate characterized by regular and frequent interaction by means of a shared body of verbal signs and set off from similar aggregates by significant differences in language use" (p. 219). Gumperz adds that speech communities may be composed of residents of a geographical region, members of occupational associations, or even compatriots of neighborhood gangs. He explains that before one can judge any speaker's intent, one must investigate the norms of appropriateness for the individual's speech community.

These norms of appropriateness, as Hymes points out in *Foundations in Sociolinguistics* (1974), comprise a discourse community's *ways of speaking*, which he defines as "a regulative idea, that the communicative conduct within a community comprises determinate patterns of speech activity, such that the communicative competence of persons comprises knowledge with regard to such patterns" (p. 45). He adds that, in his formulation, *speech* is a surrogate term for all manifestations of language, including writing.

A person becomes competent within a discourse community, therefore, by learning to use its *determinate patterns* of language—its syntax and its diction. Persons outside a discourse community—and, indeed, even some insiders—often derogate the community's use of such language, calling it merely "jargon." But jargon is not merely a stylistic feature. It grows out of writers' knowledge of subject matters and preferences for describing subject matters in specific ways. As Kinneavy (1971) points out, "Jargon . . . nearly always has good intentions—it seeks to establish accuracy and precision of reference. Jargon is often necessary in an age of increasing specialization of esoteric subject fields" (p. 176). Similarly, Lanham (1974), although he pokes fun at specialists' jargon, asserts that a community's lexicon has a binding function: "However stupefying its sound to an outsider, familiarity renders it agreeable to cognoscenti. Familiarity breeds clarity" (p. 80).

Jargon is usually described as a word-level phenomenon, but examinations of writing in different disciplines show that writers must come to know and use syntactic and intrasentential patterns as well. Smith (1979) proposes a model of scientific style in which highly specialized texts are characterized by frequent use of passives, a minimal use of conjunction between clauses and sentences, simple sentence structures, and frequent use of technical terms. Close (1965) asserts that scientific writing must be concerned with accuracy of lexical choice; expressions of impersonal activity, including use of the passive and use of nominal constructions to avoid a personal-sounding verb; and "statements of fact rather than expression through imaginative figures of speech" (p. 8).

The foregoing explanation of writers learning to use their communities' ways of speaking should not be construed as an argument that such writers should be purposefully vague or should forget their obligation to alter their language patterns when writing to those outside their discourse communities. A number of studies show the difficulties inherent in failing to adapt for a new community. For example, Heath (1979) describes the historical contexts in which doctors and lawyers have been taught to use language to hide the truth from their patients and clients. Finegan (1982) explores the difficulties brought about by lawyers who fail to realize that their clients probably do not understand the language of their wills. Campbell and Holland (1982) and Holland and Redish (1981) demonstrate a general concern for the public's ability to understand such documents as contracts, insurance policies, warranties, regulations, and instructions for form.

The communicative difficulties these studies bring to light attest to the binding power of a discourse community's ways of speaking. Successful, active writers in a discipline can become so attached to the community's accepted and expected patterns of syntax and diction that they may fail to remember that other communities have their own language conventions.

LEARNING TO WRITE IN A DISCIPLINE'S DISCOURSE COMMUNITY

Throughout the previous sections, we have repeatedly used variations of the phrase "as a person learns to write in a discipline's discourse community" to lead into our characterizations of writers' knowledge of discourse communities, subject matters, forms and genres, and ways of speaking. The question of *how* one comes to acquire such knowledge, indeed, is as important for understanding writing in academic disciplines as the question of *what* exactly writers know. Using very simple terminology, one could say that a person acquires writers' knowledge through a kind of informal apprenticeship. Certainly, when a person chooses to take specialized studies or undertake work in a discipline, he or she does become socialized into the reading, writing, and intellectual conventions of the field. We intend in this section to describe this socialization process clearly and to try to relate it to the kinds of academic disciplines a person might be exposed to at a university.

One of the most useful characterizations of the processes whereby novices in a discipline acquire writers' knowledge comes from the work of Stephen Toulmin. In *Human Understanding: The Collective Use and Evolution of Concepts* (1972), Toulmin describes how novices in any field come to know the intellectual structure of their discipline and to participate in its activities. Toulmin explains that "the content of a science . . . is transmitted from one generation of scientists to the next by a process of enculturation . . . . The core of the transmit—the primary thing to be learned, tested, put to work, criticized, and changed—is the repertory of intellectual techniques, skills, and methods of representation, which are employed in 'giving explanations' of events and phenomena within the scope of the science concerned" (p. 159). Toulmin later expands this notion of the *transmit* into one of a "constellation of explanatory procedures" which include "(1) the language (both nouns— technical terms or concept names—and also sentences, whether natural laws or straightforward generalizations), (2) the representation techniques, and (3) the application procedures of the science" (pp. 160–161). The first two elements, according to Toulmin, cover the symbolic activities of "giving explanations." The third covers the ability to recognize situations where those symbolic activities are appropriate.

We see a correspondence between our components of writers' knowledge and these elements. Toulmin's concept of language as comprising both the field's concepts and the laws and generalizations about those concepts roughly corresponds to our category of knowledge of subject matters. Toulmin's concept of representation techniques embraces our categories of knowledge of form and genre and knowledge of ways of speaking. Toulmin's concept of application procedures relates both to our category of knowledge of subjects and to our notion of knowledge of the discipline as a discourse community. Knowledge of application procedures would lead a person to understand the basic nature of intellectual transactions within the field and the kinds of treatments of subjects that are appropriate.

Toulmin makes it clear that a discipline's constellation of explanatory procedures should neither be seen as a static entity nor be considered a set of tools to be employed passively. He points out that the explanatory procedures, like the discipline itself, must evolve over time. Toulmin writes that "during his scientific enculturation, the apprentice physicist or biologist learns not only how to explain phenomena within the scope of his science by applying its existing concepts; he also learns what is involved in criticizing those concepts and so improving its current content. Indeed, learning one without the other— learning how to apply an existing repertory of concepts without learning what would compel us to qualify or change them—does nothing to make a [person] a scientist at all" (p. 165).

Most importantly, Toulmin emphasizes that the operative concepts of a discipline—that is, the core of the transmit from one generation of workers to the next—assume significance only through their use, which must be in the form of a public display (a *Darstellung*); the apprentice cannot just assume he or she has an intuitive, personal knowledge (a *Vorstellung*) of the transmitted concepts. The display, moreover, must be in the form of words and sentences: "to the extent that the content or knowledge can be specified only in judgemental or grammatical forms, that which is 'known' . . . is not an object independent of human thought, but a linguistically structured fact or proposition" (p. 196). In other words, to acquire the kinds of writers' knowledge that experienced participants in a discipline have, a novice must write about the discipline's subjects, using its genres and its preferred styles. Abstract instruction about these kinds of knowledge, although it can focus novices' attention on them, will not suffice—the novices must actually write.

Although Toulmin couches his discussion of an apprentice's enculturation into a discipline in terms of the natural science communities, he makes it clear that the process he defines can operate in any intellectual field. He points out that that nothing "limits the scope of 'disciplined' inquiry to the natural sciences. The phrase 'scientific discipline' is not a tautology; nor need the agreed goals of a collective human enterprise in all cases be explanatory ones. On the contrary, the existence of agreed, communal goals of (e.g.) a practical or judicial kind can create the basis for disciplinary activities of non-scientific kinds; to that extent, law or technology can provide fields for the rational development of improved collective procedures, quite as legitimately as science" (p. 359). No matter what field of the arts, sciences, humanities, or technologies a student chooses to enter, he or she is enculturated by writing within the discipline's discourse community.

Some kinds of disciplines obviously have more clearly defined—and more clearly communal—intellectual goals and activities than others, and this variation affects the efficiency with which, and even the degree to which, novices can come to understand and use writers' knowledge in the field. Toulmin addresses this concern by classifying disciplines—he calls them "rational enterprises"—based on the kinds of "collective ideals" they display. The most efficient of these enterprises are the *compact disciplines*, which Toulmin claims include most of the natural sciences. In compact disciplines, "activities . . . are organized around and directed towards a specific and realistic set of agreed collective ideals," which "impose corresponding demands on all who commit themselves to the professional pursuit of the activities concerned." Accordingly, "resulting discussions provide disciplinary loci for the production of 'reasons,' . . . and so improve the current repertory of concepts and techniques" (p. 379). Toulmin acknowledges that not all compact disciplines are equally compact: some develop and operate more sporadically than others.

Toulmin describes two other kinds of disciplines that differ from compact disciplines. A *would-be discipline,* he explains, "can presuppose no agreed aims, ideals, or standards." As a result, "the theoretical debate in the field becomes largely—and unintentionally—methodological or philosophical; inevitably, it is directed less at interpreting particular empirical findings than at debating the general acceptability (or unacceptability) of rival approaches, patterns of explanation, and standards of judgment" (pp. 380–381). Toulmin asserts that many of the behavioral sciences can be characterized as would-be disciplines. A *quasi-discipline* exists where "the nature of the case neither imposes an agreed body of disciplinary ideals, nor calls for a set of collective procedures, [and] the task of arriving at "rational" judgments is liable—for understandable reasons—to be subtle and debatable" (p. 396). Toulmin notes that literature and the fine arts, for example, are quasi-disciplines because the goals which direct their activities are not communal or collective, but personal.

The strength of collective ideals is, of course, only one aspect of the intellectual transmit through which novices are enculturated into a discipline. In terms of the four components of writers' knowledge we have outlined, the strength of a discipline's collective ideals probably affects most strongly a person's knowledge of the discipline as a discourse community and knowledge of subject matters. But even in what Toulmin calls quasi-disciplines, it seems that there are conventional, if not universally collective, ways of choosing and developing subjects, organizing texts, and executing styles.

Another variable that affects the ways novices acquire writers' knowledge is the extent to which professionals in the discipline believe it is necessary to train novices specifically to accomplish the discipline's work. A college or university education has many purposes, only one of which is actually to prepare students to hold some specific job. But in addition to liberally educating students, a college or university education is seen as the initial agency for professional socialization (Parsons & Platt, 1972), and students in different disciplines acquire the tools they need for working in a field in varying degrees. In some fields, labeled by Etzioni (1969) as the "semi-professions," students need only a baccalaureate degree to get an entry-level profession. One distinguishing feature of these fields—for example, nursing, elementary and secondary teaching, and business—is the "crowded curriculum" (Brier, 1985) which provides little or no opportunity for students to take courses not related to their professional training. While writing in the discipline is often not a part of the instruction students in these fields receive, they would seem to be in a better position than novices in other fields to learn the intellectual concepts— especially the knowledge of subjects, forms and genres, and ways of speaking—that writing in their discipline demands.

A METHODOLOGY FOR STUDYING WRITERS' KNOWLEDGE IN THE DISCIPLINES

To examine the consequences of our assumptions about the ways writers in academic disciplines learn and use their discourse communities' methods of choosing and developing subjects, organizing texts in forms and genres, and executing styles, we developed a task that allows us to study the relationships that prevail among these components of writers' knowledge and writers' abilities to produce texts that experienced members of their discipline deem successful. In this section, we explain how we developed this task and tested it in a pilot study.

Our task requires participants to read a characteristic text from their field, to indicate their level of experience reading and writing such texts, to evaluate a number of the text's features, and to write an abstract of the text as if they were abstracting it for other members of their discourse community. As we developed and administered the task, we were guided by the following research questions:

- What are the relationships between a writer's levels of experience and education in a discipline and his or her ability to write a successful text for the field's discourse community?
- What are the relationships between a writer's experiences specifically reading and writing texts in his or her discipline and his or her ability to write a successful text for the field's discourse community?
- What are the relationships between a writer's evaluation of a discipline-specific text's treatment of a subject matter, organization, and style and his or her ability to write a successful text for the field's discourse community?
- What are the relationships between a writer's knowledge of a characteristic subject matter in his or her discipline and his or her ability to write a successful text for the field's discourse community?

We intentionally designed our instrument to elicit what Spivey (1983) calls a "hybrid task," one that involves both reading and writing. We did so for two reasons. First, writers in academic disciplines rarely have the opportunity to write about subject matters that are strictly personal knowledge. On the contrary, they generally write about those subjects that form part of what Toulmin calls the "language" of their rational enterprise—the concept names and key terms participants in the field read and write about. Second, writers in academic disciplines, like all people, are constructive readers. As they read, they construct what Beaugrande (1980) calls a "textual world," or "the cognitive correlate of the knowledge conveyed and activated by a text in use" (p. 24). Assuming that students and practitioners in a discipline must read many of the same texts— and evidence shows that, at least in some fields, they do (Price, 1965)—this creation of textual worlds through constructive reading comprises a vital part of the process of disciplinary enculturation described in the previous section.

The reading portion of the task, thus, contained a text about one of a discipline's characteristic subject matters. The writing portion called for the participants to produce an abstract of the text. The abstract appears to be an appropriately generic, yet sufficiently discipline-specific, text type to be used in a study of writers' knowledge in academic disciplines. Bloom, Englehart, Furst, Hill, and Krathwhol (1956) include summarizing—or "the ability to translate a lengthy part of a communication into briefer or more abstract terms" (p. 92)—within the category of comprehension in their taxonomy of six intellectual abilities within the cognitive domain. Textbooks in different disciplines (e.g., Barrass, 1978, in the natural sciences; and Steward & Smelstor, 1984, in the social sciences) frequently include sections on how to write an abstract.

We administered versions of this task to groups of student writers in two fields, nursing and political science. We chose these two fields because we suspected that their processes of disciplinary enculturation differ significantly. Nursing is a clear example of what Etzioni (1969) calls a "semi-profession," a field in which students are trained specifically in a baccalaureate program to work in well defined entry-level jobs upon graduation. Programs in political science, on the other hand, usually make no claims about training students to move into specific jobs once they graduate. While the study of political science is seen as a useful prelude to working in business or government or pursuing graduate work in law or public policy, it is characteristically a field in which students can take courses, if they choose, solely to learn more about our society's political structures. One might suspect the components of writers' knowledge to be more clearly defined, and students more specifically enculturated, in nursing than in political science. Part of our results, reported below, bear out that suspicion.

We must reiterate that our application of the task with nursing and political science students amounts only to a pilot study. In both fields, the number of participants was relatively small, so the question of the statistical significance of our findings may be moot. In addition, we administered only one task to participants, so we cannot claim to have controlled for any possible differences that might have resulted had we used a second or third text. Finally, we did not attempt to control for discipline-specific knowledge by administering the nursing variant to political science students, and vice versa. Our results, therefore, are more descriptive than explanatory. Despite these reservations, and because our purpose in this chapter is to demonstrate a methodology, we see in our task a promising direction for future research on learning to write in academic disciplines.

Methods

Developing the instrument.   Our first step was to hire a faculty consultant in both of the target fields, nursing and political science. We told each of the consultants that we needed to find an article from his or her field's professional literature that met four criteria: (a) it was about a subject matter that articles in the discipline treat relatively often; (b) it represented a characteristic text type—a genre that appears frequently in the professional literature and that students might be expected to learn how to produce; (c) it represented a level of conceptual difficulty that students in upper-division undergraduate classes in the field might be expected to encounter; and (d) it was brief enough for participants to read at a normal pace in 15 minutes. Because we had to rely on volunteers in classes, our entire task could take no more than 1 hour.

In collaboration with the specialist consultants, we selected for the nursing variant of the instrument an article from the *Western Journal of Nursing Research* about a hypertension screening clinic in the Seattle schools. For the political science variant, we chose an article from *Western Political Quarterly* about characteristics of candidates in nonpartisan municipal elections. We changed the name of the authors of the articles on the outside chance that one of the participants might know the previous work of the author and therefore be biased in his or her evaluation of the text. Otherwise, we typed the article exactly as it had appeared in the journals. The participants, therefore, read a typescript version, rather than a photocopy of the article as it was published in the journal. We wanted the participants to read the text as just that—a finished text, not a published article from a journal. The nursing and the political science variant of the instrument are reproduced in Appendix A and Appendix B, respectively.

Subjects.   We administered the instruments to two groups of student writers. We administered the nursing variant to fifteen students who were taking their first group of undergraduate courses as nursing majors. These students all had completed the equivalent of two years of general undergraduate studies and were just beginning the nursing curriculum. In addition, we administered the instrument to 10 students who were taking a seminar in the Ph.D. program in our university's College of Nursing. We administered the political science variant to 20 students, mostly sophomore and juniors, in an introductory political science course for prosective majors. In addition, we administered the instrument to 10 students in a master's level seminar in political science. In both fields, therefore, we had participants relatively unaccustomed to reading and writing the discipline's texts and participants who had greater experience in the field.

Data collection procedures.   Participants in each of the four groups—beginning and advanced students in nursing and political science—completed the task during 55-minute sessions in their regular classrooms. A proctor carefully controlled the timing of each segment of the task.

In the first segment, lasting 5 minutes, partipants were asked to provide a range of demographic data: their age, the highest academic degree they hold, their current level of study, their major field, whether and how long they have held a job in their major field, and whether and how long they have taught in their major field. In the second segment, participants engaged in a free-association exercise originally developed by Langer (1981) to assess students' levels of prior knowledge about a subject before they read about it. For each of our two variants, our specialist consultants had provided us with a key term which named the main subject matter of the text and under which the article might be indexed: for the nursing article, the key term was *hypertension*, and for the political science article it was *local government form*. Following Langer's methodology, we directed participants to spend 5 minutes simply writing "the first thoughts that come to your mind when you hear the word, HYPERTENSION (or LOCAL GOVERNMENT FORM)." We instructed them not to be concerned about writing grammatically correct sentences. We then instructed participants to spend 10 minutes reflecting on their initial associations and to "write an explanation of what made you think of the words, phrases, and ideas you wrote in response to the" given key term.

In the third segment of the task, participants were given 15 minutes to read the article at their "normal reading pace." All participants in the four groups were able to complete the article in the allotted time. The fourth segment of the task required participants to report, on five-point Likert-type scales, how frequently they wrote and read articles that treated similar subject matters, had similar formats, and displayed levels of vocabulary similar to the article they had just read. The fifth segment instructed participants to evaluate the text as if they were to use it for their own study and research: they were asked to evaluate the appropriateness of the text's treatment of the subject, its format, and its level of vocabulary. Segments four and five together took 5 minutes. The final segment of the task, which required 15 minutes, directed participants to assume they were "the editorial assistant for a journal in which the text will be published" and to "write an abstract of the text that will appear between the author's name and the first paragraph of the text itself."

Data analysis procedures. The task generates a rich array of information. To reduce our data to a manageable level, we chose in this study not to examine specific stylistic features of the abstracts, such as patterns of active and passive verbs, pronoun use, nominalizations, and modification structures. We initially quantified and coded the writers' demographic data, their reports of their levels of reading and writing experiences, and their evaluations of the text's subject treatment, form, and vocabulary. Examining the remaining information required hiring and training raters from the two disciplines, nursing and political science. These trained raters—all of whom taught in the disciplines—provided three measures. First, two raters assessed the abstracts in a quasi-holistic fashion, rating them on a one-to-four, lowest-to-highest scale. The raters were trained to use two criteria: how faithfully the abstract captured the gist of the original text, and how closely the abstract resembled an abstract one would find in the professional literature of the field. Any abstract for which the raters disagreed by more than one point was given to a third rater for adjudication.

Second, two raters considered each participant's free associations and initial reflections on the key term as a single entity and rated it according to the level of prior knowledge about the subject matter that it demonstrated. Raters were given guidelines for judging responses adapted from Langer (1981):

> LEVEL ONE (little prior knowledge) responses are dominated by the following kinds of items:
> a. Prefixes, suffixes, and root words related to the concept.

b. Words that sound like the concept.
c. First-hand, but irrelevant, experiences with the concept.

LEVEL TWO (some prior knowledge) responses are dominated by the
following kinds of items:
a. Examples of the concept.
b. Attributes of the concept.
c. Defining characteristics of the concept.

LEVEL THREE (much prior knowledge) responses are dominated by the
following kinds of items:
a. Superordinate concepts that include the concept.
b. Definitions of the concept.
c. Analogies or other kinds of links of the concept with another concept.

So, for example, if a writer in political science generated a preponderance of
tautological statements like "local government form is the form of local government," or if he or she alluded repeatedly to his or her own impressions of, say,
Chicago politics, then the free association and explanation would have received a
rating of 1. A free association and explanation dominated by such statements as
"local government form can include city councils and city managers" or "local
government elections usually draw lots of candidates" would have received a
rating of 2. A free association and explanation that tried to link local government
structures to state or national structures, or that defined local government form as
any political body that provides governance of a village, town, city, county,
district, or borough, would have received a rating of 3.

Finally, two raters examined the distribution of information in the abstracts in
a manner suggested by the work of the Czech textlinguist Jiri Janos, who provides an analytic system for describing the organization of an abstract in relation
to the original text it summarizes. Janos (1979) extends the theory of functional
text perspective, which holds that a sentence can be divided into a *theme*, which
provides "given" or "old" information—the "topic" of the sentence—and a
rheme, which provides "new information"—that which is said about the topic.
Attempting to develop a procedure for automatic abstracting, Janos proposes a
"general theoretical perspective for 'Functional *text* perspective'" in which "we
can identify portions of the text as a whole which in fact summarize that 'what is
spoken about in the text' and that 'what is said about it here'" (p. 22). Janos'
theory provided categories into which raters were trained and instructed to
classify each of the t-units of the abstracts:

T (Theme). This unit refers directly to the main subject of the actual
research reported—the study involving a hypertention screening clinic
in the nursing variant and the study of socioeconomic status of nonpartisan city council candidates in the political science variant.

ET1 (Extended Theme 1). This unit characterizes a broader background of the subject, what has been written about it by other authors, what is commonly known about it, etc.

ET2 (Extended Theme 2). This unit generally characterizes the article's *general* approach to the solution of problems. This category includes such statements as "This article gives lots of ideas about hypertension" or "It provides lots of facts about local government form."

ER1 (Extended Rheme 1). This unit describes the hypothesis of the research.

ER2 (Extended Rheme 2). This unit describes the methodology used in the research.

ER3 (Extended Rheme 3). This unit describes a justification for, and shows an illustration of, the methodology used in the research.

R (Rheme). This unit describes results or conclusions of the research.

AT (Antetheme). This unit characterizes ideas for further research, based on the conclusions of the present research.

M (Metacommentary). This unit accomplishes none of the functions described above, but instead comments on the level of interest, worth, or usefulness of either the article or the author.

Janos' characterizations of portions of argumentative text structures did not include the last of the categories, metacommentary. We had to add the category to accommodate the presence of metacommentary in so many of the abstracts, a phenomenon we comment on below.

Any t-unit on which the two raters did not initially agree about which category it represented was submitted for discussion and adjudication by the two raters and the researchers. For the political science abstracts, the raters initially agreed on 66.6% of the t-units, so 33.3% were resolved through adjudication. For the nursing abstracts, raters initially agreed on 64.78% of the t-units, so 35.22% were adjudicated.

Since we were consistently interested in what kinds of knowledge successful writers use, we calculated a number of measures relative to the participants' abilities to produce effective texts, as indicated by the sum of the two holistic scores assigned to their abstracts. We determined what variables showed a significant, positive correlation with the summed holistic score. We divided the participants into groups of relatively successful and unsuccessful summarizers. Among the nursing participants, relatively unsuccessful summarizers were those whose abstracts received a summed holistic score of 2 or 3, and relatively successful summarizers were those whose abstracts received summed holistic scores of 6, 7, or 8. Among the political science participants, relatively unsuccessful summarizers were those whose abstracts received summed holistic scores of 2 or 3, and relatively successful summarizers were those whose abstracts received summed holistic scores of 5, 6, 7, or 8. We chose these values to form groups of approximately the same numbers of participants. With these groups established, we ran t-tests, cross-tabulations, and one-way analyses of variance to see how the two groups in each discipline differed. We ran multiple regression analyses to determine which of the variables that reported the participants' levels of experience with similar texts and their evaluations of the sample text significantly predicted a higher summed holistic score. Finally, we studied the distribution of thematic and rhematic material in the abstracts and tried to determine in a more qualitative fashion what constituted a successful abstract to the raters from the disciplines.

Results.   The summed holistic scores of the 30 participants in political science positively and significantly correlated with seven variables:

- the frequency with which participants wrote texts with similar formats (.3659, p = .023);
- the frequency with which participants wrote texts with similar levels of vocabulary (.4012, p = .014);
- the frequency with which participants read texts on similar subjects (.5635, p = .001);
- the frequency with which participants read texts with similar formats (.5253, p = .001);
- the frequency with which participants read texts with similar levels of vocubulary (.5505, p = .001);
- the number of t-units in the abstracts (.5505, p = .001);
- the number of words in the abstracts (.6510, p = .000).

The summed holistic scores of the 25 participants in nursing positively and significantly correlated with three variables:

- the summed score of the two raters' assessments of level of knowledge, as reflected in the free associations and explanations (.4393, p = .014);
- the number of t-units in the abstracts (.5628, p = .007);
- the number of words in the abstracts (.8094, p = .000).

The summed holistic scores of the nursing students' abstracts showed one significant negative correlation, with the degree to which the participants evaluated the article's treatment of the subject matter as appropriate for their own level of study and research (−.6121, p = .001).

T-tests showed that the relatively successful and unsuccessful writers of abstracts differed significantly in the mean number of t-units per abstract and in the mean number of words per abstract. The relatively unsuccessful writers in political science (n = 12) produced a mean 2.83 t-units per abstract (standard deviation = 1.348), while the relatively successful (n = 10) writers produced 5.6

t-units per abstract (standard deviation = 1.302); the two groups differed (t = −3.79) at the .001 level. The relatively unsuccessful writers in political science produced a mean of 53.91 words per abstract (standard deviation = 25.31), while the relatively successful writers produced 97.00 words per abstract (standard deviation = 29.36); the two groups differed (t = −3.61) at the .002 level. The relatively unsuccessful writers (n = 9) in nursing produced a mean 2.88 t-units per abstract (standard deviation = 1.202), while the relatively successful writers (n = 8) produced a mean 5.62 t-units per abstract (standard deviation = 2.118); the two groups differed (t = −3.60) at the .003 level. The relatively unsuccessful writers in nursing wrote a mean 41.77 words per abstract (standard deviation = 9.654), while the relatively successful writers wrote a mean 114.75 words per abstract (standard deviation = 27.081); the two groups differed (t = −7.59) at the .000 level.

Cross-tabulations accompanied by the Fisher's exact test showed that the two groups of participants in nursing differed signficantly in the highest degree held and the current level of study. Of the relatively unsuccessful writers, seven held an associate degree or no post-secondary degree and two held a bachelor's degree or higher, while all eight of the relatively successful writers held a bachelor's degree or higher. The two groups differed on this dimension at the .002 level. Of the relatively unsuccessful writers, eight were undergraduate students and one was a graduate student, while of the relatively successful writers one was an undergraduate and seven were graduate students. The two groups differed on this dimension at the .003 level.

A one-way analysis of variance showed that the relatively successful and unsuccessful writers in nursing differed significantly on the level of subject-matter knowledge, while the two groups of writers in political science did not. The relatively unsuccessful writers in nursing showed a mean score of 4.33 on

Table 1.   Functions and Distribution of T-Units in Political Science Abstracts

Group 1 = Relatively Unsuccessful (n = 12)			Total T-Units = 34	
Group 2 = Relatively Successful (n = 10)			Total T-Units = 56	
FUNCTION	# IN 1	% IN 1	# IN 2	% IN 2
T: Subject	10	29.41	11	19.64
ET1: Background on subject	4	11.76	6	11.11
ET2: General approach	1	2.94	4	7.14
ER1: Hypothesis	1	2.94	6	11.11
ER2: Describes methodology	3	8.82	4	7.14
ER3: Justifies methodology	0	0.00	1	1.78
R: Results	5	14.70	22	39.28
AT: Implications	0	0.00	1	1.78
M: Metacommentary	10	29.41	1	1.78

the level of knowledge measure, while the relatively successful writers showed a mean score of 5.13. The two groups differed (F = 5.791) at the .029 level.

Multiple regression analyses of the six variables reporting participants' levels of experience with similar text and three variables reporting their evaluations of the sample text showed only one significant predictor of success in writing an abstract. Among the writers from political science, the frequency with which participants read texts on similar subjects predicted a high summed holistic score (t = 2.849) at the .008 level.

The two groups of relatively unsuccessful and relatively successful writers in political science and nursing showed some noticeable differences in the distribution and patterns of thematic and rhematic material among t-units. Table 1 shows the distribution in the abstracts of the two groups of student writers in political science.

Neither the relatively unsuccessful nor the relatively successful abstracts in political science showed any distinctive patterns of thematic- and rhematic-material distribution. Among the 12 relatively unsuccessful abstracts, three showed an adjacent linkage of T-R, or subject followed by results. Two of those three abstracts put the T-R adjacent linkage in the first two t-units of the abtract. Two other relatively unsuccessful abstracts put an adjacent linkage of T-ET1, or subject followed by background material on the subject, in the first two t-units of the abstracts. Among the 10 relatively successful abstracts, two show the pattern of T-ER2-R, or subject followed by methodology followed by results.

Table 2 shows the distribution of thematic and rhematic material in the relatively unsuccessful and relatively successful abstracts of the nursing student writers.

Both the relatively unsuccessful and the relatively successful abstracts of the nursing student writers showed discernible patterns. Among the nine relatively

Table 2.   Functions and Distribution of T-Units in Nursing Abstracts

FUNCTION	# IN 1	% IN 1	# IN 2	% IN 2
Group 1 = Relatively Unsuccessful (n=9) Group 2 = Relatively Successful (n=8)			Total T-Units = 26 Total T-Units = 45	
T: Subject	7	26.92	13	28.88
ET1: Background on subject	4	15.38	0	0.00
ET2: General approach	8	30.76	1	2.22
ER1: Hypothesis	0	0.00	0	0.00
ER2: Describes methodology	0	0.00	22	48.88
ER3: Justifies methodology	0	0.00	0	0.00
R: Results	3	11.53	5	11.11
AT: Implications	1	3.84	1	2.22
M: Metacommentary	3	11.53	2	4.44

unsuccessful abstracts, three showed a pattern of T-ET2, or subject followed by an allusion to the article's or the author's general approach to solving problems. One additional abstract in this group showed the T-ET2 pattern interrupted by R, or results. Among the eight relatively successful abstracts of the nursing article, four showed a pattern of T-ER2-R, or subject followed by methodology followed by results.

Discussion

We must immediately qualify our discussion of the results of this pilot study by reiterating three reservations: We worked with very small numbers of participants; we made no effort to control for the effect of the text we used in the task; and we made no effort to control for subject-matter knowledge by assigning the nursing task to political science students and vice versa. Consequently, our results show correlations between different components of writers' knowledge and the ability to produce a successful text, but we cannot claim that the results show causal links.

Even accepting these qualifications, however, we believe the results suggest that writers who produce successful texts in these two fields apparently have internalized principles of two components of writers' knowledge described earlier in this chapter, knowledge of subject matters and investigative strategies and knowledge of formats and organization of texts. These differences, in turn, suggest a few noteworthy distinctions between the two types of academic fields we chose to examine in this study.

This pilot study clearly suggests an obvious conclusion, specifically that education and experience with a discipline's texts lead to successful writing in the field. The results from political science showed a number of significant, but relatively weak, correlations between the participants' experiences writing and reading texts similar to the one used in the task and their ability to write a successful abstract of that text. Certainly such correlations are predictable, and their absence in the results from nursing is curious. Perhaps because many of the nursing students among the novice group selected for the study already held associate's degrees in nursing, while many of the novice writers in political science were taking their first course in the field, both the novice and advanced participants in nursing had more similar levels of experience with such texts than did the political science participants. Equally predictable in the nursing results are the findings that the relatively successful writers held higher degrees and were at more advanced levels of study than the relatively unsuccessful writers.

The most noticeable differences suggested by the correlations and the t-tests are that writers whose texts apparently succeed in a discipline produce longer texts with more t-units than writers whose texts do not succeed. This finding merely reiterates similar conclusions reached by other researchers (for a review, see Nold & Freedman, 1977), who consistently find that writers who receive higher holistic scores almost always write longer texts. Moreover, this finding really contributes nothing to our effort to examine "beyond the relative 'goodness' of [writers'] texts (and) to focus on their knowledge and strategies" (Faigley et al., 1985, p. xiv).

Several elements of this pilot study's results, however, do enable us to examine the role of writers' knowledge in leading to successful writing in an academic field. Three findings in particular suggest the importance of writers' becoming enculturated into a knowledge of their field's subject matters and investigative strategies, or what Toulmin refers to as the discipline's language and application procedures.

First, the analysis of variance showed that the relatively successful writers in nursing differed significantly from the relatively unsuccessful writers in their level of prior knowledge about hypertension, the subject of the article used in the task. Using Langer's (1981) categories for assessing prior knowledge as guidelines, we can speculate that the relatively successful writers had more highly organized knowledge about hypertension. They were more able to link it to superordinate or parallel concepts, or to provide more precise definitions of it than the relatively unsuccessful writers were. For example, notice the linking, associative nature of the following excerpt from a nursing student's explanation of her free association, which received a 3 from both raters. This excerpt follows almost two pages of individually listed words and phrases about hypertension.

> The associated words have some relation to health. Physiologic health is represented via such ideas as the etiology of hypertension and some management methods. Psychologic health was also represented by words indicating affective states. Management techniques involving life style changes were documented. A consideration for the individual hypertensive's health beliefs was also shown. Essentially, looking at it in retrospect the words associated with hypertension represent an overview of the nusring process—assessment, diagnosis, plans, intervention, evaluation. In some ways, then, the supposedly free association can be seen to fit into a pattern of thinking I first learned and developed 8 years ago, as a beginning nursing student. I have used this same thinking process regularly since—not only in the direct context or application of nursing, but also in my general life as well.

This student writer is not only able to think about her subject consciously, but she is able to think about her thinking—to categorize her knowledge, to remind herself when she has found it useful in the past.

We can speculate further that the relatively unsuccessful writers in nursing had a more loosely organized knowledge of hypertension. Their responses were more likely to be dominated by first-hand experiences with hypertension, and they were able to provide many examples, attributes, and characteristics, but relatively fewer definitions or classifications of the term. The following excerpt from a low-rated explanation demonstrates these characteristics:

> The work place (hospital) and all pertinent data I have observed on the floor: i.e., physical signs in points documented to have hypertension, ruddy complexion, type A, stressed individuals, easily agitated, anxious, "hyper."

While this student clearly knows something about hypertension, she appears in her explanation to be merely recasting personal experience and playing with the morphology of the term.

Second, the nursing students showed a strong, significant, negative correlation between their evaluation of the appropriateness of subject-matter treatment in the sample text and their ability to write a successful abstract of the text. This finding may mean that, despite our best efforts to find a text that represents an average level of conceptual difficulty for upper-division undergraduate students, we may simply have found a bad article. This finding, however, does allow us to examine whether discerning readers are better writers. That is, we can speculate that, among these participants, relatively successful writers did not merely accept on faith everything the article proposed, simply because it proposed it. Perhaps they were able to weigh the subject matter treatment against their own experiences and education and examine it critically before writing about it. In Toulmin's terms, these students might have succeeded because they were able to criticize the intellectual concepts of their field.

Third, the multiple regression analyses showed that, for the political science writers, the degree to which they read texts on subjects similar to "local government form" significantly predicted a higher summed holistic score on their abstracts. This finding suggests the validity of a principle first proposed by classical rhetoricians—that speakers and writers develop arguments more frequently using the special *topoi*, or lines of investigation, from their own fields than by using the general *topoi* that can be applied to all subject matters (see Aristotle, 1932, p. 16).

The results also suggest that the relatively successful and unsuccessful writers differed in their knowledge of forms and genres, a kind of knowledge that clearly interacts with their knowledge of subject matters. An examination of the abstracts' distribution and patterns of thematic and rhematic material bears out this claim. The abstracts show clearly that the writers in the two groups in each field believe different kinds of information belong in abstracts, and the abstracts from nursing suggest that half of the relatively successful writers had internalized an organizational scheme for the genre they know as "the abstract."

As Table 1 shows, in the relatively unsuccessful abstracts in political science, writers primarily mentioned the main subject or commented on the level of difficulty, interest, or usefulness of the original article or its author. Nearly 30%

of all t-units represent statements of the main subject of the article, without referring either to the reported methodology or results. Almost 30% of the t-units, as well, represent metacommentary. Results, background material on the main subject, and methodology of the reported study occupy less important roles in the relatively unsuccessful abstracts. Notice, for example, the way this unsuccessful abstract is dominated by metacommentary:

> Lois A. Kappel, Political Scientist of the University of Vermont is a highly qualified and skillful analist. Her research on the partisanship of local government officials is highly convincing and worthy of examination.

The following unsuccessful abstract similarly is dominated by metacommentary, in this case couched in a first-person rumination on the reported study:

> A research note written by Lois A. Kappel was very interesting indeed. I really don't understand why it was written in the first place, since, at the end of the findings indicated that anticipated differences in education level, age, and proportion of attorneys on partisan and non partisan councils did not appear.

Among the relatively successful abstracts in political science, almost 40% of all t-units report results of the study, while almost 20% provide statements of the main subject of the article. Statements on background material of the main subject and explanations of the hypothesis of the reported study each account for slightly more than 10% of the t-units in the relatively successful abstracts. The following successful abstract shows the focus on subject, hypothesis, and results:

> Kappel in this study of the social background characteristics of nonpartisan city council members tests the revisionist assertion that high-SES candidates are elected more frequently in non-partisan elections. She is the first to do this with a nationwide survey. She concludes that non-partisan elections do provide higher status council members, though she observes some unusual formulations in the process.

While this abstract does show the emphases that dominate the t-units of the relatively successful political science abstracts, we should note that no clear pattern of t-unit progressions emerges in either group of abstracts in this field. Only two of eight successful texts show a repeated progression, and that is a rather odd subject-general approach to solving problems-results pattern.

What might account for these writers' lack of attention to the original text's methodology, for the predominance in unsuccessful abstracts of metacommentary, and for the lack of any clear pattern of thematic and rhematic material in either group of abstracts? The lack of attention to methodology might be attributable to the fact that only three of the 30 had ever held jobs related to their major field, and none had ever taught. If the participants in the study had never had the opportunity to work on and report research—if their focus had always been on examining the subject matters, results, and implications of others' research—they might not see the need to examine methodology very closely.

The predominance of metacommentary in the relatively unsuccessful abstracts, we would maintain, cannot be attributed solely to the participants' not taking the task seriously. Most of the metacommentary seems earnest and honest. We believe that the writers whose metacommentary caused their abstracts to receive low holistic scores simply did not know what kind of information an abstract is supposed to contain: what kinds of propositions and assertions an abstract writer is allowed to make, what kinds of lines of development an abstract is expected to manifest. A similar explanation could be offered to account for the lack of pattern of thematic or rhematic material in the abstracts of all the political science student writers. Of the 30 participants, 23 reported having read texts with similar formats as the original's occasionally or often, but only 10 reported they had written texts with similar formats as the original occasionally or often. Participants who had not written research reports may never have written abstracts either. Their lack of experience with the discipline's text types is evident.

Table 2 shows that, among the relatively unsuccessful nursing abtracts, statements of the general approach to solving problems offered by the article predominate. Other dominant elements are statements of the general subject, background material on the subject, results and metacommentary. The following unsuccessful abstract shows a number of these concerns:

> HTN is a leading killer of Americans. The article you are about to read shows how valuable nurses are in our schools. This article gives indepth attention to the problem of HTN & adolescent children in inner city schools.

Like many of the relatively unsuccessful abstracts, this sample is not concerned with the actual methodology and results of the reported *study*; on the contrary, it is concerned with what the *article* accomplishes: the article "gives indepth attention" or "provides ideas" or "talks about hypertension." This attention to the article's general approach to solving problems shows up in the suggestion of a pattern in the relatively unsuccessful abstracts. Three of the nine have the main subject-general approach pattern.

In contrast, the relatively successful nursing abstracts are dominated by specific descriptions of methodology. Other dominant elements are statements of the main subject and results. These three elements form a pattern in four of the eight successful abstracts: main subject-methodology-results. These emphases are evident in the following successful abstract:

> Keywords: hypertension, school nurse, adolescent screening, school nurse roles (communicator, health educator, health status monitor, health habit change agent, facilitator)
> The focus of this paper is a hypertension screening effort and follow-up program implemented by school nurses in three Seattle high schools. The purposes of the

research included the following objectives: identification of adolescents experiencing hypertension, facilitation of health care behaviors to obviate risks of hypertension and increased utilization of the school nurse in an expanded professional role encompassing aspects of health educator, health care liaison, and facilitator. The sample included 3031 students from three high schools, each of which was served by a school nurse. Qualitative evaluation of the study revealed a beneficial impact upon some students as well as an improved understanding of the school nurse role within the community.

Not only does this abstract suggest methodology and results, but it also benefits from the professional-looking statement of the main subjects in the "keywords" section.

The differences between the two groups in distribution and pattern of thematic and rhematic material may be attributable to the relatively successful writers' more highly organized knowledge of hypertension. An additional explanation, moreover, might be found in the successful writers' experiences and training with the discipline's intellectual activities and texts. Of the 25 participants, 24 had worked or were currently working as nurses, and eight had taught. They had probably conducted and written up actual research. They knew the importance of methodology, especially in a scientific field like theirs. They also had experience with the discipline's text types. Thirteen of the 25 reported they occasionally wrote texts with similar formats as the original article's, and 18 of the 25 reported they occasionally or often read texts with similar formats. If the abstract can be called a genre that has a specific manifestation in nursing education, many of these writers appeared to be familiar with it. This knowledge of form and genre, thus, enabled them to activate the kinds of subject-matter knowledge they know belongs in an abstract.

While we can draw comparisons between relatively successful and unsuccessful writers within the two fields, we are in no position to compare the results from nursing with those from political science, since we made no effort to match either participants or tasks. We can, however, hazard one observation about the two kinds of fields we chose to study. As we pointed out above, political science, especially at the undergraduate level, has neither a clear disciplinary definition nor a crowded curriculum. Since students take political science courses for a number of personal and professional reasons, professors and curriculum planners may not feel the need to socialize students into the language, the representation techniques, and application procedures—the knowledge of subjects, formats, and styles—of the field. But this pilot study, at least, shows the dangers of this lack of socialization. Even the more advanced writers in this study suggested little unanimity on what it means to write successfully like a political scientist.

The nursing student writers present a different picture. They are taking classes to become practitioners, researchers, and administrators in nursing. Their curriculum is crowded. While many authorities (e.g., Stromberg & Wegmann, 1981;

Pinkava & Haviland, 1984; Devlin & Slaninka, 1981) complain about what they perceive as substandard writing in nursing and nursing students, this pilot study suggests that the nurses are receiving the kind of socialization into the discipline that leads to successful writing.

IMPLICATIONS FOR FUTURE RESEARCH AND APPLICATIONS

It is a fortunate turn for writing research, we believe, that researchers have largely moved beyond their early efforts to characterize writing processes in general terms and have begun to examine how such processes—now often characterized as parallel rather than serial—are activated in specific contexts (Matsuhashi, 1987). Within these rich contexts, the writers themselves are perhaps the most intriguing focus for study. Indeed, within academic contexts, writers' knowledge might be seen as the focal point of the influences of all the other contextual components. Nearly everything that the society and the culture, the academic institution, and the instructional program have to contribute to the study of a discipline's subject matters, to the relation between writing and the advancement of knowledge, and to the teaching of writing eventually concentrates on the writer. The actual texts a writer creates give some evidence of this accumulated knowledge, but successful writers in a discipline know much more than their written products show. We make no claim that our method is the only available means for examining the interactions of writers' knowledge that successful writing demands, but we do hope it represents a beginning step.

We hope researchers in the future will adapt our methodology to study writing in different academic disciplines. Already, a group of researchers at the University of Illinois at Chicago (Jolliffe, Matsuhashi, Hare, & Rabinowitz, 1987) have begun to examine the processes of writers with varying levels of education and experience in a college of education when they are given the introduction, methods, and results section of a research article from their field and are asked to write the discussion section. Similar studies using different kinds of texts for participants to read and asking for different types of written responses hold great promise for yielding insights about the interactive nature of prior knowledge, reading, and writing.

Such studies could be profitably complemented by more observational methodologies—protocols or stimulated recall sessions from writers working on tasks in their discipline, scheduled interviews with active writers in the field, focus groups of student writers in classes that demand writing, and so on. Such a complicated topic as writers' knowledge seems to demand multiple methodologies.

When researchers begin to generate reliable insights about the kinds of writers' knowledge successful writing in a discipline demands, conscious instruction and application can begin. The results of this pilot study point to the fact that successful writers in an academic discipline possess a store of tacit knowledge that they employ, sometimes haphazardly, to produce texts for their field. Less successful writers, on the other hand, have not had the opportunity to develop this tacit knowledge. Studies like this one, therefore, suggest two specific avenues for teaching writing in academic disciplines. First, writers who are early in their studies in a discipline ought to be urged to read the kinds of research and explanations that characterize the knowledge work of the discipline, even in abbreviated forms. Similarly, they ought to be required to write—again, even in an abbreviated way—using the forms, genres, and ways of speaking of their discourse community. If instructors hope to enculturate students into the intellectual work of an academic discourse community, then students must be encouraged to read beyond textbooks and write more than multiple-choice or fill-in-the-blank examinations.

Second, experienced writers and teachers in a discipline need to talk frequently to each other and to their students about their writing. Professionals and teachers in a discipline ought to seek an awareness of their practices of developing subject matters, organizing texts, and executing styles. They need to develop a vocabulary to describe this awareness as precisely as they can. When they develop this awareness and vocabulary, professionals in a discipline—and teachers of writing—will not have to fall back so frequently on vague apprehensions such as "something about this writing doesn't seem right," or "it's simply awkward and unclear." They can rely on their own knowledge of successful writing and, in turn, pass this awareness on to their students. And isn't that what effective teaching is all about?

REFERENCES

Anderson, R. C. (1978). Schema-directed processes in language comprehension. In A. Lesgold, J. Pelligreno, S. Fokkema, & R. Glaser (Eds.), *Cognitive psychology and instruction.* New York: Plenum.

Aristotle. (1932). *The rhetoric of Aristotle.* (L. Cooper, trans.) Englewood Cliffs, NJ: Prentice-Hall.

Barrass, R. (1978). *Scientists must write: A guide to better writing for scientists, engineers, and students.* New York: John Wiley.

Bartholomae, D. (1985). Inventing the university. In M. Rose (Ed.), *When a writer can't write: Studies in writer's block and other writing process problems.* New York: Guilford.

Bazerman, C. (1980). A relationship between reading and writing: The conversational model. *College English, 41,* 656–661.

Bazerman, C. (1984). Modern evolution of the experimental report in physics: Spectroscopic articles in *Physical Review*, 1893–1980. *Social Studies of Science, 14,* 163–196.

Beaugrande, R. de (1980). *Text, discourse, and process: Toward a multidisciplinary science of texts.* Norwood, NJ: Ablex Publishing Corp.

Bereiter, C., & Scardamalia, M. (1983). Levels of inquiry in writing research. In P. Mosenthal, L. Tamor, & S. Walmsley (Eds.), *Research on writing: Principles and methods*. New York: Longman.

Black, J. B., & Wilensky, R. (1979). An evaluation of story grammars. *Cognitive Science, 3*, 213–230.

Black, J., Wilkes-Gibbs, E., & Gibbs, R. (1982). What writers need to know that they don't know they need to know. In M. Nystrand (Ed.), *What writers know: The language, process, and structure of written discourse*. New York: Academic.

Bloom, B. S., Englehart, M. D., Furst, E. J., Hill, W. H., & Krathwhol, D. R. (1956). *Taxonomy of educational objectives*. Handbook I: Cognitive domain. New York: David McKay.

Brier, E. M. (1985, July). *Breaking the writing barrier: A case of teaching writing to students and faculty in the health professions*. Paper presented at the Summer Conference on Health Communications, Northwestern University, Evanston, IL.

Bryant, D. (1972). Rhetoric: Its function and its scope. In D. Ehninger (Ed.), *Contemporary rhetoric: A reader's coursebook*. Glenview, IL: Scott, Foresman. (Original work published 1953)

Burke, K. (1931). *Counter-statement*. New York: Harcourt Brace.

Burke, K. (1945). *A grammar of motives*. New York: Prentice-Hall.

Caccamise, D. J. (1981). *Cognitive processes in writing: Idea generation and integration*. Doctoral dissertation, University of Colorado.

Campbell, L. J., & Holland, V. M. (1982). Understanding the language of public documents because readability formulas don't. In R. J. DiPietro (Ed.), *Linguistics and the professions*. Norwood, NJ: Ablex Publishing Corp.

Campbell, K. K., & Jamieson, K. H. (1978). Form and genre in rhetorical criticism: An introduction. In K. K. Campbell & K. H. Jamieson (Eds.), *Form and genre: Shaping rhetorical action*. Falls Church, VA: Speech Communication Association.

Chafe, W. (1980). The deployment of consciousness in the production of a narrative. In W. Chafe (Ed.), *The pear stories: Cognitive, cultural, and linguistic aspects of narrative production*. Norwood, NJ: Ablex Publishing Corp.

Chomsky, N. (1964). The logical basis of linguistic theory. In H. Lunt (Ed.), *Proceedings of the ninth international congress of linguists*. The Hague, Netherlands: Mouton.

Coe, R. M. (1987). An apology for form: Or, who took the form out of the process? *College English, 49*, 13–28.

Cope, E. M. (1867). *An introduction to Aristotle's Rhetoric with analysis, notes, and appendices*. London: Macmillan.

Close, R. A. (1965). *The English we use for science*. London: Longman.

Crane, D. (1972). *Invisible colleges: Diffusion of knowledge in scientific communities*. Chicago, IL: University of Chicago Press.

Crowhurst, M., & Piché, G. L. (1979). Audience and mode of discourse effects on syntactic complexity in writing at two grade levels. *Research in the Teaching of English, 13*, 101–109.

Day, R. A. (1983). *How to write and publish a scientific paper*. (2nd ed.). Philadelphia, PA: ISI Press.

Devlin, K., & Slaninka, S. (1981). Writing across the curriculum. *Journal of Nursing Education, 20*, 19–22.

Emig, J. (1971). *The composing processes of twelfth graders.* (NCTE Research Report, No. 13) Urbana, IL: NCTE.

Etzioni, A. (Ed.). (1969). *The semi-professions and their organization.* New York: Free Press.

Fahnestock, J. (1986). Accommodating science: The rhetorical life of scientific facts. *Written Communication, 3,* 275–296.

Faigley, L., Cherry, R. D., Jolliffe, D. A., & Skinner, A. M. (1985). *Assessing writers' knowledge and processes of composing.* Norwood, NJ: Ablex Publishing Corp.

Finegan, E. (1982). Form and function in testament language. In R. J. DiPietro (Ed.), *Linguistics and the professions.* Norwood, NJ: Ablex Publishing Corp.

Fish, S. (1980). *Is there a text in this class?* Cambridge, MA: Harvard University Press.

Fish, S. (1982). Working on the chain gang: Interpretation in the law and in literary criticism. *Critical Inquiry, 9,* 201–216.

Flavell, J. H. (1968). *The development of role-taking and communication skills in children.* New York: John Wiley.

Fort, K. (1971). Form, authority, and the critical essay. *College English, 33,* 629–639.

Gilbert, N. (1976). The transformation of research findings into scientific knowledge. *Social Studies of Science, 6,* 281–306.

Gilbert, N., & Mulkay, M. (1980). Contexts of scientific discourse: Social accounting in experimental papers. In K. D. Knorr, R. Krohn, & R. Whitely (Eds.), *The social processes of scientific investigation.* Dordrecht, Holland: D. Reidel.

Gross, A. G. (1985). The form of the experimental paper: A realization of the myth of induction. *Journal of Technical Writing and Communication, 15,* 15–26.

Gumperz, J. (1972). The speech community. In P. P. Giglioli (Ed.), *Language and social context.* Baltimore, MD: Penguin. (Original work published 1968.)

Gusfield, J. (1976). The literary rhetoric of science: Comedy and pathos in drinking driver research. *American Sociological Review, 41,* 16–34.

Hairston, M. C. (1978). *A contemporary rhetoric* (2nd ed.). Boston, MA: Houghton Mifflin.

Hairston, M. C. (1982). The winds of change: Thomas Kuhn and the revolution in the teaching of writing. *College Composition and Communication, 33,* 76–88.

Hartwell, P. F. (1979). Teaching arrangement: A pedagogy. *College English, 40,* 548–554.

Hawkes, T. (1977). *Structuralism and semiotics.* Berkeley, CA: University of California Press.

Heath, S. B. (1979). The context of professional languages: An historical overview. In J. E. Alatis & G. R. Tucker (Eds.), *Language in public life.* Washington, DC: Georgetown University Press.

Herzberg, B. (1986, March). The politics of discourse communities. Paper presented at the Conference on College Composition and Communication, New Orleans.

Holland, V. M., & Redish, J. C. (1981). Strategies for understanding forms and other public documents. In D. Tannen (Ed.), *Understanding discourse: Text and talk.* Washington, DC: Georgetown University Press.

Holton, G. (1965). The thematic imagination in science. In G. Holton (Ed.), *Science and culture.* Boston, MA: Houghton Mifflin.

Howell, W. S. (1971). *Eighteenth-century British logic and rhetoric.* Princeton, NJ: Princeton University Press.

Hymes, D. (1972). Introduction: Toward ethnographies of communication. In P. P. Giglioli (Ed.), *Language and social context*. Baltimore, MD: Penguin. (Original work published 1964)

Hymes, D. (1974). *Foundations in sociolinguistics: An ethnographic approach*. Philadelphia, PA: University of Pennsylvania Press.

Janos, J. (1979). Theory of functional sentence perspective and its applicatioin for the purpose of automatic abstracting. *Information Processing and Management, 15*, 19–25.

Jauss, H. R. (1982). *Toward an aesthetic of reception*. (T. Bahti, trans.). Minneapolis, MN: University of Minnesota Press.

Jolliffe, D. A. (1984). *Audience, subject, form, and ways of speaking: Writers' knowledge in the disciplines*. Doctoral dissertation, University of Texas at Austin.

Jolliffe, D. A., Matsuhashi, A., Hare, V. C., & Rabinowitz, M. (1987). *A model for curricular reform in writing in academic disciplines: A demonstration project in the College of Education at the University of Illinois at Chicago*. Unpublished manuscript, University of Illinois at Chicago.

Kinneavy, J. L. (1971). *A theory of discourse*. Englewood Cliffs, NJ: Prentice-Hall.

Knorr-Cetina, K. D. (1981). *The manufacture of knowledge: An essay on the constructivist and contextual nature of science*. Oxford, England: Pergamon.

Kroll, B. M. (1978). Cognitive egocentrism and the problem of audience awareness in written discourse. *Research in the Teaching of English, 12*, 172–185.

Kuhn, T. (1971). *The structure of scientific revolutions* (2nd ed., enlarged). Chicago, IL: University of Chicago Press. (Original work published 1962)

Kuhn, T. (1977). *The essential tension: Selected studies in scientific tradition and change*. Chicago, IL: University of Chicago Press.

Lanham, R. (1974). *Style: An anti-textbook*. New Haven, CT: Yale University Press.

Langer, J. (1981). From theory to practice: A prereading plan. *Journal of Reading, 25*, 152–156.

Langer, J. (1984). Where problems start: The effects of available information on responses to school writing tasks. In A. Applebee (Ed.), *Contexts for learning to write: Studies of secondary school instruction*. Norwood, NJ: Ablex Publishing Corp.

Mandler, J. M., & Johnson, N. R. (1977). Remembrance of things parsed: Story structure and recall. *Cognitive Psychology, 9,*, 111–151.

Mathes, J. C., & Stevenson, D. W. (1976). *Designing technical reports: Writing for audiences in organizations*. Indianapolis, IN: Bobbs-Merrill.

Matsuhashi, A. (Ed.). (1987). *Writing in real time: Modelling production processes*. Norwood, NJ: Ablex Publishing Corp.

McCloskey, D. N. (1983). The rhetoric of economics. *Journal of Economic Literature, 21*, 481–517.

McCutchen, D. (1986). Domain knowledge and linguistic knowledge in the development of writing ability. *Journal of Memory and Language, 25*, 431–444.

Medawar, P. B. (1964, August 1). Is the scientific paper fraudulent? *Saturday Review*, pp. 42–43.

Milic, L. T. (1975). The problem of style. In W. R. Winterowd (Ed.), *Contemporary rhetoric: A conceptual background with readings*. New York: Harcourt Brace Jovanovich.

Miller, C. R. (1984). Genre as social action. *Quarterly Journal of Speech, 70*, 151–167.

Myers, G. (1985). The social construction of two biologists' proposals. *Written Communication, 2*, 219–245.

Newell, G. E. (1984). Learning from writing in two content areas: A case study/protocol analysis. *Research in the Teaching of English, 18*, 266–287.

Newell, A., & Simon, H. (1972). *Human problem solving*. Englewood Cliffs, NJ: Prentice-Hall.

Nold, E. W., & Freedman, S. W. (1977). An analysis of readers' responses to essays. *Research in the Teaching of English, 11*, 164–174.

Nystrand, M. (1982). Rhetoric's "audience" and linguistic's "speech community": Implications for understanding writing, reading, and text. In M. Nystrand (Ed.), *What writers know: The language, process, and structure of written discourse*. New York: Academic.

Parsons, T., & Platt, G. (1972). *The American university*. New York: Free Press.

Perelman, Ch., & Olbrechts-Tyteca, L. (1969). *The new rhetoric: A treatise in argumentation*. (J. Wilkinson & P. Weaver, trans.) Notre Dame, IN: University of Notre Dame Press. (Original work published 1958)

Pfister, F. R., & Petrick, J. F. (1980). A heuristic model for creating a writer's audience. *College Composition and Communication, 31*, 231–240.

Piaget, J. (1955). *The language and thought of the child*. (M. Gabain, trans.) New York: Modern Library. (Original work published 1926)

Pinkava, B. P., & Haviland, C. P. (1984). Teaching writing and thinking skills. *Nursing Outlook, 32*, 270–272.

Price, D. J. de S. (1965). Networks of scientific papers. *Science, 149*, 510–515.

Quinn, K. B. (1987). *Researching the relationships between reading and writing: The generation and elaboration of ideas from reading informational prose to writing argumentative prose*. Doctoral dissertation, University of Illinois at Chicago.

Ramus, P. (1983). *Arguments in rhetoric against Quintilian*. (C. Newlands & J. Murphy, trans.). DeKalb, IL: Northern Illinois University Press. (Original work published 1549)

Rubin, D. L. (1984). Social cognitive dimensions of composing processes. *Written Communication, 1*, 211–245.

Rubin, D. L., & Piché, G. L. (1979). Development in syntactic and strategic aspects of audience adaptation skills in written persuasive communication. *Research in the Teaching of English, 13*, 293–316.

Rumelhart, D. E. (1980). On evaluating story grammars. *Cognitive Science, 4*, 313–316.

Rumelhart, D. E., & Ortony, A. (1977). The representation of knowledge in memory. In R. C. Anderson, R. J. Spiro, & W. E. Montague (Eds.), *Schooling and the acquisition of knowledge*. Hillsdale, NJ: Erlbaum.

Scardamalia, M., & Bereiter, C. (1986). Research on written composition. In M. C. Wittrock (Ed.), *Handbook of research on teaching* (3rd ed.). New York: Macmillan.

Schallert, D. L. (1982). The significance of knowledge: A synthesis of research related to schema theory. In W. Otto & S. White (Eds.), *Reading expository material*. New York: Academic.

Schank, R. C., & Abelson, R. P. (1977). *Scripts, plans, goals, and understanding: An inquiry into human knowledge structures*. Hillsdale, NJ: Erlbaum.

Secor, M. J. (1984). Perelman's loci in literary argument. *Pre/Text, 5* 97–110.

Smith, E. L. (1979). *Simplicity and complexity in scientific writing.* Ann Arbor, MI: English Composition Board.

Spivey, N. N. (1983). *Discourse synthesis: Constructing texts in reading and writing.* Doctoral dissertation, University of Texas at Austin.

Steward, J., & Smelstor, M. (1984). *Writing in the social sciences.* Glenview, IL: Scott, Foresman.

Stromberg, M., & Wegmann, J. (1981). The fine art of writing a research abstract. *Oncology Nursing Forum, 8,* 67–71.

Thorndyke, P. W. (1977). Cognitive structures in comprehension and memory of narrative discourse. *Cognitive psychology, 9,* 77–110.

Toulmin, S. E. (1958). *The uses of argument.* Cambridge, England: Cambridge University Press.

Toulmin, S. E. (1972). *Human understanding: The collective use and evolution of concepts.* Princeton, NJ: Princeton University Press.

van Dijk, T. A. (1977). *Text and context: Explorations in the semantics and pragmatics of discourse.* London: Longman.

Voss, J., Vesonder, G., & Spilich, G. (1980). Text generation and recall by high-knowledge and low-knowledge individuals. *Journal of Verbal Learning and Verbal Behavior, 19,* 651–667.

Vygotsky, L. S. (1962). *Thought and language* (E. Hanfmann & G. Vakar, trans.). Cambridge, MA: M.I.T. Press. (Original work published 1934)

White, J. B. (1983). The invisible discourse of the law: Reflections on legal literacy and general education. In R. W. Bailey & R. M. Fosheim (Eds.), *Literacy for life: The demand for reading and writing.* New York: Modern Language Association.

Willard, C. A. (1983). *Argumentation and the social grounds of knowledge.* Birmingham, AL: University of Alabama Press.

Winterowd, W. R. (Ed.). (1975). *Contemporary rhetoric: A conceptual background with readings.* New York: Harcourt Brace Jovanovich.

Witte, S. P., & Faigley, L. (1983). *Evaluating college writing programs.* Carbondale, IL: Southern Illinois University Press.

Woolgar, S. (1980). Discovery: Logic and sequence in a scientific text. In K. D. Knorr, R. Krohn, & R. Whitely (Eds.), *The social processes of scientific investigation.* Dordrecht, Holland: D. Reidel.

Young, R. (1978). Paradigms and problems: Needed research in rhetorical invention. In C. R. Cooper & L. Odell (Eds.), *Research on composing: Points of departure.* Urbana, IL: NCTE.

APPENDIX A: NURSING VARIANT OF RESEARCH TASK*

Thank you for agreeing to participate in this project.

1. What is your age? _____

2. What is the highest academic degree you hold? _____

3. What is your current level of study? (For example, a senior in undergraduate school, a second-year master's student, etc.)

_____

4. What is your major field of study?

5. Have you ever held a job directly related to this field of study? Circle YES or NO. If you answered yes, how many years have you held or did you hold this job?

_____

6. Have you ever held a teaching job directly related to this field of study? Circle YES or NO. If you answered yes, how many years have you held or did you hold this job?

_____

PLEASE STOP. Do not go on to the next page until the project leader asks you to do so.

For the next five minutes, please write the first thoughts that come into your mind when you hear the word, HYPERTENSION. Do not worry about writing grammatically correct sentences. Feel free to write just random words, phrases, and ideas. But do try to write for five minutes without interruption. You may write on this page and the blank page that follows it.

AT THE END OF FIVE MINUTES, THE PROJECT LEADER WILL SAY "STOP" AND ASK YOU TO GO ON TO THE NEXT STEP. PLEASE DO NOT GO ON UNTIL THE PROJECT LEADER SAYS TO DO SO.

For the next ten minutes, write an explanation of what made you think of the words, phrases, and ideas you wrote in response to the word, HYPERTENSION. In other words, explain the thinking processes underlying your free associations on the word. You may write on this page and the blank page that follows it.

AT THE END OF TEN MINUTES, THE PROJECT LEADER WILL SAY "STOP" AND ASK YOU TO GO ON TO THE NEXT STEP. PLEASE DO NOT GO ON UNTIL THE PROJECT LEADER SAYS TO DO SO.

For the next fifteen minutes, read the following text at your normal reading pace.

_____

* Spratlen, L. P. (1981). "Using research in practice: Extending school nursing roles and services in a hypertension screening and follow-up program." *Western Journal of Nursing Research, 3,* 50–453. Copyright © 1981 by Sage Publications. Reprinted by permission of Sage Publications, c.

AT THE END OF FIFTEEN MINUTES, THE PROJECT LEADER WILL SAY "STOP" AND ASK YOU TO GO ON TO THE NEXT STEP. PLEASE DO NOT GO ON UNTIL THE PROJECT LEADER SAYS TO DO SO.

[Note: The following article is reprinted from *Western Journal of Nursing Research*, 3 (1981), 450–453. In the research task, the author was named "Jill Smith Michler" in case any of the participants had heard of Lois Price Spratlen and would, therefore, be biased in responding to the article.]

Extending School Nursing Roles and Services in a Hypertension Screening and Follow-up Program.

Lois Price Spratlen

Hypertension screening and follow-up programs in public schools offer unique opportunities for extending the roles and the health services delivered by school nurses. Health education, health habit change regimes, student referral and follow-up activities can all be combined with carefully planned and executed mass screening for hypertension. These conclusions are supportd by the results of a research program between December, 1978 and April, 1979, in three Seattle, Washington inner-city schools.

Background and Description of the Study.   The research examined the pattern of occurrence and related characteristics of blood pressure among adolescents in the inner city. It also added to our knowledge about ethnic and inner city aspects of hypertension among adolescents.

A total of 3,031 students (54 percent of enrollment in the three schools) were screened for hypertension. Abnormal elevations were defined on the basis of the 95th percentile of systolic and diastolic blood pressures adjusted for age and sex. Once students were identified with respect to this standard, school nurses were involved in the referral and follow-up phases of the research. The research led to some practical, preventive applications that were incorporated into school nursing. Liaison with families and community providers, teaching for health habit change and community outreach were some of the other important contributions of the research.

School Nurse Roles.   Freeman (1970:309) groups the school nurse's roles under three headings: "1) to contribute to the personal health care and health education of the school populations; 2) to contribute to the improvement of the physical and social environment in which the school population spends its school hours; and 3) to relate these efforts toward health improvment to those of the family and of the community at large." These headings are sufficiently broad to include the activities carried out by the school nurses in the Seattle hypertension screening and follow-up study. The above grouping, however, does not address specifically newer dimensions in primary and long-term care giving (Committee to Study Extended Roles for Nurses:1971). The roles emphasized in the Seattle hypertension screening and follow-up study were those of the communicator, health educator, health status monitor, health habit change agent, and facilitator for student, family, school and community cooperation.

Communication was critically important for carrying out the research. Parents or guardians had to be notified that their son or daughter had an elevated blood pressure that should be evaluated by the family's health provider. The school nurse indicated to parents that she would continue to monitor the adolescent's blood pressure at school on a regular basis throughout the academic year. The nurse also informed the parent or guardian that she would make recommendations for personal changes in health habits that seemed appropriate for each student.

The health educator role involved providing students with basic information about the relationship between diet, weight management, and regular exercise and blood pressure. Since each student with an elevated blood pressure did not require change in all three areas, the school nurse completed a personal assessment of the adolescent's health status. In consultation with the student, the nurse developed a personal plan by which the student could become more aware of and responsible for personal health maintenance.

The school nurse served as a health status monitor throughout the remainder of the academic year. In one of the schools the nurse was familiar with many of the families and aspects of the their health history. This made it possible to personalize long-term follow-up activities.

For hypertension the health habit change agent role was given special attention, recognizing that dietary practices, smoking and, for females, use of oral contraceptives are contributing factors to elevated readings. The change agent role involved programs of counseling and related assistance in health habit behavior change. The school nurse maintained frequent and personal contact with the students in small groups, providing encouragement and reinforcement. Some progress was noted for a number of students. The exact results of this aspect of the study are being analyzed separately.

The facilitator role is also a very valuable one. Cooperation was linked to the interest and skill exhibited by the school nurses. One example includes how nurses encouraged parents and guardains without health care providers to seek blood pressure evaluation in community clinics. Adolescents were encouraged to assume responsibility for meeting their own health care needs by scheduling and keeping clinic appointments.

Summary.   Research activities and results from the Seattle hypertension screening and follow-up were of immediate benefit to the school nurses. The study was compatible with the nurse's knowledge base, role as a primary health provider, and her willingness to extend these functions in conjunction with the screening study.

The study benefited from the school nurses' professional relationships with school administrators; they were well known by many parents and health providers in the community as well. Personal rapport and concern could be expressed to the students. Both roles and services were extended in the process.

A coincidental aspect of the study should also be noted. Shortly after the study was completed a school district budget problem developed in which a large scale reduction in the services of school nurses was considered. The discussion of the extended roles of the nurses helped policymakers become more aware of the contributions of school nurses beyond traditional services to students. The results of sharing the information and experiences from the study were constructive and modestly persuasive in the situations. The case for continuation of the three nurses involved were strengthened as a result of the study.

The Seattle hypertension screening and follow-up study involving three inner city high schools and the nurses assigned to them provided ample evidence that research and school nursing can be quite compatible. School nurses' roles can be extended and health services for student and families can be increased through well-planned collaboration and cooperation between nursing researchers and practitioners in the public schools.

References

Brink, Susan G., et al. 1981. Nurses and Nurse Practitioners in Schools, *Journal of School Health* 51(1):7–10.

Buser, Bess N. 1980. The Evolution of School Health Services: New York and Nationwide, *Journal of School Health* 50(10):475–477.

Committee to Study Extended Roles for Nurses. 1971. Extending the Scope of Nursing Practice. *American Journal of Nursing* 71(12):2346–2351. (Report to the Secretary of the U.S. Department of Health, Education, and Welfare.)

Damiane, Mary Lou, et al. 1980. Hemophilia: The Role of the School Nurse, *Journal of School Health* 50(10):451–454.

Freeman, Ruth B. 1970. *Community Health Nursing Practice*. Philadelphia: W. B. Saunders Company.

Gilman, Susan, et al. 1979. Task Differentiation Among Elementary, Middle and High School Nurses, *Journal of School Health* 49(6):313–316.

U. S. Bureau of the Census. 1980. *Social Indicators III — Selected Data on Social Conditions and Trends in the United States*. Washington, D.C.: U.S. Government Printing Office.

Warren, Rueben, C. 1980. A Community Approach — School-Based Health Care Delivery, *Journal*

PLEASE STOP. Do not go on to the next step until the project leader says to do so.

In the next five minutes, please respond to the following nine questions by circling the number on the five-point scale that *best* describes your experience with texts of the kind you have just read.

1. I write pieces on similar subjects as this text's.

NEVER	ONCE	SELDOM	OCCASIONALLY	OFTEN
1	2	3	4	5

2. I write pieces that have a format similar to this text's.

NEVER	ONCE	SELDOM	OCCASIONALLY	OFTEN
1	2	3	4	5

3. I write pieces that use a level of vocabulary similar to this text's.

NEVER	ONCE	SELDOM	OCCASIONALLY	OFTEN
1	2	3	4	5

4. I read pieces on similar subjects as this text's.

NEVER	ONCE	SELDOM	OCCASIONALLY	OFTEN
1	2	3	4	5

5. I read pieces that have a format similar to this text's.

NEVER	ONCE	SELDOM	OCCASIONALLY	OFTEN
1	2	3	4	5

6. I read pieces that use a level of vocabulary similar to this text's.

NEVER	ONCE	SELDOM	OCCASIONALLY	OFTEN
1	2	3	4	5

GO TO THE FOLLOWING PAGE FOR QUESTIONS 7, 8, AND 9.

7. For purposes of your own study and research, the level of treatment this text gave to its subject was:

HIGHLY		NO		HIGHLY
INAPPROPRIATE	INAPPROPRIATE	OPINION	APPROPRIATE	APPROPRIATE
1	2	3	4	5

8. In your opinion, the format this text employed was:

HIGHLY		NO		HIGHLY
INAPPROPRIATE	INAPPROPRIATE	OPINION	APPROPRIATE	APPROPRIATE
1	2	3	4	5

9. In your opinion, the level of vocabulary this text employed was:

HIGHLY		NO		HIGHLY
INAPPROPRIATE	INAPPROPRIATE	OPINION	APPROPRIATE	APPROPRIATE
1	2	3	4	5

PLEASE STOP. Do not go on to the next step until the project leader says to do so.

Imagine you are the editorial assistant for a journal in which this text will be published. In the next fifteen minutes, write an abstract of the text that will appear between the author's name and the first paragraph of the text itself. You may write on this page and the blank page that follows it.

THIS IS THE LAST TASK IN THE PROJECT. THANK YOU AGAIN FOR AGREE-
ING TO PARTICIPATE.

APPENDIX B: ARTICLE USED IN POLITICAL SCIENCE VARIANT OF RESEARCH TASK*

[Note: The political science variant of the research task is identical to the nursing variant presented in Appendix A, except that political science participants were asked to associate on the phrase, LOCAL GOVERNMENT FORM, and to read the following article. This article is reprinted from *Western Political Quarterly*, 38 (1985), 495–501. In the original research task, the author was named "Lois A. Kappel" of the University of Vermont in case any of the participants had heard of Carol A. Cassell of the University of Alabama and would, therefore, be biased in responding to the article.]

Social Background Characteristics of Nonpartisan City Council Members
A Research Note

Carol A. Cassell
University of Alabama

In roughly two-thirds of U.S. municipal elections, candidates run for office without party labels. Such nonpartisan elections are a product of the municipal reform movement of the

---

early twentieth century, which attempted to limit the power of corrupt party machines, insulate local elections from the influence of state and national party government, and encourage recruitment of superior candidates, who might be reluctant to associate themselves with party organizations (Lee 1960). Nonpartisan elections provide an interesting contrast with elections where party labels are present.

Behaviorally oriented political scientists of the mid-twentieth century questioned the validity of the reformers' good government theory of nonpartisan elections. A revisionist theory developed based on observations of nonpartisan elections in practice and a theoretical recognition of the functions of political parties in politcal systems. The classic reassessment was made by Adrian (1952), who hypothesized that nonpartisan elections weakened political parties, tended to be issueless in nature, advantaged incumbents and made them less accountable to the public, and restricted recruitment to higher political office. Subsequent studies of California cities (Lee 1960; Hawley 1973) also asserted that nonpartisan systems tended to over-recruit members of the business community and Republicans, thus reducing the representativeness of local government. This is plausible on any of several grounds: high-SES candidates (and Republicans) may be more willing to run for office in nonpartisan systems; high-SES candidates may be more likely to have the resources to win without the aid of a party label; or lower turnout in nonpartisan elections may bias the voting electorate in favor of high-SES candidates.

To date, none of this has been tested with a nationwide survey. This paper makes a beginning toward remedying that omission. Drawing on a survey of all U.S. cities with a population of 2,500 or more, I test the revisionist assertion that high-SES candidates are elected more frequently in nonpartisan elections. In addition, I examine the relationship between ballot form and several other characteristics previously found to be related to it.

The survey from which I take my data, *Form of Government-1981*, was conducted by the International City Management Association, Washington, D.C. Using a mail questionnaire, the ICMA surveyed all U.S. cities size 2,500 and above, with a response rate of 69 percent. The survey items include measures of municipal government structures and of social background characteristics of incumbent council members, including occupation, education, and age.

Background.   As a Progressive reform of the early twentieth century, the nonpartisan ballot is strongly related to region for historical reasons. Cities in the Northeast, formed early in U.S. history, are only 32 percent nonpartisan. Younger cities in the West were more likely to be influenced by the Progressive movement. Thus the proportion of nonpatisan cities in the West is over twice that in the Northeast. Given this geographic and historical basis it is not surprising that ballot form, when considered nationally, has little relationship to other demographic factors. Despite assertions that nonpartisan elections occur more frequently in smaller and more middle-class cities, we find no evidence of significant relationships between ballot form and city size or income. The proportion of nonpartisan ballots is the same among large, medium, and small size cities. Nor does income seem to make any difference. In 1980, the median annual income in nonpartisan cities was $10,355, while that in partisan cities was $10,260.

A majority of all forms of government (mayor-council, council-manager, etc.) have nonpartisan elections, although the nonpartisan ballot is more frequently associated with the reform model of government (council-manager). Likewise, the nonpartisan ballot is used in a majority of all council constituency types but occurs most frequently with the most common reform model constituency type (at-large). When the three reform structures are considered together, the nature of city government is characterized more by diversity than by the "reformed" or "unreformed" model. Only 28 percent of U.S. cities have adopted all three reform structures (nonpartisan ballot, council-manager form of government, and at-large elections), and only 5 percent use all three unreformed structures (partisan ballot, mayor- council form of government, and ward elections).

Since ballot form is not associated with city size or income, comparative studies such as the analyses presented below need not control for these factors. The relationship between ballot form and other municipal reform structures, however, suggests a need to control for other municipal reform structures to assess the relationship between ballot form and other variables.

Previous Studies of Social Background.   Despite the revisionist claim that nonpartisan systems are biased toward higher SES officeholders, only a few studies have examined social background of elected officials in nonpartisan systems. Lee (1960: 171) found the nonpartisan system "pretty bad" in terms of the representativeness of local elective officials. Affluent white Protestant males were clearly advantaged in California municipal elections (all nonpartisan). As Lee noted, however, there was no evidence to determine whether successful candidates in cities with partisan elections would be any different. Rogers and Arman (1971) found that officials elected in nonpartisan systems in Ohio have high status occupations and higher income than officials elected in partisan systems there. Their study was based on a 1967 questionnaire sent to all mayors and council members in Ohio cities with populations of 25,000 or more. Since nonpartisan systems tend to co-occur with at-large elections, which also may produce more affluent council members, at-largism is a potential confounding factor here. In another study, Feld and Lutz (1977) compared background characteristics of individuals recruited to run for the nonpartisan Houston City Council and the partisan Texas legislature from approximately the same electoral area. They found the nonpartisan city council to contain more members of the business community than the partisan state legislative seats from the same geographic areas. This difference cannot be attributed to varying district size, although the nature of the office being sought may be a confounding factor.

Related to the thesis that nonpartisan elections benefit high SES candidates is the thesis that nonpartisan elections benefit Republican candidates, on the assumption that high SES candidates tend to be Republican. Alternatively, the lower turnout that seems to characterize nonpartisan elections may help explain the apparent Republican (and high SES) advantage. Hawley (1973), who tested the thesis most systematically, found that nonpartisanship does benefit Republicans, although the bias is substantial only in cities with a populations of 50,000 or more.

Previous studies also have found that officials elected in nonpartisan elections are generally older and are more often attorneys than those elected in partisan systems (Rogers and Arman 1971; Feld and Lutz 1977). In explanation, Rogers and Arman suggest that it may simply take longer to develop the notability necessary for electoral success without a party label. Another pssibility is that nonpartisan offices have lower career utility for ambitious politicans. If so, one might expect to find fewer young members and attorneys on nonpartisan councils. Feld and Lutz conclude that nonpartisan councils may attract "an older, more established man seeking a prestigious diversion," whereas partisan councils may attract "a young breed of politician" (1977: 927).

Analysis.   The present data enable us to test some of these hypotheses more definitively than previously had been possible. To address the proposition that nonpartisan city councils contain a higher proportion of persons of high socioeconomic status, Table 1

Table 1.   Percent High Occupational Status and Average Education in
Nonpartisan and Partisan City Councils by City Size

City Size		Percent High Occupational Status*	Average Education†
2,500 and above			
	nonpartisan	51.1 (2636)	14.5 (2139)
	partisan	44.4 (1131)	14.3 (962)
25,000 and above			
	nonpartisan	53.9 (529)	15.4 (430)
	partisan	45.7 (214)	15.0 (162)

Note: The figures in parentheses are the number of cases on which percentages are based.
*High occupational status = professionals, business executives and managers. The remainder are business or industry employees, homemakers, teachers and other educational personnel and clergy. Farmers or ranchers, retired persons and other are excluded.
†The survey item measuring education is categorical. The actual years of schooling are estimated by coding under high school graduate = 10, high school graduate = 12, post high school technical = 13, 1 to 3 years of college = 14, bachelor's degree = 16, master's degree = 17, doctor's degree and medical degree = 20, law degree = 19. Other is excluded.

compares the occupational status and education of council members in nonpartisan city councils. The data show occupational but not educational differences. The occupational differences are consistent and significant, although not dramatic: 51 percent of nonpartisan council members but only 44 percent of partisan council members have "high" occupational status.

Since the association of the nonpartisan ballot with at- large constituencies leaves a suspicion of spuriousness (more affluent candidates may be better able to afford a citywide campaign). Table 2 adds controls for council constituency. Without these controls, high occupational status is 7 or 8 percent greater in nonpartisan than in partisan cities (Table 1). With council constituency controlled, it remains 6 or 7 percent greater, on average, within each category of constituency (at-large, combination, or district). At the

Table 2.   Percent High Occupational Status by Council
Constituency in Nonpartisan and Partisan Cities by City Size

City Size	Council Constituency	High Occupational Status	
		Nonpartisan	Partisan
2,500 and above			
	at large	53.8 (1189)	47.5 (684)
	combination	45.8 (413)	40.9 (230)
	district	43.8 (413)	37.7 (203)
25,000 and above			
	at large	56.7 (361)	50.0 (98)
	combination	48.1 (120)	44.0 (74)
	district	47.6 (45)	36.9 (40)

Note: The figures in parentheses are number of cases on which percentages are based.

Table 3.   Average Age and Percent Attorney in Nonpartisan and Partisan City Councils by City Size

City Size		Average Age*	Percent Attorney
2,500 and above			
	nonpartisan	47.9 (2650)	3.8 (2672)
	partisan	47.3 (1106)	4.1 (1145)
25,000 and above			
	nonpartisan	47.8 (528)	7.9 (532)
	partisan	46.3 (205)	7.7 (214)

Note: The figures in parentheses are the number of cases on which percentages are based.
*The survey item which measures age is categorical. Average age is estimated by coding under 22 = 21, 22–29 = 25.5, 30–39 = 34.5, 40–49 = 44.5, 50–59 = 54.5 and 60 and over = 65.

extremes, reformed cities with both nonpartisan and at-large elections have a majority of elites on their councils (54 percent); and unreformed cities with both partisan and district elections have clear minority of elites on their councils (37 percent). This difference does not vary with city size.

Previous findings that officials elected in nonpartisan systems are older and less likely to be attorneys find no support here. Table 3 shows that the average age of city council members is virtually identical in nonpartisan and partisan cities, even for cities with a population of 25,000 or more, where such differences may be more important. Similarly, there is virtually no difference in the proportion of attorneys elected in partisan and nonpartisan systems.

Conclusions.   This paper provides more conclusive evidence that nonpartisan elections produce higher status council members than partisan elections. The combination of nonpartisanship with at-largism, as opposed to the combination of partisanship with ward elections, exaggerates this difference. On the other hand, anticipated differences in education level, age, and proportion of attorneys on partisan and nonpartisan councils do not appear.

These findings may help clarify the role of local partisan elections as providers of access to political office for non-elite candidates. They also afford a firmer empirical basis for the revisionist critique of nonpartisan elections as tending to produce less representative municipal legislatures.

References

Adrian, C. 1951. "Some General Characteristics of Nonpartisan Elections." *American Political Science Review* 46 (September): 766–76.
Cassel, C. 1985. "The Nonpartisan Ballot in the United States," in B. Grofman and A. Lijphart, eds. *Electoral Laws and Their Political Consequences.* New York: Agathon.
Engstrom, R. and J. Pezant. 1975. "Candidate Attraction to the Politicized Councilmanic Office: A Note on New Orleans." *Social Science Quarterly* (March): 975–82.
Feld, R. and D. Lutz. 1972. "Recruitment to the Houston City Council." *Journal of Politics* 34 (August): 924–33.
Hawley, W. 1973. *Nonpartisan Elections and the Case for Party Politics.* New York: Wiley.
Karnig, A., and B. O. Walter. 1977. "Municipal Elections: Registration, Incumbent Success, and Voter Participation." *The Municipal Yearbook 1977*, pp. 65–72. Washington, D.C.: International City Management Association.

Lee, E. 1960. *The Politics of Nonpartisanship: A Study of California City Elections*. Berkeley: University of California Press.

Lee, E. 1963. "City Elections: A Statistical Profile." *The Municipal Yearbook 1963*. Chicago: International City Management Association.

Rogers, C., and H. Arman. 1971. "Nonpartisanship and Election to City Office." *Social Science Quarterly* 51 (March): 941-45.

Sanders, H.T. 1979. "Governmental Structure in American Cities." *The Municipal Yearbook 1979*, pp. 97–112. Washington, D.C.: International City Management Association.

Sanders, H.T. 1982. "The Government of American Cities: Continuity and Change in Structure." *The Municipal Yearbook 1982*, pp. 178–86. Washington, D.C.: International City Management Association.

3 A Model for Investigating the Functions of Written Language in Different Disciplines*

Michael M. Williamson

Indiana University of Pennsylvania

INTRODUCTION

As the introduction to this volume notes, recent interest in writing across the curriculum has developed along two broad lines. Both approaches to writing across the curriculum have emerged from scholarly traditions with research programs intended to generate principled theories of written discourse and the composing process, but neither has developed a clearly defined model of the meaning of learning to write in specific disciplines (Jolliffe, 1984). Because no coherent theory linking the act of writing with the function of writing in specific fields exists, Jolliffe calls for a principled theory of the acquisition of communicative competence (Hymes, 1972) in specific disciplines as a basis for future instructional practices. This criticism does not deny the value of either text-centered or person-centered composition research. However, as Faigley (1985) observes, researchers in rhetoric and composition have not been sensitive to the social context in which they collected data. Jolliffe, recognizing that the context of writing in each discipline is different, asserts that the meaning of learning to write in academic disciplines may depend upon systemic contextual differences that influence instructional practices and the use of writing in instruction in each discipline in ways unpredictable from decontextualized theories of writing.

The purpose of this chapter is to present a research methodology for investigating the relationship between the social context of specific disciplines and the

---

*I would like to thank my colleague Pat Hartwell, who commented on an early version of this chapter and provided me with many valuable suggestions for revision.

89

acquisition of communicative competence by student writers. I will illustrate that methodology by presenting a study of the function of academic writing for undergraduates in three college curricula. The chapter is divided into two sections. The first section will discuss the functional perspective on social issues as a basis for contextualized research and present the application of functional inquiry to research in academic disciplines; the second section will report the research study and discuss its implications for developing writing instruction across the curriculum.

FUNCTIONAL RESEARCH AND THE ACADEMIC DISCOURSE COMMUNITY

The Functional Perspective

Function, as a general term in social sciences research, has been defined by Garvin (1977) as the meaning of human behavior to the participants in a social network. For Garvin, function refers to two aspects of a social system, "the function of the system as a whole," and the way in which "the elements of a system function with respect to one another" (p.6). Function, then, is "the role that a given behavioral system plays in the life of the people" (p.6). Garvin (1977) and Diesing (1971) share the view that function cannot be investigated outside its natural setting, because the meanings of public events lie in the participants' understanding of the relationship between an event itself and the context in which it occurs. Garvin characterizes functional inquiry as event-centered as opposed to person-centered, because it attempts to explain the social meaning of behavioral events rather than psychological traits. As such, functional inquiry is an explanation of human behavior against the background of a social system or culture as a whole. Diesing terms this perspective on human behavior *holistic,* because it preserves the unity of personal, psychological events and their public, social functions. The relationship between behavior as both personal and public event is one aspect of Vygotsky's psychological view of the social and historical origins of language acquisition (Wertsch, 1983). In one sense, as Saussure (1960) points out, the relationship between symbols and their referents is essentially arbitrary. However, as Vygotsky notes, the child acquires language, among other human cognitive functions, in a social and historical context. In the case of language, the reference and meanings of symbols have been conditioned through conventional usage. Part of the task of the child in language acquisition is to discover the adult meanings of words (Vygotsky, 1962; 1978). According to Wertsch, Vygotsky did not distinguish a clear boundary between the social and psychological processes in human cognition, because such a boundary would be theoretically artificial and would obscure the important interactive influences of one set of processes on the other. In essence, a functional approach to social sciences research assumes that the social and psychological perspectives on human behavior are so intertwined that they cannot be meaningfully separated.

Diesing (1971) also claims that an understanding of the function of behavior depends upon observation of and participation in the behavioral system, affording the observer an understanding of the target behavior or behavioral subsystem in its natural setting. Holistic research includes a range of qualitative research strategies, subsuming ethnography and qualitative case studies. Garvin believes that holistic or qualitative research strategies are best suited to functional inquiry, because they allow a view of the total scope of behavior in its natural setting and a view of the functioning of individual elements within the whole system, a wholeness lost in other research paradigms that Diesing describes, such as formal modeling procedures and experimental research designs.

The Academic Discourse Community

Borrowing a term from Toulmin (1972), Jolliffe (1984; Jolliffe & Brier, this volume) labels the process a student follows as he or she enters an academic field, *disciplinary enculturation.* His concern for the meaning of learning to write in a discipline raises questions about the function of writing in the field itself as well as in the process of enculturation. The major questions that must be answered are: What is the meaning or function of writing in specific disciplines, and how does this influence learning to write in the discipline? Thus, to begin to understand disciplinary enculturation and the acquisition of communicative competence in an academic discipline, it is necessary to understand the broader context for academic writing.

Members of academic disciplines participate in a social setting that is defined by two powerful contexts. The first is the discipline itself as a context for teaching and research, involving a community unified by the interest of its members in a specific object of study. The second is the specific college or university as a context for daily activity, involving participants from a variety of disciplinary communities. In Bazerman's (1982) view, writing is the primary channel for communicating knowledge in an academic setting. Students learn to write, as he suggests, because it enables their participation in the academic community. However, written language has a variety of important influences on the lives of academics, some related to their discipline and some related to their lives in a specific institution. Thus, written language is likely to have a variety of functions for college teachers, and these functions are likely to influence their views of the meaning of learning to write for their students. In turn, their view of the meaning of learning the discipline and learning to write should influence their uses of writing in the classroom.

Registers, Discourse Communities, and Linguistic Functions

Halliday (1978) has proposed a model of communication which provides a delineation of the various functions of language. He has stated that an understanding of the social functions of language provides a clue to the meanings of texts that the participants in a discourse can be said to know prior to the opening moves of their texts (Halliday, 1970). This theory is a starting place for an investigation of the function of writing in specific disciplines because it provides a broadly based analysis of the social context of communication.

Like Hymes (1968), Halliday views language as having both social and referential meanings, distinguishing the ideational content of a text from the social context of the discourse. Halliday (1978) calls this social or contextual meaning *register,* which he defines as semantic patterns determining participants' use of social information to structure to predict the meaning of a text through gathering meaning from the situation itself, as opposed to the surface structure of the text. Registers also include knowledge of the conventional structures of discourse for particular situations, forming the basis for generating texts. Register is comprised of three variables, *field* (the activity and the function of language within that activity), *tenor* (status and role relationships of participants), and *mode* (transmission characteristics and text typology).

Applying this scheme to writing in academic disciplines, academics read and write in two fields, their disciplinary community and their college or university, each with its own particular customary linguistic functions; however, these fields interact with one another. Successful writing for the discipline may be one foundation of success in the local setting, since it may be the basis for promotion and tenure as well as the basis for recognition within the discipline. When writing about their discipline, academics need to adjust the tenor of their discourse for each context. A local interdisciplinary committee is a very different audience than a national committee constituted from members of a single discipline. In addition, the daily life of a university is likely to require different text types than the larger profession. The quantity of face-to-face interaction at an institution authorizes more informal modes of discourse (notes, memos, etc.) than the disciplinary community that only meets infrequently in highly formalized settings such as annual symposia or colloquia.

Another conceptualization of the different functions of writing for academics is that they participate in two different discourse communities. Nystrand (1982), explaining the effects of the social aspects of language, claims that individuals who communicate on a regular basis or who could communicate because they are from the same social group, form a *discourse community.* Gumperz (1971) first employed the term *speech community* to designate social groups that share a common language and interact frequently. According to Faigley (1985), in theory all readers of the same language could constitute a single discourse community, but writing is never addressed to "everyone capable of deciphering the words" (p. 238). Instead, he points out that some individuals, because of their social activity, participate in groups that come to have "specialized discourse competence" (p. 236). In this sense, academics have specialized discourse competence in two settings.

Student writing has also been shown to be an aspect of a specialized discourse competence. Britton, Burgess, Martin, McLeod, and Rosen (1975) in a study of school sponsored writing by 11- to 18-year-olds in England, and Applebee (1981) in a similar study in America, found that writing to display knowledge is the dominant function of school writing. But not all students find this dominant function of language in school, knowledge display, natural. Heath (1982), for example, reports that some young children experience difficulties with oral display questions when first confronted with them, if they do not have cultural models for recognizing the validity of such questions. Cazden (1983) found that children have social adjustment problems in school when their model of the function of language at home conflicts with teachers' perceptions of the function of language in school lessons.

The sensitivity of students to the context of writing in schools is illustrated by Freedman's (1984) study of teachers' responses to student and professional writing. She found that English teachers, unaware that texts by professional writers were mixed with texts by student writers, assigned consistent holistic ratings to student texts, but holistically rated texts by professional writers extremely inconsistently. She explained that the professional writers in her study answered *real* questions, responding to typical college essay topics by exploring their relevance to a reader and their appropriateness as a subject for communication. On the other hand, she found that the students in her study answered *exam* questions, responding to the topics by showing what they knew about them. In English classrooms, teachers raise essay topics to get students to show what they know about written language. Students are not expected to question the validity or explore the relevance of the essay stimulus. Because students are familiar with the context in which exam questions are raised, they are familiar with the appropriate register for their response. Because the professional writers did not use the register of school writing, they received inconsistent ratings from the teachers who read the papers, indicating that teachers have different thresholds of tolerance for violation of their expectations about the register of school writing. Professional writers, more fluent than the novice student writers, could be considered to have failed the assignment in one sense, because they did not understand the social setting of the school, the context in which their texts would be read. Of course, as novice writers, some students failed and some succeeded, depending upon their relative fluency with the register. Teachers could rate student essays consistently, however, as successes or failures because the students were attempting to communicate within the appropriate register. Freedman also observed that student writers tended to address the reader as a superior adult; the professional writers tended to address the reader as a peer. She noted that a peer role relationship is not appropriate for student writing, because it violates the status and role expectations of teachers. Thus, the social context of school dictates what can be written about, how it can be written about, and how the writer should interact with the reader. Just as the children in Heath's study who found oral display questions an unfamiliar and even nonsensical use of language, some of the professional writers in Freedman's study, when treating the topic of the essay she asked them to write as a real question, imposed their own understanding of the context of the discourse on their texts. The teachers who read their essays believing they were written by students did not consistently validate the professionals' approaches to the topic.

Thus, membership in a discourse community facilitates communication because it bestows familiarity with the registers that are used by other members of the community in speaking and writing, empowering the individual to act on and through that community, in effect, to display membership. Participation in a community through language is also a sign of membership; it signals that the speaker or writer is familiar with the customs and mores that bind the community. Use of the register of school writing signals the student writer's membership in the community at the same time it signals his or her role and status. Messages, although linguistically well formed, that violate the conventions of the expected register are misunderstood because they violate the customary ways of communicating, displaying unfamiliarity with the context that is a sign that the speaker is not a member of the discourse community. In this sense, registers appear to function like regional, social, or ethnic dialects. Fluent communication in a register or dialect is a sign, a social semiotic, as Halliday (1978) puts it, of group membership.

This special function of language as a social signal of group membership has special implications for communication within any community and for outsiders who wish to communicate with members of the community. Labov (1972) has analyzed Black English Vernacular (BEV) and has suggested that it is structurally suitable to convey meanings as complex as those carried in messages in Standard Written English (SWE). Following this line of reasoning, Baugh (1983) observes that academic physics could be communicated as logically in BEV as in SWE, except that the discipline is customarily communicated through a specialized register of SWE. Baugh's analysis of the structural differences between BEV and SWE suggests that these differences are minimal, leading him to the conclusion that the failure of speakers of different dialects of English to comprehend one another is functionally determined. The physicist would not recognize his or her discipline expressed in another dialect of English because he or she would not recognize discourse about physics outside its customary register as a meaningful communication, even though he or she would be hearing it in an intelligible dialect. Thus, communications about physics intended to advance physicists' understanding of their subject in BEV are only historically impossible. Thus, the social function of language would appear to dominate the ideational function.

Similarly, most English teachers claim that student writing is not meaningful communication because of the errors that obscure its meaning. Strict adherence to the mechanical formalities of SWE is one characteristic of the register of the composition classroom. Yet teachers must reach beyond the errors and process the meaning of the text in the act of correcting the error. Errors in the college composition classroom function as a signal of relative fluency with SWE and are one basis for judging the relative merits of texts. Thus, the social function of errors dominates the ideation of a text in that context, even though the reader can easily process them for their ideation.

Writing in educational settings is a complex and interesting subset of the problem involved in relating language as communication of ideation and language as a social signal. Besides mastering a written dialect of English that identifies the writer as a literate and educated person, students, as they progress in a field, have to begin to master specialized registers that govern communication in the discourse communities of their disciplines. Membership in a discourse community is both a problem of learning the language and accepting the social values of the community that lie behind the use of language and drive discourse in the language (Bartholomae, 1985; Bazerman, 1982, 1983).

Recently, several writers have explored the problem of language as both vehicle for communication and for values in the context of college composition courses and, more generally, for all academic discourse. Bizzell (1984, 1985, 1986) explored the implications of attempting to enter the academic discourse community, in particular—the problems faced by basic writers as they are confronted with a new discourse community with unfamiliar norms. She hypothesizes that membership in the academic discourse community requires that basic writers repudiate their native speech communities, because of the conflict resulting between the values of the academic discourse community and their home speech community (Bizzell, 1984). For Bizzell, the academic discourse community exists, as a fact of the social context of higher education, before the student arrives on campus. In her latest contribution (Bizzell, 1986), she grapples with the problem of the enlightened English composition instructor who would permit the student to compose in his or her own dialect and not impose the norms of academic discourse and its accompanying values on that student. Unfortunately, she observes that such a separate peace is not possible. The enlightened composition instructor does not impose the register or registers of academic discourse as a norm in the English classroom. Some of Freedman's teacher-readers gave positive ratings to the nonconforming professional writers. However, the use of academic discourse is a systemic norm imposed by the social and historical conventions of postsecondary education. Failure to master academic discourse must finally result in failure in the academic context because of the unpredictable responses of other members of the community to nonconforming discourse.

Bartholomae (1985) complicates the problem raised by Bizzell. He claims that each time a student writer composes, he or she is forced to invent the academic discourse community, a process of building a communication upon the conventions of that discourse community, conventions unfamiliar to many undergraduates. Bartholomae's analysis suggests that all social norms do not have an independent existence. Instead, they are created by individuals each time they act in the social setting. This position is consistent with Vygotsky's theoretical position, because social processes such as register are not aspects of a context independent of the participants' understanding of the context; the social context of human behavior is not independent of the individuals who create the context through their interactions. Indeed, the functional perspective, as a view of the meaning of human behavior, is not posited as independent of the behavior; it is the meaning that humans themselves imput to their behavior.

Bartholomae complicates the situation for beginning college writers when he suggests that the real problem for all students entering the university is the need to write through the conventions of a variety of academic discourse communities, pointing out that a university student fulfilling liberal education requirements, "must learn to try on a variety of voices and interpretive schemes, to write, for example, as a literary critic one day and as an experimental psychologist the next" (p. 135). The conventions that govern a particular discipline, for Bartholomae, are "both problems of finish (social) and problems of substance (ideation)" (p. 157). Thus, mastering the conventions of a particular discipline requires both knowledge of the customary ways of writing in the discipline and knowledge of the discipline. While student writers struggle against their limited awareness of the knowledge of the discipline, they have to produce writing to be evaluated by senior members of the disciplinary community.

Bazerman's (1982, 1983) research confirms that professional texts in different disciplines are driven by different discourse communities, because their texts follow different discourse pathways. His research also uncovered procedural differences in text generation in different disciplines. For him, text generation is particularly enlightening about the writing in a discipline, because it lies in the act of formulating a written message and mastering the substance of the discipline, echoing Bartholomae's view of the problem for student writers.

Jolliffe (1984) summarizes the complexity of understanding writing as an aspect of disciplinary enculturation when he claims that learning to write in a discipline is a multifaceted investigation of the writing of both students and professionals. For professionals and apprentices (graduate students), a mastery of the disciplinary register is clearly a measure of their success in communicating with their peers. Undergraduate writers may very well be confronted by a different set of contingencies imposed upon their writing. Of particular concern is the relationship between the two divergent social contexts for written language, the specific discipline itself and the local institution, as well as the manner in which these two influences interact in determining the uses that faculty make of writing in their teaching.

If academic disciplines constitute a larger discourse community or sets of discourse communitites that share common purposes, individual colleges are as varied as the disciplines they house. This variation might influence the purposes for learning and the manner in which knowledge is transmitted, in turn influencing some of the local functions of writing for both teachers and students. As broad classes, the small liberal arts college, the comprehensive university, and the large research university are likely to have different goals for students' learning. At the same time, each institution has developed its own model for undergraduate education, subject to the special circumstances that govern it.

But educational institutions are also places of convention. Since academics meet one another in the disciplinary setting as well as the local institutional setting, writing in undergraduate education, if undergraduate writing is perceived as a different activity from professional writing, may have a set of functions that are common to all disciplines and may govern its uses, regardless of the disciplinary affiliation of a teacher.

Clearly, the complexity of issues surrounding writing as an aspect of disciplinary enculturation cannot be settled without careful consideration of the range of issues raised in this brief and highly selective review of the scholarship. The issues raised here are important, because a clear understanding of the function of writing in disciplines will affect composition research and composition instruction. In the description of the research methodology that follows, I will illustrate the value of contextualized or qualitative inquiry as a tool for examining the variety of influences on the function of writing in different disciplines and for understanding the depth of interaction between these influences. Quantitative research methodologies such as formal modeling and experimental studies are not adequate to trace the complex interaction of the issues outlined in this review, nor are they suited to functional inquiry, because they do not examine the meaning of behavior in the process of explaining it.

THE RESEARCH METHODOLOGY

Stages of Qualitative Research

Diesing (1971) outlines three stages for qualitative research: preparation, observation, and explanation. The first stage is prior preparation, when the researcher becomes acquainted with the proposed subject before beginning direct study of the subject itself, including reading information in published reports and examing any existing theories. In this stage, the basic activity of the researcher is bound to the library. The second stage is observation and participation. Dividing participant-observation into two types, the scheduled and the unscheduled, he views activity at this stage as the beginning of data collection in the field.

Scheduled activities are preplanned data collection activities; unscheduled activities are any data collection strategies which are not planned in advance as part of the design of the study. The third stage of qualitative research is explanation, involving the generation and testing of themes that emerge in the data. The third stage is a change of perspective on data collection, unlike the change of venue from the library to the field that occurs between the first and the second stage. The researcher begins the explanatory stage by generating the themes that appear to be emerging from the data collection and categorizing them. Then he or she cross checks one data source with another, a process also known as triangulation (Miles & Huberman, 1983).

After the researcher has discovered several themes and begun to test them, he or she begins to build a model of the behavioral system, connecting the themes into a network or pattern specifying causal or functional relationships between the themes. The process of tracing a pattern yields the explanation of the relationship. This process of generating an explanation is recursive, because the researcher returns to observation and participation to confirm explanations and test their limitations. This process of confirmation and testing yields additional themes which have to be incorporated into the network. The explanatory process stops when the researcher has exhausted plausible explanatory relationships and further attempts at validation do not reveal additional themes.

THE RESEARCH STUDY

Preliminary Activities

Following Diesing's outline, I began the study of the function of writing for undergraduates by exploring the available scholarly literature relevant to the function of writing in learning and exploring the limited scholarly literature on writing instruction in disciplines other than English. I read theoretical discussions, research studies, and student texts. To organize my knowledge, I began keeping field notes in which I explored my growing understanding of the issues. In addition to field notes, Miles and Huberman (1983) suggest that a researcher develop a conceptual framework to help organize the knowledge gathered before data collection begins. The building of a conceptual framework is an extremely useful technique for focusing and bounding data collection as well as specifying the researcher's preliminary bias toward the subject of the study. It provided a formal framework to structure the overwhelming mass of information that resulted from my preparation activities. By focusing the research questions, the conceptual framework bounded a potentially unlimited data set. From this conceptual model, I began to draw up sets of research questions that focused my interest on the subject of this research and the data that I had to collect.

The discussion of academic writing in the first part of this chapter delineates the conceptual framework for this study. The research questions that grew out of this framework focused upon the teacher and the teacher's perceptions of writing and learning in the discipline. Therefore, formally designed data collection was bounded by limiting it to instructors. This decision followed from Miles and Huberman's (1983) suggestion that data collection be bounded by sampling from the available data, because the data from a single social setting are so varied and numerous that they preclude mere collection, not to mention analysis. Sampling is identifying the *"people* to observe or interview . . . (as well as the) *settings, events,* and social *processes"* (p. 37).

The decision to limit the investigation to a single site and to limit formal data collection to interviews with teachers grew out of my sense that working with other types of informants as part of my scheduled activities would not reveal data as rich in participant explanation relating the two contexts of concern, the local institutional setting and the profession. Administrators are often too distant from the classroom. Administrators also must engage in public relations as one aspect of their work, making them potentially unreliable informants. Students, on the other hand, do not have reliable access to a discipline beyond the local setting. Ultimately, because college faculty are accorded a larger measure of freedom in planning the content and process of instruction, their explanation of the function of writing for students represents the dominant view.

The most important use of formal interview data from student informants and administrator informants would have been to provide a preplanned procedure to cross check of the reliability and validity of the themes that emerged in faculty interviews. Therefore, I included interviews with students and administrators as unscheduled and informal data collection. In designing the scheduled aspect of the study, I built cross-checking procedures into the data collection and model-building stages such that each of two informant served to cross check another in each discipline. Each discipline that was examined in the study served as a cross check for the two that were studied. Informants' statements in one interview were cross checked in a second interview. Informal data collection with students and administrators throughout the study revealed little useful information. While the contact with college administrators was an absolute prerequisite for permission to conduct the study and for orientation to the site, most were reluctant to comment on the basic research questions, deferring to the English department, in particular, for answers.

Identification of the Target Site

Because functional inquiry concentrates on the holism of a single system, this study was conducted at a single university. In one very important way, this limits the generalizability of the findings to the context of this institution. Because I was able to concentrate on the data from this single behavioral system in depth, I believe that I was able to build a more complex and satisfactory explanation.

Because this type of in-depth work is difficult with a larger sample, a suitably representative sample is impossible.

The actual target site for the study was selected because it has an explicitly stated strong commitment to undergraduate education as well as some graduate programs. The graduate programs, I hoped, would provide a richer diversity of views than I expected to find in an insitutuion without them. The college catalog suggests that effective teaching is the primary orientation of faculty, but also suggested that research is a consideration in the daily life of many of them.

Acculturation to the Target Site

The initial period of contact with a behavioral system, according to Diesing (1971), is a time of acculturation when the observer acquaints himself or herself with the daily lives of the participants. At a college or university, acculturation is simplified to some extent, because descriptions of daily life are available in written documents. To speed acculturation, I read any written documents from the site, spoke informally with administrators, and observed daily activity from locations such as the student union building. At this stage, I also spent time mapping and graphing data from the site. For instance, I computed the ratio of Ph.D.s to master's and bachelor's degrees among the faculty, as well as the ratio of graduate faculty to undergraduate faculty in specific departments. I also gathered comparative data, such as the average SAT score of entering classes, to allow for later comparison with other campuses. The results of this activity allowed me to revise my initial conceptual framework and research questions against a variety of contextual aspects of the site and further refine the research questions in light of the stated goals and mission of the college (Miles & Huberman, 1983).

Selection of Informants

My informal and unscheduled acculturation activities led me to believe that the site was suitable, and I obtained permission to conduct the study from the college president through the dean responsible for the humanities, who referred me to the dean responsible for social and natural sciences.

In the selection of informants, my goal was to pick departments that represented the central tendency of each of the three major divisions of learning generally accepted at most colleges: natural sciences, social sciences, and humanities. This variety of informants was solicited partly because the study was designed to compare the functions of writing in different disciplines and partly because the process of comparing the explanations of informants in one discipline with the others served as a form of cross checking.

The cooperation of faculty for the interviews, the scheduled data collection activity of this study, was solicited through telephone calls. Based on telephone conversations with the chair of each of three departments, biology, sociology, and English, I contacted two faculty from each department recommended by their chair as good teachers who also utilize writing in upper level courses for majors. The purpose of having two informants was to provide a basis for cross checking the views of each with the other. At the very outset of the process of identifying participants, the focus of the study as an examination of written language was explained to all individuals, producing some bias in the recommendation of instructors by department chairs.

Data Collection

Scheduled data collection was based upon two interviews with each participant, the first as a data collection session and the second as a confirmation session. Comparison of data collected in the first interview with data collected in the second interview, comparison of data collected with the other informant in each department, and comparison of the data collected in other departments allowed for a cross-checking strategy which triangulated each informant, as a data source, with at least three other data sources. I conducted the first interview with all participants before conducting any confirmation interviews, to be sure that I had an opportunity to gather all possible themes.

I tape-recorded both of the scheduled interviews, because it allowed for a permanent record of everything said, but left me free to concentrate on the substance of the interview itself (Mosher & Kalton, 1972). Belson (1967) reports that the accuracy of responses in his sample was not affected by the use of tape recorder, although upper social classes tended to have slightly reduced linguistic accuracy when taped, possibly because they are monitoring their speech. On the other hand, Diesing cites a study by Clark (1965) which reports that informant responses tend to be more elaborate in the presence of a tape recorder. Thus, the responses of academics are likely to be more carefully considered and formal when they believe that their statements will be recorded verbatim and transcribed. Since most academics are used to having students record their lectures, I do not believe that the taping was intrusive. While most of the informants expressed a conscious awareness of the recorder by pausing in their speech while I changed tapes or expressing a concern that the microphone was close enough, only one informant expressed any initial discomfort with talking into the microphone.

The first interview with each informant was planned around a loose schedule which began with my clarifying the purpose of the study. I then asked the instructor to describe a course he or she had just taught for majors in the department and to explain the relationship of the course to the departmental major. When I felt that I clearly understood this information, I asked the instructor to describe the course requirements as if he or she were talking to a student. If necessary, I asked for clarification of the role of writing requirements in the course and asked the instructor about the methods he or she uses to present assignments, help the students perform them, and evaluate them. From there, I asked each informant to discuss the role of written language in the discipline and in the student's career after completing the bachelor's degree. Finally, I asked each informant to discuss his or her own scholarship. During this interview, I also solicited documents, in the form of course syllabi, assignment sheets, and student papers. These I examined with the informant at this interview.

In the second interview with each informant, I showed tentative models of the role of written language in his or her course and his or her scholarship as these models related to the discipline and the university and invited him or her to confirm, reject, or revise these models with me. At the same time, I cross checked information from other informants and solicited further information to clarify details. As the informants helped me to revise the models, I encouraged them to discuss their ideals as well as the situation confronting them at their college. I hoped, during this second interview, that the informants would become an integral part of the model-building process (Goetz & LeCompte, 1984; Heath, 1983). I described my efforts in building an initial model explaining the uses of written language in the discipline and the classroom to the informants as tentative. Since they were all described as good teachers by at least their department chairperson, I must assume that they believed they had nothing to hide; there was no reason for them to avoid honesty in responding to the models.

Model Building

The model building stage of the study between the first and second interview requires further explanation, since it was the primary mode of data analysis in this study. While the transcripts were being typed, I reviewed the tapes several times. Each time I listened to a tape, I began by reviewing my field notes from the beginning of the study to that time. As I was listening, I added to my notes and extended them. I began to notice categories of functions for student writing, leading to modifications of the revised conceptual framework. In the final stages, before I returned for the second interview with each participant, I drew out a model for each discipline which included all of the relevant classroom language variables suggested by all the participants. This model was framed in the context of the university as a whole and each discipline as a separate department.

As I constructed the models, I interviewed other administrators and other faculty informally to cross check the statements of the teacher-informants and to validate the accuracy of specific bits of information. These meetings were unscheduled data collection and were not tape-recorded. In all, 28 hours of scheduled interviews were conducted with the six participants and one additional English instructor, resulting in 640 pages of transcripts.

The exploration of the data from preliminary interviews was conducted according to Pike's heuristic procedures (1959, 1967, 1982). These discovery procedures have a researcher select a unit of analysis and classify it as an independent unit, which Pike labels a *particle*. From there, the researcher moves to comparison with other contrasting units, placing these units in temporal, spatial and logical sequences. Pike labels this level of analysis a *wave*. Sequences of waves create the *field* which is the larger context of the study. In my initial model, writing assignments were the unit of analysis. Courses became waves and departments became fields. Because the system is recursive, this initial field view then becomes the particle for a larger view. Thus, departments themselves become particles, and the institution becomes a wave within the field of postsecondary education. I also examined the individual teachers as particles within a wave represented by their academic department, which lies within the field of their affiliation to their discipline.

RESULTS OF THE STUDY

The results of the study are reported by department to provide a context for the discussion which follows. The results of qualitative research have more in common with narrative as a discourse mode than the abbreviated mode of reporting the results of quantitative research. In this sense, the results of data analysis in qualitative research are confounded with the analysis procedures that generated the results.

Biology

The primary goal of the biology department in undergraduate education, as conceived by both participants, is to train students for entry into graduate school. Writing in biology appears to be affected by two factors, class size and the participating biologists' conception of the nature of biology as the object of undergraduate study. Class size was reported to be one major deterrent to use of written assignments in the lower levels of undergraduate study in biology, with sections of one hundred or more students common.

> Participant: . . . it (is) basically just giving out information. They are learning the language is what they are doing. I refuse to give multiple choice tests. I do give fill-ins, which is as far as I can go. There's about 106 in the class; and even if I gave one essay question, trying to grade 106 essay questions is more than I can handle.

The participating biologists did not perceive a relationship between learning biology for the undergraduate and writing, as the following analogy suggests.

> Observer: . . . science courses . . . (are) communication of factual information to undergraduate students?

Participant: Particularly in the lower level courses. . . . What are they going to write about? They don't know enough yet to write. And that's not a criticism of the students. It's like learning a foreign language, your German I class. You don't write essays in German I, you are just trying to memorize the verbs and grammar, and that is what undergraduates in biology courses are, many of them, learning a language, memorizing terms, getting the basic information.

This statement implies that biology, for the undergraduate, is a matter of memorization, learning the facts that have been accumulated by the discipline. Students' mastery of that knowledge is then tested by objective measures. The teacher's role in learning emerged in this context as well.

P: . . . Some of mine (lecture notes) are brown around the edges . . . I can revise them as I'm lecturing. If something doesn't go well, I write a little note on the lectures to rewrite this section . . . most of my courses are basically presenting information. It's quite different from English literature, for example, where you are dealing with concepts and interpretations. Most undergraduate biology courses tend to be presenting information.

The importance of the teacher, and the centrality of spoken language in biology, emerged in discussion of the use of textbooks.

P: We have a textbook which is, I think, more of a guide than as a complete . . . I lecture on things that aren't in the textbook, I cover things in more detail . . . so the textbook is just kind of a crutch to fall back on really. It gives them (the students) a place . . . they can use as a beginning point.

Thus, in one sense, the participating biologists rely very little upon written language, since they do not depend upon student writing or textbooks. However, in another sense, writing has an important function for both teacher and student. Lectures are written out in advance, and class notes record the information delivered through lectures. The importance of class notes as a part of learning biology was discussed by the participants.

P: Good students have good notes, bad students have bad notes . . . They are generally sloppy, they don't write them down, you know if I write something on the board, they won't bother writing it down or they will abbreviate to the point where it doesn't make any sense . . . Quite a few students . . . go back and recopy them (their notes) . . . some students use that as a study aid, the act of rewriting their notes is the way they learn . . . I find that certainly the way to learn something is to prepare a lecture. To think about how you are going to tell somebody else what you are reading about, you really learn . . . I guess you concentrate more when you are thinking about communicating it.

Here, the function of writing as a tool for learning biology emerges. Writing lectures is an aspect of the instructor's mastery of biology; notetaking is an aspect of students' mastery. Again, the emphasis in learning is mastering factual information, since revising class notes is a reconstruction of what was said.

A second type of learning identified by the biologists, the laboratory experience, was termed the *hands-on* approach by one of the participants. Laboratory courses are also intended to teach students specific information. In addition, the laboratory is where the student learns the process of being a biologist.

> P: . . . Even the data, if the numbers that they are supposed to get are not correct, and I know what numbers they are supposed to get, if they get the wrong numbers and they make the right conclusions from those numbers, that's fine.

Laboratory work, thus, is learning through discovery. The student replicates established experimental procedures to learn the reasoning processes and lab techniques of the practicing biologist. In the lab, students are expected to master the skills of manipulating equipment and the logical process of relating data collection to explanation. They are also given a graphic demonstration of biological concepts. The participants believe the results of this demonstration are fundamentally different than classroom learning. Both stated that learning in the lab is less efficient than the classroom, because an experiment demonstrating a single concept might take students several weeks to conduct. Despite this inefficiency, they both believe the laboratory experience is essential to student learning, even in courses for nonmajors, because it demonstrates that biology is not as absolute as a lecture might make it appear, an interesting contradiction of their view that learning biology is primarily a matter of memorizing facts.

Written language has a reporting function in the context of the laboratory course. Students follow a predetermined form to report the results of their work to the teacher.

> P: I have them write an introduction, very brief methods (section in their papers) because the methods are usually on the handout for the experimental part of the lab you do. I don't want them to repeat that. The results (section), which is where they take their data that they collect and explain that data, and then the discussion (section), which is an interpretation of that data . . .

This participant said that he took this general format from the professional journals in which he reports his own research. Thus, writing functions in the lab experience as the lab functions in student learning, as a mirror of the activity of the professional. In the lab, students not only learn the process of biology, they also learn how one communicates about biology.

One of the participants described the sequence has uses to train students into the customary ways of writing about lab work in biology. After students write up their experiments, he corrects the paper to help them understand how they had deviated from acceptable laboratory procedure, proper logical derivation of their conclusions, and the model for reporting their work.

> P: . . . The intent is that the first time through they make the mistakes and they are identified by me and then the second time they are supposed to not make those mistakes and improve. They do not write the second lab until the first one has been edited by me . . . in pointing out what's wrong, what's right, what they didn't do, why they didn't follow the format, why their reasoning is wrong, why the conclusions they've come to weren't warranted by the data that they showed. . . . Ninety percent of the time, the reason students make mistakes is because they don't know what is right and they don't know what is correct.

Of further interest in this discussion was the status accorded grammar in the discussion of students' problems. Both participants in biology stated that lack of knowledge of grammar is at the heart of the problems students have when something goes wrong with their writing.

> P: I would say that poor students, certainly their grammar is poor and their choice of words and syntax is bad. Frequently sentence structure just has no meaning . . . And when that happens, you can't correct it; the meaning is so nebulous, there is no way to correct the meaning. Many times, I'd say that is true of the worst students. The moderate students or the average students commit fewer errors, their grammar is better, they normally make sense of the information that they are trying to say, but frequently their word choices are poor. In other words, there are better ways scientifically of explaining something to make meanings clear, and frequently you will catch students writing a sentence that has double meanings in it and those are the things that take more time to correct. . . . I expect spelling, coherent sentences, something appropriate in paragraphs. . . . If I pick it up (a deviation from standard usage) my own grammar isn't that good. Within the limits of my own knowledge, if I see it, I'll correct it on the paper. I wouldn't take off for it . . . students don't like that, I get nasty comments from students who don't do well. They say, "He graded us on our writing ability, not the experiment in the lab."

The biologists appear not to see knowledge of biology and laboratory skills as separate from a student's ability to write. Like knowledge of biology, knowlege of a language is broken down into components to be mastered. But writing ability is only one of several symptoms of the weak student. Other symptoms are weak lab technique, weak reasoning, and failure to master the material adequately. As undergraduate students in biology begin to learn the conventions of communicating with other biologists, they learn a format for and a process of written commununication that is highly conventionalized, as it is conceived by the participating biologists. Their discussion of the importance of correctness in technique and reasoning as well as English usage emphasizes this interpretation. Because scientific communication rests on special meanings for words, neither of the participants believes that written communication in biology, at any level, can tolerate deviance from standard English usage. Because of the necessity of precision in communication between scientists, according to both participants, usage is narrowly restricted. In effect, both participants suggest that the dialect employed by biologists located in widely divergent geographical and temporal locations requires the use of a standard register, governed by the specialized interests of biologists.

Research and publication are high priorites for the participants. They relate publication to participation in the discipline, both as a way of achieving status and as a way of achieving their goals as teachers. While publication was seen by both participants as a way of contributing to the field, it also provides status at their home institution. Besides improving their knowledge of the discipline, a road to better teaching, their professional activity, acccording to the bioligists, increases students' chances for admission to better graduate programs.

Writing, as a professional activity, is therefore a basic assumption for participation in departmental life. One background informant discussed a recent tenure decision involving a biologist who was judged to have an insufficient record of professional activity; he was not granted tenure by the department. While this situation suggests that all biologists do not agree on the need to publish, this biology department appears fairly unified about the need for publication, since it grows directly out of the undergraduate teaching mission and the views of individuals about the necessity of formal participation in the larger disciplinary community.

Sociology

Sociology at the target institution is a discipline with explicitly drawn general intellectual goals beyond the mastery of sociological content. Because there are few majors in sociology and only a small percentage of them go on to graduate school, the participating sociologists report that their department's curriculum is organized around a series of highly structured concentrations of courses in specialized aspects of sociology. Some of these concentrations are in applied areas, intended to provide a minor in applied sociology for majors in other departments to enhance their knowledge of their own field and to improve their employment opportunities on graduation. In addition, the concentrations provide a curriculum for students in other majors to study sociology for its own sake. The quality of teaching must be very high to sustain a continued interest from students outside of the department.

> P: . . . very few people come here declaring a sociology major . . . many people come saying, "I want to major in computer science . . . (or) business." We get students because we're largely a service department. We, this fall, had the second largest FTE in the college, it was like 25 and you're budgeted for 18. That is because our intro sections and our social problems sections are very full, but it also means that we have a series of courses in the upper levels that draw very well. . . .

And now we are in the process of revising (the curriculum for the major) . . . because we don't send anybody to graduate school. . . . Concentrations are inter- disciplinary groupings of courses that students tack onto a major. These were started about six or seven years ago with a grant that was administered by one of our sociology faculty. The major concentrations are social work, criminal justice, they have them in labor, industrial management, in six or seven other areas. . . . I just started one in social gerontology. You will have the major, and then that concentration is essentially that bridge to the applied world.

In this context, the participants conceive undergraduate study of sociology partly as mastery of content and partly as evidence of work with that content.

P: I want them to do two things basically in any class I teach: I want them to demonstrate to me that they have new knowledge that they didn't have before they took that course, number one. Number two, that they've done something with that new knowledge; they've thought about it . . . in other words they've done some kind of analytic work in their heads about that new information. . . . And I don't care how clumsy they are. . . . Oh, they want the truth. And unfortunately we sociologists, and a lot of other disciplines, present them with an overabundance of riches when it comes to the truth, because we say, "You want a truth. I'll give you four truths, each one contradicting the other one!" It just scares the shit out of them.

This statement suggests the difficulty of learning sociology. From the instruc- tors' point of view, sociology is a matrix of theoretical overviews and empirical studies. One participant discussed the apparent contradictions of teaching her students interactionist theory, a phenomenologically based theory, as the under- pinning for a course and then examining research findings derived from a positivistic theory of social research.

P: Well, you know, I'm a hypocrite because in Deviant Behavior (her course), you know, we put down the positivistic approach and then we go through all the statistics.

It became clear, quite early in the interviews, that the selection of participants was quite fortunate. The other participant was a demographer who stated that his initial training was in the positivistic side of sociology.

P: Formal demographers only essentially study birth, death, and migration, and they are really only interested in measuring and documenting those particular phenomena . . . generally speaking, demographers tend to be people who work more with numbers, tend to quantify, by the nature, I think of the very data they work with.

Both participants recognize their own views as a choice emerging from a common field of study. The differences between their approaches depend on the questions raised about a social event and the type of data collected.

> P: I present them with alternative definitions, one is the positivist definition and the other is the interactionist and, as you might well surmise, I am an interactionist, and show the different assumptions of each. They also lead to different methodological preferences, they look at different kind of data. Clearly, they develop very different kinds of theories . . .
>
> P: . . . sometimes it's very beneficial to take a particular situation and say, "Now how would a symbolic interactionist describe this? What things would he or she look at, what method of analysis would he or she find, and what questions would he or she ask?" And you run the same thing through conflict theorists or functional theorists. You get them (students) to realize that any phenomenon can be looked at . . . (through) these different theoretical perspectives . . . each time you have been analytic. I guess I tend to see analytic as being a broader kind of, I would call it, a skill or a broader kind of approach, and theory being the specific framework, the specific assumptions that you are making . . .

Analysis, as a label for the work they expect students to do with knowledge, was a recurrent theme in the statements of both participants. Clarifying the meaning of analysis was difficult, even in the follow-up interviews. The word *analysis* occurred, without prompting from the observer, in both of the initial interviews.

While the participants see undergraduate study of sociology as both a matter of content and a matter of analytic work with that content, the chief problem for the undergraduate lies in the lack of certainty which results from this approach to learning.

> P: . . . the social sciences have bitten very deeply of the fruit of relativism, as we know, have moved sharply away from determinism. A lot of students come in, you know these little wide-eyed people, and they want truth . . . they clutch, and they get frightened. They want to come down, and "I want the truth, one through ten." And you present them with this view of the truth . . . and we're talking about models, two or three, and then you begin to poke holes in each one, and I sometimes wonder are they really at the point of intellectual sophistication that they can handle that. The impression I have is that many cannot, and they just decide, "It's all bullshit anyway; I'm gonna go take mathematics or biology, they know what they're talking about."

This conceptualization of sociology is reflected in a distinction that one of the participants makes between two of the different types of writing he sponsors in his teaching, the research paper and the thought paper. These two writing activities reflect the two styles of learning that students in sociology undertake.

> P: . . . the term paper (research paper) is meant to be, unfortunately an exercise, but it really comes down to an exercise in them (the students) defining a problem,

identifying the appropriate variable, finding information, reading the information.
. . . They have got to come up with some hypothesis, some notion that they are
going to test . . . the thought paper I see as a more free flowing, less structured,
nonempirical kind of process. Hopefully, they will take some ideas that they've
have been exposed to in a given area and be able to extrapolate and tease some
meaning and show some kind of analytical ability to that particular body of material
with another issue. . . . They are not going to the library and look this stuff up, and
they only get a little bit of guidance. . . . So it is an attempt to see how well they
are, at this stage, able to apply some ideas beyond what they have been more or less
spoon-fed.

Sociology also has a variety of compartments of knowledge, and the subfields
of sociology are potentially as confusing to students as the variety of theories.
Unlike the differing theoretical perspectives, which arise out of different assumptions about social processes in general, the specific branch of sociology addressed in a particular course depends on the orientation toward knowledge.
Students are expected to learn distinctions that appear to be difficult for them. In
extending his view of the function of the term paper, this same participant also
explained the problem of getting students to write papers that are from the
appropriate field within sociology.

P: Sometimes a student will come up and say, "I'm interested in looking at
changing patterns of family formations." Now demographers do look at that. . . .
And I'll say, "Fine, but remember," and this is probably the hardest thing for them
to do and its the most satisfying when they do it and the most exasperating to try to
teach them because it's not something you can very readily teach, "Remember, it's
got to be a population paper, and not a family paper."

Part of the problem with teaching students to grow beyond their egocentric
perspectives and understand the tricky variety in sociological knowledge is that
the subject matter of sociology is life itself.

P: . . . (in studying death) as a sociologist, we study the routine, we study the
common occurrence, my God, everybody dies. . . . I don't think that they (the
students) realize that there are all these variations, cultural variations. . . . The
whole thrust of the course all the way through is to dissuade them from thinking
individualistically and psychologically and to begin thinking sociologically.

The other participant also discussed this problem:

P: . . . what I was describing to you was this battle of getting students to turn . . .
what they see as purely private experience into what a sociologist would call either
public experiences or experiences that can be looked at in terms of social causes.
. . . I don't want to hear what you think. I want to hear what . . . you observe to be a
legitimate, scientific kind of question. I really don't care what you feelings are

because we're talking about analyzing and observing and documenting and thinking through and trying to determine which line of argument is most supported by the facts . . . you get a lot of, "Well I think," and "I feel." These are issues that are very important to people, (fertility, contraception and abortion) and one thing I'm trying to do in some cases is teach them that these are issues that, while it is of value to look at them from a philosophical or moral point of view, when you look at them as a demographer you are looking at them from a scientific point of view. You make a distinction.

Since sociological processes are part of their everyday lives, students have to be tricked into taking a new perspective, adopting a new view of reality.

P: . . . it's a lot of fun dealing with the concept of norms with students because the fun comes in when you talk about breaking norms . . . they all go, "I can't see a norm, I can't touch a norm; what do you mean norm?" . . . . I dress, usually start out dressing very informally . . . for three or four weeks after we've talked about norms and then I come in just dressed to kill. And they all laugh and applaud and say, "Oh, you're breaking your norms." Then I go, "Great, you've got it."

In the response to the variety of perspectives and the need to go beyond an egocentric view, students want to learn the correct answers.

P: And they want to know what's right of course, and you want to say, "Wrong question. Don't ask which one is right." . . . if you get them to appreciate the relativeness of their society, their customs, of their ideologies, of their behaviors, and you can do this through historical analyses of all kinds of things, you know, sexual behaviors . . . you want to get them to the see . . . (anything) to get them to understand . . . that norms are time bound and situation bound and place bound and culture bound and age bound.

Sociology also has a laboratory component that assists students in making the shift from the personal to the sociological perspective, guides them in learning the nature of analysis, and helps them to see the direct application of their learning. One participant talked about involvement with students who were doing internships in the community.

P: . . . it has been a perfect laboratory for students. I teach a course in urban sociology, and I've had interns who worked with an agency down there on this housing issue. And they have been exposed to this kind of living laboratory of what the textbooks talk about when they talk about community conflict. . . . And these were people who I never thought would have . . . understood it . . . (or) applied it, but they have and they've come out with this new analytical ability that they didn't have before . . . they've been totally changed . . . .

The internship is where all three of the major goals of the study of sociology merge. The first goal is knowledge of sociological theory and research. The second is a personal connection to this knowledge through an ability to analyze both theory and social processes in action. The third is professional training that prepares students for employment. The theory coalesces into a body of knowledge which provides a basis for understanding the larger issues involved. The personal connection helps students to understand that the patterns they see are essentially individual events. The internship itself represents the first time that students actually gain experience in the daily work of sociology outside of a classroom.

Writing functions in the sociology curriculum to assist students' learning in very much the same way that the lab/internship component does.

> P: So it's a real challenge to get any student in sociology to take what they see as really personal issues, personal troubles, and show them that there is a social level to that. . . . I think sociologists tend to be a very critical, questioning group of people. Our business is to explore everything around us and I think when you have students who just don't get excited about doing that and don't seem to care . . . that is a hard attitude for me to accept . . . it's really great to see students who go from mixed-up, freshman adolescents who are worried about getting laid and what's going to happen in the bar to juniors and seniors who are out in the community doing internships, talking abut graduate school and want to be x, y, z. . . . And I think that having students write in analytic ways is probably one of the most effective ways to bring about that transition.

This statement reflects the goals of the sociologist as a teacher and the function of writing in the curriculum because it explicitly ties students' writing to facilitating intellectual growth. The participant cited an experience with two students that demonstrates this change.

> P: . . . I had two students who started out with me in the school problems courses . . . who were in school because their parents had sent them . . . definitely groping, they were lost . . . they were total screw-ups the first time they were in my classes; you know, they would come to class hung-over and obviously had their minds on other things. . . . And I think they finally found themselves in a state where they were getting terrible grades. . . . And they came to me and said, "What can we do? . . . I think they began to realize that they had to make some changes. . . . And the next semester I had an opportunity to look for students for an internship locally with an organization that is among other things an advocate for the housing rights of low-income and minority people . . . and I approached them (the two women) with the idea and they thought it was great. . . . And the reason I thought this was good for them was because now they became the object of discrimination. Nobody wanted anybody around to hear what they were doing, and here you have these two young college girls showing up at these meetings. They legally had a right to be there because these were meetings that had to be open to the public. . . . And they found themselves being treated rather rudely, gruffly . . . it was kind of, "Well,

what do you little girls want and who the hell sent you here, who are you working for?". . . . They became very passionate workers, and they jumped into this internship, and they did three times more than what they should have or had to, and they went on after that internship to become involved in a number of community kinds of issues . . . and they're going on to law school . . . and I found this out when I got their journals that they wrote over the semester. . . . I used to look at this periodically . . . I'd say, "Now don't react that way (personally), react to it as a sociologist; I want you to tell me sociologically what's going on here, what's the interpersonal and interpolitical dynamics here, what actors are involved, what conflict. . . . " And probably in that process was one where I think they had a really good chance to experience this going beyond the individual reaction to the notion of the social reality of what it was they were involved with. And I think they did that pretty well because I think since they were doing other projects like reading background material and looking at information enabled them to put their personal experience in.

This example displays the subtle interrelationship of informal student writing and the internship as a tool for learning the complex perspective of sociology. Writing functions as an expressive tool for students to examine their experience in the internship, and under the guidance of a teacher, move from a personalized perspective to a sociological perspective.

Both informants reported that writing functions in their professional lives in a similar fashion.

P: It (writing) forces a kind of discipline on your thoughts. . . . A lot of redundancies drop out. . . . I think it highlights the logical sequence of your ideas."

The two informants seem to be writers with very different styles, however.

P: The writing I have done . . . just seemed to develop in a very natural way out of the data. . . . when I decided to do a study. . . . I went out and read all I could. . . . So I had a certain set of assumptions I went into the field with. And what I found, it was a really wonderful part of the process, is that like excess baggage you shed these assumptions as you go along. . . . So what happened was I get all my information, I sat down with it, and the data itself suggested the relevant categories that would become the topics that had to be dealt with. As far as the actual writing goes, all I can say is all my life I've had a facility with writing.

This first statement, emphasizing natural process, is in distinct contrast to that of the second participation, emphasizing social experience.

P: There are two types of writers and the one type is the guy who it just flows out of and the other is the guy who works on it and reconstructs, and reconstructs, and I'm really that second type so what I try to do with my students is just give them what I think are the basic ingredients that I use in terms of writing. . . . None of those things (communicating in writing) come easy to me. I'm one of those people who got through graduate school on the basis of persistence . . . and the same thing has been true of my writing. . . .

In the follow-up interview, this same participant elaborated on the difficulty of the writing process.

P: . . . when I tend to write a first draft of an article or paper, I tend to be pretty bombastic, not in the sense of using big words, but I'm usually pretty critical and I always have to go back and rather than say, "This research doesn't tell us anything about the question," you have to say it a little nicer, otherwise people who review your paper are going to say, "Now what do you mean, I wrote two articles on that. . . . " I always have to tone down my things.

This apparent inconsistency between the writing habits of the two sociologists was cleared up when the first participant discussed the use of field notes while collecting her data. The manner in which she writes these notes is very similar to the journal writing that the other instructor requires of students, suggesting that the precedent for the student's journal is the ethnographer's field notes. The field notes are ideas and impressions collected throughout the day. This daily activity of keeping field notes seems to function as both a record of activities and as a form of prewriting. Since the initial conceptual work is undertaken during the research activity, drafting becomes a matter of transcribing previously formed concepts.

Two problems inhibit the use of writing in the sociology curriculum: the number of students in a class, and students' difficulty with expressing themselves in formal writing assignments. The problem of student writing leads one of the instructors to a distinction between English composition classes and sociology classes.

P: What I would like to see is an effort to standardize their composition classes. It's like several people teach introduction to sociology, and it doesn't matter much who teaches it. There's core material that everybody teaches. Otherwise it's just crazy to call it introduction to sociology. Again, there's that common body of knowledge and any survey course, any intro course like that, as you and I know, is basically learning vocabulary anyway. And the vocabulary really doesn't change all that much . . . there's a core of material you have to go through and I think that certainly true in terms of English composition courses also, but the people over there (in the English Department) apparently don't think that . . .

This sociologist also believes that students are unable to write well because they have not mastered grammar.

P: Students can go through this program, and you see this in advising, and the only English course they have to take is composition; a three credit composition course, that's the only God-damned English course they must take. When you add to that the fact that everybody in the English Department, you know, takes a crack at English composition, there is no standardization of that course. Some people go on and teach poetry criticism, some people go on and teach the twentieth century novel; they teach what they damn-well want. Then they pass these kids on to us, of course many of them I doubt, have ever diagrammed a sentence in their life . . . .

The other participant stated that any teacher has to work with students' writing skills, if only to preserve daily sanity at the job. Although suggesting that teaching writing and analytic skills in large sections is difficult, this participant went on to say:

P: . . . if every course a student takes works on those kinds of skills (writing), then every other course (he or she) takes that student will do better (than) in (the previous one) and they will get more out of (it). And in a way, if every course did that, every faculty member would be helping every other faculty member have a more successful course and the college would therefore produce a better product, and in the end, the college community as a whole will benefit. . . .

This statement reflects the notion that fluent writing is fostered by attention to writing in all disciplines. Thus, the belief that poor writing results from lack of knowledge of grammar is contrasted with the recognition that only writing itself helps students to become better writers and thinkers. The second sociologist continually reinforced the notion that writing and other intellectual skills are valuable in their own right, that students should master writing and analytic skills as an important aspect of their education, regardless of their major. The other participant, while condemning the apparent inability of students to write adequately and the English department for failing to train them properly, values writing for both herself and students as an important intellectual tool also. In this context, both participants express regret that some of the written work in classes had to be reduced because of increasing enrollments, reporting a reduction of the amount, not the quality, in both examinations and papers.

The sociologists also differ slightly from one another in their uses of writing. One uses such tools as the journal and the "thought" paper as a method of fostering analytic skills; the other, while emphasizing the intellectual clarity that grows from writing, combines writing as a learning activity with evaluation in final examinations. Although the explicit goal at the root of both teaching practices is to have students use language to explore their knowledge, final examinations require students to master the knowledge transmitted in class before entering the examination room. Journals allow students to experiment with learning without the penalty of a poor grade if they do not achieve understanding at their first try. In this sense, the essay exam is simultaneously the exploration of learning and the evaluation of learning.

The curricular goals of the sociologists are diverse, reflecting differences in their theoretical approaches to their discipline, reflecting differences in their work habits approaches to education. The orientation of their department also reflects this diversity. The variety of perspectives that form the core of their discipline seems to dictate and support this curricular variety.

English

Both participants in English alluded to the split in the profession over the teaching of writing, referred to by Hairston (1982), following Kuhn (1970), as a *paradigm shift*. One of the participants described his training as emerging from the "new paradigm." The other described a critical transformation in his professional life that lead him into it.

> P: I think about the time I came here I was going through a critical pedagogical transformation and I think that it was primarily the influence of colleagues here, namely (another English instructor at the site), a couple of other people, that I began to move away from the, well if it's English comp then we'll write in-class themes and to write five set themes and then I began to move over into other approaches to writing. Then I team-taught a graduate writing workshop with (another English instructor at the site) and that just exploded all the previous Neanderthal notions I had about approaches to writing. And so, I became much more committed to various kinds of writing and using writing for purposes other than measurement of standard English usage skills and coherent paragraphs and such like.

Unlike participants in the other two departments, the rationale for the uses of writing was so intertwined with descriptions of the curriculum and descriptions of the actual writing assignments that I have preserved the integrity of their responses by reporting assignment types and written language functions together. The writing required by both participants in English falls into three categories, expressive, transactive, and poetic, as they consciously follow Britton (1978). The log-journal is the first type of writing that is used by both participants in English. One of the participants reported that he uses a journal in a course in media criticism for several reasons.

> P: (The journal) has a kind of supervisory function for me . . . it's a direct feedback to the pedagogy of the course (and) how the various contents of the course are going. It's a direct feedback to me on how I'm coming across with the content of the course, and also it's a direct expression of what a student will say in the first four weeks of a course. . . . The secondary purpose is I want them to make a status report of their own weekly progress. . . . Sometimes in the journal I've included a word for every day that is both specific and general; a word dealing with terminology, which even though they're communications majors, they're not very acquainted with . . . and then I want them to keep a log which is just a notation without comment, unless they want to make one, of what they're reading and particularly what they're watching (on television for the course).

The journal has four basic functions. It is a record of the student's response to the instructor and the course content, a record of daily activity, a place for students to explore their learning, and a tool for evaluating, but not grading, the student's progress on a regular basis. As a teaching tool, it functions generally for students both to record and to examine their learning through the use of writing. The journal also serves an important private function for this teacher, as a monitor of the television program choices of college students. He stated that he was able to predict the current surge in college students' interest in daytime soaps several months before this be came an object of national attention. As he put it, "Long before it became *Newsweek* knowledge that students were hooked on afternoon soap operas, I knew where they were at 3:00 every afternoon." This last use of the journal reflects the types of logs used by the television rating services to monitor the viewing habits of selected individuals for use by the television industry in planning programming.

The other participant in English discussed the use of the journal in a literature course. His statements imply that he employs it as an expressive tool for students, within a broad spectrum of classroom writing activities. He intends to foster one kind of learning by having students keep journals.

P: They'll also do a journal, and they'll write at least one entry on each work that we read. If we spend a whole week on something like Othello, they'll probably do two or three. . . . And those entries will take all sorts of forms, and I'll have them just explore the variety of kinds of writing you do in response to literature. . . . I stress heavily learning to ask questions about literature and try to convince them that good readers are very uncertain people; they're full of questions and they don't insist on answers right away. That's the exact opposite of the sort of, you know, typical anthology approach where kids are immediately confronted with the hardest question of all, "What is the theme of this story?" That requires that you answer 70 other questions before you can even imagine what the theme is . . . so sometimes in the journal I simply ask them to write questions. I sometimes ask them to speculate about answers. . . . They'll also write quite personal kinds of reactions telling me about characters that they like or dislike and why, that they identify with or don't and why, comparing events in works we read to things that happened to them. I sometimes will give them the beginnings to things and ask them to . . . you know, like the first paragraph of a Hemingway story, and just simply ask them to continue it in that style. I'll ask them to retell episodes from the points of view of one or more characters. And then I (ask students to) take on a task that an author faces like . . . characterizing through dialogue, and I will present that very same task that an author faces at some point, say in a story perhaps to a class, and I'll say, "Now, two people who are total strangers find each other face to face under these sorts of circumstances and talk about this subject. Try to give us an idea of the personality of each in only so many sentences of exchange," and then they will try and then I'll say, "Here is how Ernest Hemingway, for instance, faced that same problem and solved it."

In this case, the journal becomes a tool for students' exploration of their own responses to literature and the act of literary creation. The participant encourages students to look at their own response as a private act, growing out of their own experiences with the literary text, necessitating the expressive use of the journal. The journal is not a private record, as students are often asked to read their journals to the class.

In discussing the journal, both participants suggested that some students are upset by the quantity of writing required in their English classes, because they do not perceive the value of writing. They also reported that those students who willingly become involved with writing assignments do so because they are perceived as low-risk activities, believing the writing itself will not be the focus of evaluation, implying that students do not enjoy writing and believe that they are unable to write with sufficient skill. According to the participants, other students appear to resent the quantity of writing, because the course is about literature or media criticism, as opposed to composition, suggesting that some students believe writing is unrelated to the English curriculum.

Both participants also stated that the journal is a prewriting activity and an instructional tool for developing what they call analytical thought about literature. As with prewriting, the analytical mode of thinking culminates in the critical paper about a literary work. The critical paper is the second mode of writing required of undergraduates. It has a transactional function, relating the private experience of literary response to communication with another person. The term *analysis* was used by the participants in English to describe the special mental activity of literary criticism that lies beyond the expressive record of the journal. As one participant stated it:

P: . . . and it (the journal) also, I think, is a chance to do something different, something that's not critical, analytical, and something I will not go through and pick over, you know, disagree with. . . . The critical writing, I ask them to do in order to think with a kind of closeness about literature that only writing elicits and do that independently of a teacher standing up there asking a whole bunch of questions which sort of supply the thinking structure for them. I think only writing does that about experience. There's a kind of depth of thought about one's experience that writing will generate and so I do it for that reason. I also, I just like the habit of mind that the care and attention that critical writing encourages, fosters, and again I like requiring students to do something well, very carefully. . . . I (also) encourage kids to write the sort of literature that they read, partly because I agree with Donald Graves in the report to the Ford Foundation that our whole educational system encourages passivity, that is valuing the ideas of others over producing one's own, valuing the art of others over producing one's own . . . and I also think again one of the best ways to understand any art is to practice it, to try it. So, I suppose there's a sort of dual rationale, learning appreciation through doing. Appreciation of what an artist is doing by becoming the artist, at least a little bit here and there.

O: Is there some sort of distinction in the kind of thought that occurs between the two types of writing we're talking about now (transactional versus poetic)?

P: Yes. Analytical vs. sort of imaginative, intuitive kind of thought that creates literature. I know it's just a sort of sampling of that kind of thought, the kind
of thinking that a poet does, but I think it's a very useful, helpful one. I think it does
sort of educate the imagination in a way that straight analysis doesn't.

This statement clarifies the role of critical, expository writing in English and
introduces the third mode of discourse in English, contrasting its function with
the explanatory mode. This participant views literary criticism as having two
parts, analysis and appreciation, giving rise to his uses of writing and teaching.
The first, analytic mode requires readers to look closely at their own reaction to a
literary work. When writing transactively about this mode of response to literature, students have to maintain the integrity of their response against the demands
of communication with an audience. The second mode of literary response,
appreciation, is synonymous with enjoyment or pleasure. This mode grows out
of both a breadth of acquaintance with literature and an understanding of of the
creative process itself. He believes that appreciation is fostered by writing in both
expository and poetic forms.

While the other participant does not require that students utilize poetic forms
of writing, he also explicitly joins analytic thinking with critical writing, which
he sponsors in two ways. His discussion of the purpose for having a midterm
conference with individual students about the course illustrates this merging of
knowledge and writing.

P: . . . it's not a composition conference; it's much more the interrelationship of the
writing and the development of knowledge in the area that are working together,
which is my overall objective, that is that the writing be coextensive with the
knowing and that neither writing or knowing be for its own sake . . . the experience
that I've had is that at a certain point the strategies for critical and analytical
thinking, in general, will begin to make sense with what they know, and there will
be an almost perceptible light bulb.

Students awaken to the fact that analytical thinking and critical writing demand a
special perspective, requiring a more decentered perspective than they are accustomed to taking.

P: . . . for some students it's a very, very slow process. They cannot, in some
cases, articulate either verbally or in writing what it is they say they know and
frequently they're blocked or they come in telling me that they're poor writers; I
mean they're already convinced that they're poor writers. Someone has already
convinced them that they're poor writers and it's up to me to try to persuade them
that they aren't poor writers and they aren't poor thinkers, they're just unpracticed.
. . . I will say something at a certain point, and their eyes will glisten and the
corners of their mouths will go up, and they do understand . . . there will be some
people who will still, at that moment, be sitting there and they've only got about 10
or 15 watts, and the other ones are going three ways at once.

The other English teacher also discussed the value of transactive writing about the analytic experience as a means of facilitating the transition from a self-centered perspective on knowledge to a decentered one. Both participants believe that the transition does not occur without writing and, more importantly, direct knowledge of the process of writing.

> P: . . . if some sort of substantive writing isn't required of them and writing that really evolves through a process, then they really have no notion of what really hard won success and the well-developed idea is like . . . and it helps since reading literature is a a very slow and thoughtful process and very few people, I think, come up with dazzling insights into literature instantly. They read, and they reread, and they think, and they ponder, and they ask questions. They arrive slowly at insights that are rich. Writing, in particular, encourages that kind of, you know, rich insights into literature because writing is a slow process and so is reading.

Both of the participants in English utilize an explicitly developmental model for the writing assignments in their courses, one that supports the development of individual pieces of writing through the entire process of text generation, relying heavily on peer responses to help with the problem that reading several drafts of several papers from each student would cause. Although unified in their beliefs about the functions of writing and the need to sponsor the entire process of writing, both participants have slightly different approaches to teaching. One sets up a series of class activities intended to foster writing at different stages of the composing process. The other participant uses two kinds of transactional writing assignments, the Short Writing Assignment (SWA) and the Laboratory Paper. Each assignment has a different function in learning about the subject matter and a different function in learning about writing.

> P: Then, what I call the SWA, is the short writing assignments are essentially peer discussion, editing sessions. I set a topic. Everyone writes on the same topic. I divide the class into small groups and devote one class period to the small group discussion. . . . That has a number of purposes, but the one that is most important to me is that they begin to write some genuine kinds of media criticism, that they get immediate feedback on what they've written from their peers, and that they . . . report to a general in-class discussion of what the topic was. The topics tend to be more global and less specific than the lab assignments, which are very, very specific.
> O: So this is an exploratory kind of thing to look at their own background in the course content without a lot of direction from you about what the output is supposed to look like.
> P: I do, on the handout, tell them they should evaluate each other's papers in terms of four or five specific things which are sort of traditional English composition elements . . . and that they give that kind of feedback to the student. They are required to . . . they've run the papers off, sufficient numbers for everyone in their small group and for me..they are required to give the author of the paper feedback

and when the author of the paper has all the feedback from all of the members of his or her group, he reports that to me.

O: Would the author of the paper do any revision and then hand it in for a grade?

P: I haven't done that. . . . The evaluation of the SWAs is something I try not to get involved with.

O: So the students would actually be responsible for evaluating each other's papers?

P: Right. But, see, the students want to know how come you have something which counts . . . I forget what it is, let's see, 20 percent of my grade . . . and all you get is a copy.

O: Makes them feel a little bit uncomfortable that you are not looking at it and partly that other students have control over the outcome?

P: Well, it's that, plus they want . . . you know, anything that's going to count 20 percent of their grade, they're going to want to know that I have seen it and I have evaluated it, and what I resist is having it become another lab assignment. The lab assignments come directly to me; they don't go to anybody else, and I give them feedback on that, and that's very much one-to-one. Most of the conferencing that I do with them is on their lab assignments. And, the lab assignments are a different kind of activity. I pose essentially lab questions for them, and they have to go and use the videotapes in the lab library and choosing the program, respond, or programs, because I have multiple versions most of the situation comedies and domestic comedies for them to use.

This participant also delineates the two exercises largely in terms of the quality of the assignment itself. The SWAs are guided by a broad question that the students have to approach and evaluate independently. The SWA also forms the primary basis for this instructor's sponsorship of the entire process of writing. The goal for a lab assignment is much more specific and direct, based upon a narrow goal for student learning and less instructor-sponsored writing process activity. Since the SWA is entirely student evaluated, the lab assignment becomes the primary basis for instructor evaluation of student learning, along with the journal. Troubling to the students is the fact that a significant portion of learning in the class is peer directed. This departure from the norm of the teacher-directed evaluation is unique to this participant.

The other participant in English, although he also uses peer responding and peer editing, does not leave the final evaluation of any student writing to students. Like the former participant, he also sponsors production of writing assignments from start to finish.

P: . . . roughly, there'll be a prewriting day in which the topic is open, the topic will be open on the last analytic paper. Part of the assignment is picking a topic to do. And more so on the second, probably less on the first. And, on the first one, I'll give them choices and I want the paper to be an experience that teaches them how crucial in a great story like that every detail can be, to develop an atmosphere, sort of a pervasive feeling, and that that feeling spills over into a theme. And I'll have them on the first day just look at those images separately and talk about the feelings that they generate and then frame a thesis independently. . . . Then we'll list details through the story that sort of develop that and do that independently and then they'll do a draft, come back with it, and they'll help each other, and I'll probably give them guided questions. And they'll help each other with questions . . . then usually there's some stylistic things I have them do too . . . but on the last day they'll bring the typed paper and right in class . . . they'll correct it, that'll be sort of an editing day, and they'll go through and correct spelling and improve transition and all. . . . Then we'll have our one required conference; I hope they'll come for others and I'll invite them to revise it or in some cases just require that they revise it if . . . they can do better.

In this case, the instructor includes topic development in his approach, assuming that students are not able to pick suitable topics for literary papers without training. While he consciously steps students through the entire writing process with class activities, he also helps them see the importance of the process in their developing conceptions of their topics.

P: . . . another strategy I have to encourage their interaction . . . (is to) number all the different kinds of input that went into the writing of a piece. Number it in the margin and make a key for it in the final piece of writing so that scattered through the margins of the final piece of writing . . . were things like "number 1" meant my idea from the first draft, "number 2" idea from conference with student, somebody said add this or delete this or something . . . and so on, and I tell the students, the more they make use of each other and these things that we do, the better it goes over with me in the final paper. That really seems to encourage them to take us seriously. If the conference leads to an expansion of the paper or something and it's clear that I'm going to look to see that they use the conferences with each other to do something with the paper, then it seems to help. . . . And so the sort of sullen, passive kids find themselves reading five things or else . . . because I collect it and grade it, you know, if they haven't got it then it's a real problem.
O: Now would you typically read both drafts together?
P: And I make a great fuss over people whose papers go through all sorts of stages and strategies, you know, and throw away things and so on. Make a great fuss of praising them and that sort of thing.

His approach to writing integrates the written work students do with peers into the whole of the course. Although the two participants in English differ in some aspects of their use of student peer group activity, one depends completely upon peer involvement, including evaluation, the other upon peer input to assist students in preparing for the teacher's evaluation, their differences represent small distinctions without a real theoretical difference.

Perhaps because I was recognized as a college English teacher by the participants in English, they discussed the grammatical formalities of written English very little. They both focus their main efforts on the processes of writing and thinking, with editing in advanced courses handled by peer groups, suggesting that students are expected to have mastered SWE before enrolling in the course. While they both underlined the importance of SWE as the appropriate dialect for writing in college, they stated that grammatical problems in student writing are primarily a manifestation of students' problems with the material, finding that mechanical problems usually disappear if students spend sufficient effort on the meaning they wish to convey in their writing.

The participants in English also expect that the thinking and writing skills students learn in English courses will have broader implications, relating literacy and learning in a more general orientation across disciplines.

> P: . . . those papers are exercises in close reading that I hope will spill over into their reading of everything. They're sort of doing in slow motion what I hope they'll do when they go on and read . . . (I) want them to read analytically as they're going, in order to write analytically. . . . I think that, at least in writing generally, that kids can go all the way through here and perform satisfactorily in a major, and if some sort of really substantive writing isn't required of them, and writing that really evolves through a process, then they really have no notion of what really hard won success and the well-developed idea is like. . . . And this whole notion that good thinking is exclusively of the kind that you can demonstrate on an opscan form, that there's no such thing as the very slow, painstaking discovery of and refinement of and development of good ideas, that you can think well if you don't ever have to do that sort of thinking, I think is wrong and so that's another reason that I believe in writing.

Thus, the uses of writing in the curriculum are tied to the participants' belief that writing and thinking have to be fostered as basic intellectual functions of the individual. They have a central concern for the overall growth of the student and a sense of the responsibility for providing experiences that will help students' intellectual development by fostering an analytic approach to thought and writing more general than a specific knowledge of literary analysis.

The participants in English also discussed the relationship between their own writing, their profession, and student writing. One discussed the revitalization of his current research after a period of scholarly inactivity, because he has been spending more time on his teaching. While he had previously been a very active scholar, the amount of writing that he required of students interfered with the completion of some projects. The other participant discussed his writing both as a scholar and in his interests outside of teaching. While he stated that he does not write very much for a professional audience, he recently completed a book chapter based on his dissertation research. Most of the professional writing that he discussed was connected to the writing of his students. When they write, he writes with them. He also discussed his correspondence with colleagues as an important aspect of his professional writing, stating that this writing, in particular, was of special importance to his growth as a teacher, suggesting that his use of peer writing groups writing to stimulate the development of thought in his classes may mirror his own experience with writing. His dissatisfaction with professional research and publication grows out of his dissatisfaction with the register of literary criticism.

> P: . . . someone who's pleased with that sort of critical voice, and I don't know if I should be pleased with it because most people can't take it on effectively. It's usually stuffy and labored and unpleasant when kids do it and I think of my own undergraduate papers in English, you know, and I think it is a limiting kind of writing . . . I think it does teach that sort of close thinking and some appreciation, but it has problems I hope to improve. . . it does (professional critical writing) represent, it seems to me, a different experience and an experience in the hands of some of these people who are so complex and just unreadable that most people don't understand it unless you're required to read it in graduate school, the way we all were, and an experience that most of us don't even want . . . on the other hand, C.S. Lewis was able to write things like the *Preface to Paradise Lost* so that an undergraduate could read it and appreciate the richness of his ideas . . . and yet understand them too . . . if you say, "Well, this is a great study in English, it tells us a lot, but it's very poorly written," that communicates a very mixed message . . . you can be an English educator without being a good writer or you could be a sociologist without being a good writer.

Professional writing in literary study is problematic for this participant, because he is able to identify much that he does not want to emulate in his perception of the dry persona of the professional literary critic. Yet he admires the special quality of certain preferred works of criticism which breathe life into the literary work they examine.

The participants' beliefs about professional writing may grow out of the fact that English teachers are particularly self-conscious writers. Because they teach writing, they have very high stylistic standards. They also seem exceptionally concerned about the problems created for the discipline by the need to publish, because, in their view, this need encourages rapid publication of ideas that are not fully developed or publication of ideas that are only marginally original. In addition, they do not enjoy the formal register of critical writing, divorced as it is from the primary process of reading. The need to write is not satisfied by their professional writing alone. The role of the department is primarily training secondary English teachers in the departmental majors courses and training undergraduates to write in general education English courses. Reflecting the orientation of the department, these English instructors seemed less interested in writing for publication. While they do not publish frequently, they are busy writers who practice the notion that one must be a writer to teach writing effectively.

DISCUSSION

All participants in this study had explicit beliefs about the uses of writing in their disciplines and in their teaching, grounding their views of the function of student writing in the classroom in the relationship between writing and learning. Some of the participants' statements in each discipline suggest the need for discipline-specific models of learning and writing, confirming Jolliffe's (1984; Jolliffe & Brier, this volume) concern about the function of writing in disciplinary enculturation. However, two factors underlying the models of the function of writing in each of the disciplines unify them and allow the construction of a single model of learning and writing across all three disciplines. Representing broad interrelated continuums on which each of the disciplines can be located, these factors are the nature of the knowledge that the undergraduate has to master and the teachers' methods of communicating that knowledge.

Related to Bartholomae's (1985) observation that the problem the undergraduate has to face is not mastery of a single academic discourse community but of several disciplinary discourse communities, each discipline presents the student with varying degrees of certainty about knowledge. Faculty tailor their approaches to teaching based on their conceptions of knowledge in their discipline. Their views of the potential uses of writing as a teaching tool are subject to this constraint as well. Participants in each of the disciplines also appear to differ about the specifiability of the casual relations between their teaching and student learning. More simply, when faculty see their discipline as matter of memorization, they perceive a direct connection between their actions as teachers and student learning. When faculty see the nature of learning requiring the student to go beyond collecting facts, they are less able to tie their teaching directly to student learning.

Three other factors play a significant role in the participants' approach to teaching and their uses of writing in teaching: their commitment to scholarship, the viability of their departments as training grounds for scholars, and their view of the general function of writing in learning and teaching. These factors confound the previous two, because they are not discipline-specific aspects of teaching. Instead, they grow out of the local context of the institution and the place of the individual department in that setting. The participants' committment to scholarship affects their approaches to instruction because of the limits it sets to their involvement with students. The number of majors, a determinant of class size, also dictates the amount of writing that can be used. Finally, the informants differed within disciplines on some functions of writing for undergraduates, related to their own experience as writers. Thus, this study confirms that the function of writing in specific curricula is indeed subject to both disciplinary factors and local factors.

Teaching and Learning in Different Disciplines

Student learning.   The primary contrast in the differing perspectives on student learning in the disciplines is the locus of certainty about the substance of the discipline for the undergraduate. In biology, both participants characterize the substance of mastering the discipline as a matter of memorization, growing out of their view that scientific knowledge is fixed, at least for the undergraduate. In sociology, the emphasis of both participants was on the uncertainty produced by the conflicting views on sociological knowledge. Both of the sociologists, like the biologists, expect students to have acquired new information. But they believe the very nature of that knowledge requires students to move beyond any particular piece of it in the process of learning. Unlike biology, the knowledge of sociology that confronts the undergraduate is not fixed and unchanging, forcing students to an analytic mode of learning as opposed to memorization. Dealing with the conflict is inescapable, because it is this conflict that defines sociology as a discipline. The other feature of scoiology is that it forces students to confront their own adolescent egocentrism as they master the discipline (Erikson, 1968; Perry, 1970). The participants in English also described the need for students to decenter as they studied literature and also employed the term *analysis* to characterize the student's learning. At no time did they discuss, however, a body of knowledge that they expected students to master. Instead, they suggested that knowledge in English lies in analysis and appreciation, the process of reading a literary work.

This description captures the poles of the learning factor. Biology has a fixed content that is represented to the undergraduate as built on a foundation of certainty. The metaphor of learning a new language, suggested by one of the biologists, seems to be appropriate, because the undergraduate is faced with mastering new sets of labels as well as new processes of thinking and writing. Even in the case of the laboratory experience, learning is the repetition of previously established procedures. Biology, in the conception of the biologists in this study, is based on clearly defined territory that must be mapped out for the student. The primary function of student writing in biology is to record the survey of the terrain. The orientation of the biology curriculum toward preparing students for graduate study appears to influence the participants when they include writing assignments in laboratory work that require learning the disciplinary voice of biology.

It is worth noting that this view of biology has been challenged. Myers' (1985) examination of professional writing in biology does not confirm the fixed view of knowledge as an accurate one. A number of other writers have suggested that the belief that science is a fixed and unchanging body of knowledge is not reflected in the history of science (Kuhn, 1970) or the beliefs of some scientists in a variety of scientific disciplines (Thomas, 1974, 1983; Zukav, 1979).

Because there is no formal content to reading literary works apart from response, knowledge in English cannot be specified apart from the acts of reading and writing about reading. Undergraduates have to learn a characteristic mode of thinking about literature as they read. The participants in English in this study believe that literary response begins in an inherently personal act and use writing as a mode of exploring response. In addition, they also sponsor more formal writing activities that are intended to provide the basis for students to begin communicating their response to others. In one sense, this communication is a beginning of students' participation in the literary experience. They also ask students to explore literature through creation of literary discourse. The purpose of this type of writing is to teach students more about how to respond to literature, as opposed to teaching them how to write literary discourse more effectively. In contrast to biology, little attention is paid to training undergraduate students to write in the disciplinary voice. Again, this stance toward the disciplinary voice seems to be conditioned by local factors, since the department's curriculum is more oriented toward preparing teachers of English for secondary schools than preparing students for graduate school.

Sociology lies between biology and English, because the nature of knowledge is grounded in the conflict between theoretical orientations and the student's need to master the substance of those orientations. Like English and unlike biology, knowledge is not in the knowing but in what the student has done with it, the analytic framework created for it. Unlike English and like biology, sociological knowledge is believed to be codified and is understood to have an independence from student learning. But the student is expected to go beyond substance and both evaluate and apply it. The orientation of this sociology department toward the disciplinary voice in student writing is probably quite unusual. Because they have few majors and send few students to graduate training, a local condition, they are not particularly concerned with teaching students to master the disciplinary voice of sociology.

Teaching methodology. If learning biology is primarily a matter of memorization, teaching biology is primarily giving out information. Teaching is predominantly lecturing; evaluation of student learning is viewed as an objective procedure. In sociology, lectures were combined with class discussion as a method of conveying knowledge of sociological theory and encouraging students to apply it analytically. The focus of evaluation for both of the sociologists was on the objective demonstration that students had new knowledge and a more subjective evaluation of students' work with that knowledge. In English, the teaching of literature and the evaluation of student learning are intimately tied to the use of writing. Teaching is indirect. The use of peer activity as a regular part of class activities demonstrates this conclusion. Evaluation is based upon a subjective view of the student as an individual reader of literature, depending not on how much he or she has learned, but instead upon the teacher's assessment of the student's private act of reading a literary text through his or her ability to recast it in writing. Possibly to counteract the potential subjectivity of their judgments, the English instructors utilize a variety of modes of writing to assess students. This variety provides them with an indication of the effort that students put into their work, guarding against the possiblity of prejudicial judgments based upon a disagreement about the substance of response as oppposed to the quality of response.

Thus, the undergraduate studying literature faces a teaching methodology that can only be defined in the process of doing it. Biology is at the other extreme, with a public knowledge base and an externally defined teaching methodology. Sociology lies somewhere in between biology and English, because it has a fairly clearly defined body of knowledge for students to master and an implicit curricular goal of moving students beyond their egocentric perspectives toward one that views everyday occurrences as public events.

Analysis, as employed by the English and sociology instructors, is a mystical term used to define a teaching/learning process that cannot be described independently from students' demonstrations of their ability to perform it. While these participants are able to say what they want students to be able to to, they did not believe that the analytic perspective was something that could be readily taught. In English, the term *analysis* is also a code word suggesting the participants' identification with the school of literary study known as New Criticism. Their view of literary study is also overlaid with more recent developments in literary response theory described by Bleich (1978), Holland (1975), Petrosky (1985), and Rosenblatt (1978), among others. This contrast accounts for their emphasis on the subjective nature of the act of responding, and their need to move this private act to the public act of communicating about it.

Also worth noting is the belief of both sociologists and English teachers that the analytic perspective and writing itself are skills with value outside their disciplines. This perspective suggests that they see themselves participating in a larger college community. This institutional perspective was not shared by the biologists, perhaps because their primary orientation for students is toward the discipline itself.

The Function of Writing in Three Curricula

Clearly none of the participants could be held to ascribe to either the general writing approach or the discipline-specific writing approach as defined by Jolliffe (1984). For the most part, the functions of writing in all three curricula, according to the participants, are involved with both writing as a mode of learning and as a mode of disciplinary participation. Writing as disciplinary participation is related to the particular curricular goals of the individual department. Because the biologists' main goal at this institution is to train students to enter the apprentice level of the profession, they include writing in the disciplinary voice. The participants in English emphasize personal uses of writing as a tool in learning over discipline-specific uses, because they, like the sociologists, are working with a variety of students, some of whom will go on to advanced study or careers in the field and some of whom are interested in the study of the field for its own sake.

Thus, disciplines, from the perspective of the undergraduate, could be said to have two primary types of registers, those related to learning and those related to disciplinary uses of writing. Registers related to learning are the functions of written language commonly used by teachers in the process of instruction and will not form a part of the registers of the disciplinary voice. However, student registers are no less a part of disciplinary enculturation than discipline-specific registers, because both are parts of the path toward acceptance into the discipline as a mature participant.

As Garvin (1977) observes, behavior has multiple functions when it is viewed in its natural setting. Clearly, writing has several important functions for undergraduate students. As Jolliffe (1984) surmises, the meaning of learning to write is indeed an aspect of disciplinary enculturation, when viewed from the context of the discipline. When viewed from the context of a particular curriculum at a particular college or university, the multiple functions of writing are subject to local factors that determine the extent to which faculty teaching in a department see the need for undergraduates to participate directly in the discourse community by writing texts conditioned by the disciplinary voice. As departments see themselves participating in the training of scholars, they emphasize the enculturation function of writing and focus on the disciplinary voice. As departments see themselves apart from the training of scholars, the function of writing in learning appears to be governed by factors which emphasize more general uses of writing. While the orientation of teachers toward knowledge itself is the other dominant factor in the function of student writing that they sponsor in their classrooms, the picture of learning and the function of writing in the three curricula in this study implies that any real conclusions about the writing and the teaching of writing will be bound inextricably to that context, despite the influence of disciplinary factors.

This confounding of local contextual factors and discipline-specific factors validates the necessity of holistic research methodology in further explorations of writing in academic disciplines, because only qualitative research can capture the variety functions that writing can take on in a college or university setting with its two, often conflicting, contexts. This observation has broader implications for research in rhetoric and composition, indeed in any research on the teaching of language. To the extent that such research is decontextualized as Faigley (1985) and Harste, Woodward, and Burke (1984), among many others, observe, it contributes to the split between teachers and researchers. Because decontextualized research is not sensitive to the many local factors that affect the daily lives of teachers, despite their connections to their profession, they will have some difficulty perceiving the potential applications of such research. Classroom language research conducted through a laboratory model simplifies too many of the contextual factors through its very attempt to isolate and manipulate specific variables. This simplification causes language teachers, who live in the very complicated context of the classroom, to perceive the conditions behind the research to be underdetermined, resulting in their rejection of the practicality of the recommendations for teaching that grow out of the research (Bolster, 1983).

I suspect that researchers will ultimately have to become more accustomed to addressing the issue of audience as they design and report their research. While I have been advocating holistic methodology as the soundest basis for research that leads to direct application, I do not want to deny the validity of basic research on language and language teaching. Such research may well be conducted in a laboratory-like setting and not have immediate applications to language teaching and learning. But researchers will have to understand that the extent to which they wish to have a direct impact on teachers and learners will determine the extent to which they will have to go beyond a decontextualized research methodology and examine the validity of their findings in contextualized research which preserves the complex interaction of variables in actual classrooms.

This study also suggests the reason for the variety of models of writing across the curriculum that has emerged in the literature. Each institution, indeed each department in each institution, may have its own perspective on what students must learn in a writing course that addresses the needs of writing in the discipline. This diversity is a sign of a healthy and robust profession. Researchers in writing and teachers of writing would, perhaps, be a little more patient with each another in disagreements about models if they took the time to understand and acknowledging the influence of local factors on curriculum design.

REFERENCES

Applebee, A. N. (1981). *Writing in the secondary schools*. Urbana, IL: National Council of Teachers of English.

Bartholomae, D. (1985). Inventing the university. In M. Rose (Ed.), *When a writer can't write* (pp. 134–165). New York: Guilford.

Baugh, J. (1983, March). *The English of American Blacks and Chicanos*. Paper presented to the Graduate Group in Semiotics of the Linguistics Department, State University of New York at Buffalo.

Bazerman, C. (1982, December). *The discourse paths of different disciplines*. Paper presented at the Annual Meeting of the Modern Language Association, Los Angeles.

Bazerman, C. (1983). What written knowledge does: Three examples of academic discourse. *Philosophy of the Social Sciences, 11*, 361–387.

Belson, W. A. (1967). Tape recording: Its effect on accuracy of response in survey interviews. *Journal of Marketing Research, 4*, 253–260.

Bizzell, P. (1984, March). *What happens when basic writers come to college?* Paper presented at the Annual Meeting of the Conference on College Composition and Communication, New York.

Bizzell, P. (1985, March). *Separation and resistance in academic discourse*. Paper presented at the Annual Meeting of the Conference on College Composition and Communication, Minneapolis.

Bizzell, P. (1986, March). *Academic discourse: Taxonomy of conventions or collaborative practice?* Paper presented at the Annual Meeting of the Conference on College Composition and Communication, New Orleans.

Bleich, D. (1978). *Subjective criticism*. Baltimore, MD: John Hopkins University Press.

Bolster, Jr., A. R. (1983). Toward a more effective model of research on teaching. *Harvard Educational Review, 53*, 294–308.

Britton, J. S. (1978). The composing process and the functions of writing. In C. R. Cooper & L. Odell (Eds.), *Research in composing: Points of departure* (pp. 13–28). Urbana, IL: National Council Teachers of English.

Britton, J.S., Burgess, T., Martin, N., McLeod, A., & Rosen, H. (1975). *The development of writing abilities (11-18)*. London: Macmillian Education Limited.

Cazden, C. B. (1983). Peekaboo as an instructional model: Discourse development at home and school. In B. Bain (Ed.), *The sociogenesis of language and human conduct* (pp. 33–58). New York: Plenum.

Clark, K. (1965). *Dark ghetto*. New York: Harper.

Diesing, P. (1971). *Patterns of discovery in the social sciences*. New York: Aldine.

Erikson, E. H. (1968). *Identity, youth and crisis*. New York: W. W. Norton.

Faigley, L. (1985). Nonacademic writing: The social perspective. In L. Odell & D. Goswami (Eds.), *Writing in nonacademic settings* (pp. 231–248). New York: Guilford.

Freedman S. (1984). The registers of student and professional expository writing: Influences on teachers' responses. In R. Beach & L.S. Bridwell (Eds.), *New directions in composition research* (pp. 334–347). New York: Guilford.

Garvin, P.L. (1977, March). *An empiricist epistemology for linguistics*. Inaugural Lecture at The Fourth Annual LACUS Forum, Montreal.

Goetz, J.P., & LeCompte, M.D. (1984). *Ethnography and qualitative design in educational research*. New York: Academic.

Gumperz, J. J. (1971) *Language in social groups: Essays selected and introduced by Anwar S. Dill*. Palo Alto, CA: Stanford University Press.

Hairston, M. (1982). The winds of change: Thomas Kuhn and the revolution in the teaching of writing. *College Composition and Communication, 33*, 76–88.

Halliday, M. A. K. (1970). Language structure and language function. In J. Lyons (Ed.), *New horizons in linguistics* (pp. 140–165). Baltimore, MD: Penguin.

Halliday, M. A. K. (1978). *Language as social semiotic*. Baltimore, MD: University Park Press.

Harste, J. C., Woodward, V. A., & Burke, C. L. (1984). Examining our assumptions: A transactional view of literacy and learning. *Research in the Teaching of English, 18*, 84–108.

Heath, S. B. (1982). Questioning at home and at school: A comparative study. In G. Spindler (Ed.), *Doing the ethnography of schooling: Educational anthropology in action* (pp. 102–131). New York: Holt, Rinehart, & Winston.

Heath, S. B. (1983). *Ways with words: Language, life, and work in communities and classrooms*. New York: Cambridge University Press.

Holland, N. N. (1975). *5 readers reading*. New Haven, CT: Yale University Press.

Hymes, D. (1968). The ethnography of speaking. In J. A. Fishman (Ed.), *Readings in the sociology of language* (pp. 99–138). The Hague: Mouton.

Hymes, D. (1972). On communicative competence. In J. Pride & J. Holmes (Eds.), *Sociolinguistics* (pp. 269–293). Harmondsworth, England: Penguin.

Jolliffe, D.A. (1984). *Audience, subject, form and ways of speaking: Writers' knowledge in the discipline.* Unpublished doctoral dissertation, University of Texas at Austin.

Kuhn, T. S. (1970). *The structure of scientific revolution* (2nd ed.). Chicago, IL: University of Chicago.

Miles, M. B., & Huberman, A. M. (1983). *Qualitative data analysis: A sourcebook of new methods.* Beverly Hills, CA: Sage Publications.

Labov, W. (1972). *Language in the inner city: Studies in the Black English Venacular.* Philadelphia: University of Pennsylvania Press.

Mosher, C. A., & Kalton, G. (1972). *Survey methods in social investigation* (2nd ed.). New York: Basic Books.

Myers, G. (1985). The social world of two biologists' proposals. *Written Communication, 3,* 219–245.

Nystrand, M. (1982). Rhetoric's "audience" and linguistics' "speech community": Implications for understanding writing, reading, and text. In M. Nystrand (Ed.), *What writers know: The language, process, and structure of written discourse* (pp. 1–30). New York: Academic Press.

Perry, W. G. (1970). *Forms of intellectual and ethical development in the college years.* New York: Holt, Rinehart and Winston.

Petrosky, A. R. (1985). Response: A way of knowing. In C. R. Cooper (Ed.), *Researching response to literature and the teaching of literature: Points of departure* (pp. 70–86). Norwood, NJ: Ablex Publishing Corp.

Pike, K. L. (1959). Language as particle, wave and field. *Texas Quarterly, 2,* 37–54.

Pike, K. L. (1967). *Language in relation to a unified theory of human behavior.* The Hague, Netherlands: Mouton.

Pike, K. L. (1982). *Linguistic concepts.* Lincoln, NE: University of Nebraska.

Rosenblatt, L. M . (1978). *The reader, the text, the poem: The transactional theory of literary work.* Carbondale, IL: Southern Illinois.

Saussure, F. de. (1960). *Course in general linguistics* (W. Baskin, trans.). London: Baskin. (Original work published 1916.)

Thomas, L. (1974). *The lives of a cell: Notes of a biology watcher.* New York: Viking.

Thomas, L. (1983). *Late night thoughts on listening to Mahler's Ninth Symphony.* New York: Viking Press.

Toulman, S. (1972). *Human understanding: The collective uses and evolution of concepts.* Princeton, NJ: Princeton University Press.

Vygotsky, L. S. (1968). *Thought and language* (E. Hanfmann and G. Vakar, trans.). Cambridge, MA: M.I.T. Press. (Original work published 1932.)

Vygotsky, L. S. (1978). *Mind in society: The development of higher mental processes* (M. Cole, V. John-Steiner, S. Scribner, & T. Souberman, trans.). Cambridge, MA: Harvard University Press.

Wertsch, J. V. (1983). The role of semiosis in L. S. Vygotsky's theory of human cognition. In B. Bain (Ed.), *The sociogenesis of language and human conduct* (pp. 17–31). New York: Plenum.

Zukav, G. (1979). *The dancing Wu Li Masters: An overview of the new physics.* New York: Bantam.

4 Teaching, Writing, and Learning: A Naturalistic Study of Writing in an Undergraduate Literature Course*

Anne J. Herrington

University of Massachusetts at Amherst

The pioneering work of James Britton and his colleagues (1975), particularly as reported in *The Development of Writing Abilities (11–18)*, has been a major force in focusing writing research and pedagogy on the relation between writing and learning in school. Their work raises a question of import not only for writing classrooms, but for classes in all disciplines where teachers ask their students to write: When we ask students to write, what educational function is it serving for them?

Theoretical and practical scholarship identifies a number of functions that writing in school might serve. Some scholars argue that writing can function to help introduce students to the intellectual and social conventions of the academic communities they are participating in at school and the professional communities they will enter after school (Maimon, 1983; Bizzell, 1982; Bazerman, 1982). Related to this last function, Toulmin (1972) argues that writing can be a means of demonstrating one's knowledge in the sense of showing one is "learning to perform the relevant collective activities" of a discipline. Other scholars shift the focus to the immediate function writing can serve for students as a means to engage in independent thinking, exploring and shaping their own ideas about their reading and other data they encounter (Britton et al., 1975; Fulwiler, 1982; Knoblauch & Brannon, 1983). The assumption underlying all of these claims as to function is that writing in school plays a central role in the intellectual life of students, both while in school and after.

If one accepts this assumption, then it is important for researchers to examine

* This study was supported by a grant from the National Council of Teachers of English Research Fund. In addition to thanking NCTE, I wish to thank the professor and students of the course I studied for sharing their time and insights with me. I thank also my research assistant, Linda Ferreira-Buckley, for her careful and insightful work.

whether and how any of these functions are realized. Such studies are important for two reasons. First, they would help clarify misconceptions of functions. Too often, as popularly used, functions are distorted in ways that have negative consequences for teaching. For instance, *exploring ideas* and *demonstrating knowledge* (and the broader terms *expressive* and *transactional* functions) are often treated as mutually exclusive, with the former term associated with true learning and the latter with parroting back information. Further, a given function is often identified with a given type of writing (e.g., journal writing with exploring ideas and term papers with demonstrating knowledge) as if function resided in texts, instead of in writers' and readers' intentions. Such distortions not only obscure what may be fruitful interrelationships among functions, but also may lead teachers to choose certain types of writing assignments and not others because they are assumed to embody certain functions.

Second, such studies would further our understanding of the way the social situation in which one writes influences the function writing will serve. Recent naturalistic studies of elementary and secondary classrooms that have begun to explore these influences have shown that the teacher, as initiator and sole audience for most writing, has a particularly strong influence in determining functions (Florio & Clark, 1982) and the general intellectual activities reflected in students' writing (e.g., summary versus analysis, Applebee, 1984; reproduction versus reconstruction, Mosenthal, 1983).

The study reported on in this chapter continues this line of research, but in a college course whose aim is to introduce students to some of the methods and texts of the discipline. By studying this course, my aim was to explore how a teacher by her words and actions in class influences the specific interpretive approaches students use in their papers. The study considers as well a factor other research (Dyson, 1984; Faigley & Hansen, 1985) has shown is important: individual students' own backgrounds and interests and how they may influence those students' perceptions of functions and how they respond to the teacher. The specific questions that guided this study are as follows:

- What functions does writing serve for learning within the class studied?
- How are those functions shaped by the professor's manner of conducting class (i.e., the nature of the assignment, the way she conducts class sessions and projects her role)?
- How are those functions and the professor's manner of teaching linked to students' writing and learning (i.e., the interpretive strategies used in their writing and the way individual students interpret functions and approach the writing assignments)

METHOD

The study uses a combination of methods associated with naturalistic research, including both quantitative and qualitative approaches and such specific methods as a survey questionnaire, participant-observation, interviews with students and professors, and text analysis (Schatzmann & Strauss, 1973; Doheny-Farina & Odell, 1985; and Denzin, 1970).

Course Studied

The study was conducted in an undergraduate literature course, *English 222: British Literature from 1798*, taught at a large state university. The course is one of four British and American survey courses required of English majors as introductions to literary studies. As described in the *Undergraduate Bulletin*, each course is to be "an introduction to literary history and analysis." According to the professor who teaches the course, her primary aim was to "teach the students how to read like English majors." The secondary aim was having them learn about the major periods and authors covered. For the course, students were expected to take two exams, keep a reading journal all semester, and write two formal papers. Although I do not discuss these journals in this chapter, I believe they were one factor in establishing an atmosphere conducive to using writing with an expressive intent. Here, I focus on the papers.

I chose to conduct the study in a literature course primarily because I believe those of us in English interested in the role writing can play for learning in any discipline should begin to examine practice in our own discipline as well as others, particularly some of our as yet unexamined assumptions about the functions various types of writing assignments serve and how those functions are determined.

Participants

The primary participants in the study included the teacher of the course and seven students enrolled in the course (total enrollment of 45). The professor, Dr. J., an associate professor, is an experienced teacher of this course. She is also a rhetoric scholar and experienced teacher of writing, so there is some reason to believe she applies sound rhetorical principles in using writing in this course. She received a distinguished teaching award from the university's College of Liberal Arts in 1986.

The seven students chosen for the intensive study represented the range of students enrolled in the course. Four were beginning literature students in their second through fifth semester who had taken only one or no college literature courses before this course. Three were more experienced literature students in their sixth through eighth semester who had already taken five or more literature courses. They also represented a range of abilities from average to superior, as determined by their performance on the first exam in the course and the instructor's and my own judgments of their participation in class discussions during the first 5 weeks of the semester.

From these seven, I have selected three to present as illustrative case studies. I describe their backgrounds in the full case study reports at the end of this chapter.

In addition to the primary participants, a larger sample of students and faculty was also consulted to obtain information about the larger community of which the primary participants were a part. The students included 35 members of the class who completed a survey about functions and audiences for the writing assignments, and three other literature professors who completed the survey and were interviewed. All three professors teach similar introductory survey courses for majors.

INSTRUMENTATION

Writing Questionnaire

The questionnaire administered to the larger sample of students and faculty asked respondents the purposes they perceived for doing each writing assignment. Respondents were given a list of six possibilities and asked to rate each on an ordinal response continuum. (See Table 1.) They also completed open-ended questions asking about primary and secondary audiences, characteristics of the primary audience, and their own definitions of the purposes they had indicated were primary (e.g., What does 'demonstrating knowledge' mean to you?). Students completed the questionnaire twice, immediately after finishing each major writing assignment. The faculty completed it once.

Participant-Observation

Throughout the 15 weeks of the course, I attended at least one of the two weekly class meetings, taking field notes and participating to a limited degree in discussions. The aim of my observations was to identify characteristics of the professor's manner of teaching, the way she interacted with students, and the way assignments were presented. Excerpts from the field notes were used in the interviews.

Interviews

Each of the primary participants was interviewed twice. During the first interview, completed after the first writing assignment had been evaluated by the professor, the students were asked to elaborate on their questionnaire responses and interpret the professor's in-class explanation of the assignment (e.g., What did Professor J. mean when she said, "It should have an interesting issue to explore"?).

In the first interview, they also completed discourse-based interviews about their first papers. These interviews were conducted to elicit the students' interpretations of the assignment, particularly the issue, purpose, and interpretive strategies appropriate to it. The interview procedure involved asking each student about specific sections (each ranging in length from one word to a sentence) of his or her paper (Odell & Goswami, 1982; Odell, Goswami, & Herrington, 1983). The sections I chose were of the following three types (the brackets denote the specific section I asked students about):

> *Statements of Elaboration:*
> Example: "One concerns Hardy's concentration on cycles—[both natural cycles that bring harvests and frosts, and unnatural cycles that produce strawberries and roses out of season.]"
> *Statements that set up some dissonance:*
> Example: "Oscar Wilde's 'The Importance of Being Earnest' [can be deceiving. Ostensibly only a light comedy, it actually] explores serious questions about an individual's relationship to his society."
> *Statements that make an inference or judgment:*
> Example: "[An introduction which sends the reader on a voyage in "a bark of dead men's bones" . . . leads the reader to expect a story of violence and adventure, not a statement in spiritual terms about human psychology.]"

In the interviews I would ask whether the interviewee would be willing to delete or alter the bracketed section, and why. I explained that I was not in any way implying that the bracketed section should be deleted or altered, and that I was most interested in the reasons the interviewees gave for whatever decision they made.

The second interviews, conducted after the second assignment was returned, included a second discourse-based interview on this assignment and questions about interviewees' perceptions of the professor's manner of teaching. As one part of the interview, interviewees were given transcripts of the beginning of two class sessions I had judged to be typical. (See Figure 1 for an example.) They were asked first whether they agreed they were typical, and then to comment on the professor's manner. They were also asked about Professor J.'s manner of conducting class (e.g., "Would you characterize it as directive or nondirective?")

The three other literature professors were interviewed once. In these interviews, I asked them to complete the Writing Questionnaire, interpet the assignment as Professor J. had given it, and complete discourse-based interviews about the second writings of the three case study students.

Analysis of Students' Writing

For the analysis of students' writing in this class, I used the first and second papers written by the seven primary participants. While these papers are a small sample of the full class, the professor felt them to be representative of the class.

To analyze lines of reasoning, I analyzed the issues and claims appearing in these papers. For the initial analysis of types of issues, *issue* was defined broadly as the primary problem or question that a paper tried to address. A stricter definition, following rhetorical and argumentation theory, would have stipulated that only problems in dispute or questions for which an answer was not yet known be termed issues. Further, they would have had to be of interest to an audience. (See, for example, Aristotle, *Rhetoric*, line 1357a25; Toulmin, Rieke, & Janik, 1979, pp. 267–76). I did not use this stricter definition because it would have meant excluding some papers, since they did not have an apparent issue, at least not for the audience, the professor. My aim was to be more inclusive in order to analyze characteristics of both the less and the more successful papers. I identified the issues in all papers by my own critical analysis of the introductory sections.

Claims were defined using Toulmin et al.'s definition: "assertions put forth with the implication that there are underlying 'good reasons' that could show them to be 'well founded'" (1979, p. 29). I identified claims using the procedure I developed for an earlier study (Herrington, 1985), using such explicit cues as logical connectives indicating a conclusion (e.g., so, therefore) and adjectives of evaluation (e.g., good, incongruous). For this study, I also included the following types of interpretive statements:

> *Classificatory statements: Noun1 is Noun2.*
> Example: "Here, Keats is a confident and intensely capable master."
> *Statements that identify an attribute: Noun is adj.*
> Example: ". . . he paints for us a picture that is so vivid that we can almost smell it."
> *Inference statements that explicitly or implicitly refer to an effect.*
> Example: "Using this technique, Joyce allows the reader to see what Eveline cannot see . . ."

Using these cues, I identified specific claim sentences and excerpted them from the papers for subsequent analysis.

DATA ANALYSIS

Questionnaire

The questions about purposes were analyzed using descriptive statistics. The open-ended questions were analyzed using methods of content analysis. This analysis was done by my research assistant and then checked by me.

Participant Observation

My field notes consisted of written transcripts of the class sessions that I attended. I analyzed these notes to identify the issues most frequently raised, the way the professor typically conducted discussions, the ways assignments were presented, and the role the professor projected in class. I checked the validity of my analyses by comparing them with information from the participants, both the students and the professor.

Interviews

To analyze the open-ended portions of the interviews, I read all responses to a given question, looked for patterns in these responses, and excerpted specific interview responses to illustrate each generalization.

For the part of the study reported on in this chapter, I used only the discourse-based interviews relevant to the case studies: those of Sandy, Sheila, and Kerri, and the professor. These interviews are an additional source of information regarding these students' and the professor's understanding of the demands of the assignment, specifically issue, purpose, and appropriate lines of reasoning (e.g., claims and data).

Analysis of Students' Writing

I analyzed issues in two ways. First, I classified them according to types (e.g., a question about theme, a question about narrative technique). I also analyzed the way the issues were formulated in the less- versus the more-successful papers. (The evaluations of how successful the papers had been was based on Prof. J's grade and on my own and two research assistants' judgments.)

Claim statements were analyzed using a categorization scheme to classify types of reasons. I developed the scheme by reading the papers and inductively formulating classifications for all the types of claim statements made. I referred also to Purves and Rippere's (1968) classification scheme, "Elements of Writing about a Literary Work."[1] As Table 2 indicates, the scheme I developed has four primary categories: Personal Reaction, Interpretation of Meaning, Interpretation of Technique, and Evaluation.

Second, two readers (Ph. D. students in rhetoric and composition) and I used the scheme to classify the claim statements, with two readers for each paper's set of claims. In those instances where the first two readers did not agree, the third

---

[1] The scheme I developed differs from Purves and Rippere's in two primary ways: (a) Since my research aim was to identify claim statements only, I did not include statements of fact or paraphrases or plot summary that would be included within the Purves and Rippere Perception category. I did, however, include as interpretive claims inference statements of the kind they classify as perception (e.g., "Jonas' use of paradox reflects the confused situation in which he finds himself." See Purves & Rippere, 1968, p. 22). (b) My category of Personal Reaction differs from their category of Engagement-Involvement primarily in that it includes only personal reaction claims that refer to "I." Personal reactions statements referring to "the author" or "we" were classified as either II.E. Interpretation of Meaning based on effect on readers, or III.E. Interpretation of Technique based on effect on readers.

reader read and rated the claim also. The claim was then classified on the basis of agreement by two of the readers. The overall percentage of agreement was 81%.

RESULTS

Functions

The Writing Questionnaire results show that both the professor and the students perceived that the papers served multiple functions. More specifically, the professor's response to the questionnaire showed that she wanted these papers to serve three main functions, all related to her primary aim for the course (to have students learn "how to read like English majors"). As Table 1 indicates, the primary function was "exploring and shaping the writer's own ideas," with "proving a point about something," and "convincing someone" as dominant as well. "Demonstrating your knowledge of something" was a secondary purpose. She explained this last purpose as follows: "Not specific knowledge, [but] interpetive skills. . . [for example] knowledge of *how* the imagery of a poem combines to make a certain effect."

The students' responses to the questionnaire showed that they shared the professor's perception that the primary function was "exploring and shaping one's own ideas." They saw three functions as secondary: "demonstrating knowledge," "proving a point about something," and "convincing someone." Further, their interview responses indicated that many perceived "demonstrating knowledge" as the professor did: that is, as showing they knew *how* to interpret something, instead of showing that they could parrot back *what* was said in class or a scholarly article.

These findings are of note because they suggest that this class differs from the situation that much writing-across-the-curriculum scholarship finds is too often

Table 1.   Perceived Functions for Students' Literature Papers

	Professor	Students (n = 34)	
Perceived Function		M	SD
Exploring one's own ideas	6	5.5	.89
Demonstrating one's knowledge	4	4.8	1.02
Proving a point about something	5	4.8	1.21
Convincing someone of something	5	4.4	1.29
Informing someone	3	4.1	1.26
Instructing someone	4	3.0	.96

Note. The professor's rating and students' mean ratings are based on a scale of 1 (not a function at all) to 6 (very much a function).

Data from the Writing Questionnaire completed after the second paper.

the case: In too many classes, writing serves only as a means of parroting back given information (Knoblauch & Brannon, 1983; Freisinger, 1982). Other research suggests that one reason writing serves this limited function is that some writing assignments pose no genuine issue for students (Herrington, 1985). Instead of perceiving "demonstrating knowledge" in this negative sense, students perceived it in the more positive sense of learning interpretive approaches. Further, the findings show that the writings were perceived to serve simultaneously both transactional functions (to demonstrate and convince) and expressive functions (to explore one's own ideas). The question is why? I believe the answer is to be found not only in the nature of the assignment, but also the way class was conducted.

TEACHING

The Assignment

The assignment, which was the same for both papers, left students a good deal of latitude to write on something that interested them, and encouraged them to rely on their own interpretations instead of resorting to published criticism.

The professor presented the assignment orally. Before the first paper was due, she commented on the assignment on three separate days. Each day she stressed that the papers were not to be a "regurgitation of class discussions." On the first day of class she explained that students were to do two 3- to 5-page papers. The first was to be a "close analysis of one of the assigned poems." When asked what this meant, she said they might focus on "voice, theme, or narrative technique."

Three weeks before the first paper was due, she gave more specific instructions. This time she repeated the word *issue* three times. She defined it only implicitly, however, by saying she wanted "an argument of some sort" and by citing examples: e.g., look at another pair of Blake poems from "Songs of Innocence and Experience" to see "how the two poems talk to each other." A student asked if she wanted an "explication." The professor responded that the paper "should have a purpose and an interesting issue to explore. Work your explication into a framework where you are focusing on some issue."

Two weeks before the paper was due, she mentioned it again, reminding students that they were to cover "some point we haven't talked about in class" and characterizing the audience as follows: "Think of yourself as delivering this paper to your classmates and me which means you have to establish the context. Don't expect that the teacher knows all this and has all these lines in her head."

Before the second paper was due, she commented on the assignment two more times. First, when she returned the first papers, she spent about 15 minutes discussing the difference between effective and ineffective papers. She said that it was not enough just to have a theme (e.g., "Nature in Wordsworth") and to point to what Wordsworth says about nature. "That's not an adequate purpose. You haven't said anything." They had to have a thesis (e.g., "Wordsworth points to three stages in human development"). That sort of generalization she said was "one step up" from "just pointing." Beyond that, the most effective papers "explored relationships and contrasts (e.g., "The stages in the development of youth parallel the development of the poet's mind and the development of the poem"). To get to this end, she advised students to ask themselves "Why am I talking about this topic? What does it help me to understand?" and to "incorporate into yourself a sense of a reader pushing you to say, 'So what? What use is such knowledge?'"

Two weeks before the second paper was due, she suggested three basic ways to approach the paper: as a thematic study (e.g., "A topic like free will and determinism in *Tess*), a study of narrative technique (e.g., "What did Hardy do to give us a sense of what characters think?), or a study of social conventions and how they operate in a work (e.g, in *Pride and Prejudice*, what is the code of manners these people operate under?).

The students responded positively to the assignment. When asked whether they would rather do the papers or exams, 86% of them (30, n = 35) chose the papers. One explained that she preferred the papers because "the thought process is longer, more extensive; therefore I learn much more from writing papers." In comments representative of other students, one student said she viewed the papers as an occasion for "finding out how the work impressed you," and another said, "I can be more creative." Many noted specifically that they valued these papers because they could choose their own topic. As one explained, "a paper gives you the chance to examine what interests you." These comments suggest that having a choice of topic and approach was conducive to students' feeling that the aim was to explore their own ideas. More specifically, they suggest that the assignment encouraged students to explore what was an issue for them: some question they wanted to resolve for themselves.

The Teacher as Audience

The role this professor projected of herself as an audience also encouraged their perceiving this exploratory aim as primary, as well as a communicative aim ("to convince") as secondary. With one exception, the students I interviewed said they found plausible the professor's characterization of herself as one who does not know it all. As one student reflected, "I don't think you could teach the same thing year after year if you didn't expect to learn anything. I remember when we were doing Shelley in class, someone said something that really struck her. Yeah, I definitely think so." Further, all perceived her to be open-minded, nonjudgmental, and interested in their ideas. In a characteristic comment, one student explained the professor's manner in terms of its influence on her: "It makes me feel less intimidated. It's sometimes like she doesn't know anything about the story and she just wants us to tell her what we're thinking. I think that's really good because, in my other class, I sit there and feel really intimidated because sometimes you'll come out with things and if he doesn't agree with them, then he says we're wrong."

Manner of Conducting Class

As these students'comments reflect, that students had these perceptions of the professor related to the way she conducted class. The professor rarely lectured, except for short 10- to 15-minute context-setting introductions to each author. Instead, she ran the classes as discussions. While she was clearly shaping the direction of these discussions, she did not do so obviously. Instead, she would remain in the background, paraphrasing comments, posing questions, remaining nonjudgmental. One student commented, "She's probably directive and we don't realize it. She seems to lead it, to encourage the discussion to where it should go, but she doesn't come out and say this is what this means."

Further, the class was conducted in a way that demonstrated the inductive exploratory process the professor wanted students to learn to use. My observations indicated that she would most frequently begin discussions of a work by asking students what puzzled them or struck them as "odd" or an "issue." She would elicit a number of comments, settle on one as a focusing question for the discussion, then turn to the work to explore the question. (See Figure 1.)

When the students I interviewed reviewed this transcript and another similar to it, they agreed they were typical. In characterizing the professor's role throughout a typical session, one student explained, "she starts out a little nondirective—I think to get everyone participating—then she gets directive." As the transcript illustrates, she would begin by letting them introduce questions. The students I interviewed thought this manner of beginning was effective because, as one commented, "A major thing is what questions are you left with. That's a good way to go about interpreting." Another commented, "It's a lot easier to say what you didn't understand, than to say some brilliant revelation that you got. It takes the pressure off people so they'll maybe feel more comfortable about speaking up."

Once a few questions were out, the professor would be more directive in pushing them to test out their ideas. The last comment shows her being quite directive in setting up the way they would pursue the broader question of why Mabel tried to kill herself. The students I interviewed found this directiveness about method to be useful. One commented, "She's very good at pointing out what to look for in a text. A major thing is what questions are you left with— that's a good way to go about interpreting." One student ended her comments by saying, "I kind of like the way she lets us discover the story instead of telling us outright, 'This is what it is.'"

As these comments indicate, this manner of conducting class helped students

Professor:	What strikes you as odd or an issue?
Student 1:	The title. It suggests a relation between the daughter, but the father's not in it.
Student 2:	I can't understand why she killed herself.
Professor:	What possible motives?
Student 3:	She didn't have any other choice. She couldn't go to her sister.
Professor:	Was it suicide?
Student 3:	I thought so.
Professor:	Are you satisfied with that? Other possible motives?
Student 4:	To call attention to herself?
Professor:	Satisfied with this?
Student 5:	No.
Student 6:	She seems right from the start to know what she was doing.
Professor:	Does she know she's going to commit suicide from the beginning?
Student 6:	I think so. She seemed to know that.
Student 1:	I don't think so. She just seemed to be out of her head.
Professor:	So, she did it without motive? So, big questions here about motive. All right, help. Let's not start with the end. Let's go back to the beginning. I want to start by seeing how she's presented in relation to her brothers. How are they contrasted?

Figure 1.   Typical opening of a class discussion, this one focusing on "The Horse Dealer's Daughter."

learn to trust their own reactions to works and see that being puzzled is often the beginning point for identifying an interesting issue that arises from the work. In essence, by her inductive, exploratory manner of conducting class, the professor was demonstrating what it meant to her "to read like English majors." That this is so is evident from her comments—made after reviewing the transcript— explaining what she hoped students would learn from the class:

> I think the notion of, in the first place, not being afraid to indicate what sounds strange or odd or confusing or disturbing to you. . . . Interpretation here would involve taking in the whole, having an impression of being disturbed or uneasy about something and then going back and looking for what creates a coherent pattern in the story. So that seems to me the method I'm trying to teach and that's what I'm trying to do there in these transcripts.

As Figure 1 illustrates, this method was implicit in the way the professor conducted class, although she never explained it explicitly to the class.

Class discussions also demonstrated implicitly the three approaches the professor said students might take for their second paper (studies of theme, technique, or social conventions). Discussions of thematic issues dominated, which is perhaps not surprising given that the professor invited students to begin with what struck them as odd or what they did not understand when they read the work. So, for example, after having read "Kubla Khan," one student noted two lines ["Ancestral voices prophesying war!" (1.30) and "And all should cry, Beware! Beware!" (1.49)], asking if Coleridge was saying that the poet has the potential to be dangerous. He said, "The poem seemed to come out with a strange note about what we should think about paradise and the poet." Another student said she thought the poem was saying that if, the poet had the chance, he would rebuild paradise. To get students to pursue these questions, the professor directed their attention back to the beginning of the poem and had them work through it stanza by stanza, focusing on the images and what she called the "movement" of the poem. She did not try to lead them to any neat resolution of the issue. Instead, the discussion of this issue opened up discussions of two other issues. This discussion illustrated the same pattern implicit in other discussions: The professor would focus the class on some problem in interpretation that the students identified; she would then lead them to try to resolve it through a close reading of the work. Further, it shows how the discussions served more to open up issues and possible readings than to try to identify a single correct reading.

Assuming that this professor's aim was to influence her students' behavior, the question arises of what relation we see between this professor's teaching and students' writing and learning: What do the students' papers show about how students are reading literature, and how do their readings correspond to the approach the professor modeled in class? What do the case studies show about how individuals responded to the professor's manner of teaching?

WRITING: LINES OF REASONING

The lines of reasoning used in the students' papers mirror the class, not only in the types of issues addressed, but also in the approaches used to resolving those issues. An analysis of the lines of reasoning evident in the more successful versus the less successful papers also shows that the writers of the more successful papers seemed to follow more closely the method of interpretation that was implicit in the conduct of class discussions. That is, they focused on a relationship, often on some dissonance they sensed, and they answered questions that led them to integrate their interpretations to answer the question "So what?"

In this section I first discuss the issues and then the claims. As I discuss each, I summarize common characteristics of all papers and then report on differences between the more and the less successful ones.

Issues

Although students were free to choose the issues they would write on, the issues addressed in the papers still corresponded generally to those the professor focused on in class discussions. All except one were interpretive instead of evaluative. Further, they were either studies of theme, narrative technique, or social conventions. Of the 14 papers I examined, nine were studies of theme (e.g., How does "Sleep and Poetry" reflect Keats' personal struggle to understand the relation of the philosophical realm to his poetry?), three of technique (e.g., How is it that Keats' three-stanza poem, "Ode on Melancholy," seems to be a better poem without the fourth stanza that was in the original version?), and two of social conventions (e.g., Is "The Importance of Being Earnest" just a "light comedy," or does it say something more serious about "an individual's relationship to his society"?).

The issues students chose, even the thematic ones, varied a good deal from one another. These variations reflect not only individual interests, but also differences between the more and less successful papers. From these papers, I identified three characteristics that distinguished how the writers of the more successful papers formulated issues: (a) they focused implicitly on a question that led them to focus on a relationship; (b) they narrowed the scope of their inquiry, focusing on a particular aspect of a work, often on some "dissonance" they sensed; and (c) they answered questions that led them to examine that aspect or dissonance in more depth. These characteristics help explain how one might follow the professor's advice that they should do more than explicate; they should "work explication into a framework where you are focusing on some issue."

First, a number of the more successful papers were implicitly focused on a question that led them to focus on a relationship, asking "how does x relate to y?" or "what effect does x have on y?" instead of "what is x?" For example, instead of asking "What is Joyce's narrative technique in 'Eveline'?", one student asked "How does the change in narrative point of view in the story affect our experience of reading the story?" By posing the issue in this way, the student focused on a relationship—here, technique to theme—and set herself up to address the questions the professor suggested they try to answer: "So what?" "What does this help me to understand?" Papers that focused on thematic issues also implicitly addressed a "how" question that focused on a relationship. For example, one of the papers that dealt with the theme of separation in Chapter 2 of D. H. Lawrence's *The Rainbow* explored how the various manifestations of that theme in the chapter affected our reading of it. Other successful papers asked how a poem or story is a reflection of something else, say, of an artist's personal struggles or artistic beliefs.

Second, the more successful papers were narrowed in scope, focusing on a particular aspect of the work, often on some dissonance the student sensed about the work. For instance, the paper on Keats's "Sleep and Poetry" focused on the apparent anomaly of Keats, "perhaps the most intensely physical poet," writing a poem where he seemed to question "dwelling on the physical." The other Keats paper, on "Ode on Melancholy," explored why the poem "seems more satisfying and coherent" without the fourth stanza, when "at first glance it is not apparent why this is true." In focusing on issues of this sort, the writers of these papers seemed to be starting with what Prof. J. identified as "having an impression of being disturbed or uneasy about something."

Third, as they explored the central issue, the writers of these papers seemed to be trying to answer other questions that led them to examine the work in more depth. For example, the student who wrote on the theme of separation in Lawrence's *The Rainbow* examined how that theme operates not only at the physical, but also the psychological level, and how separations apparent at the beginning of the chapter change as the chapter progresses. In doing so, she seemed to be guided by questions that helped her stay focused and integrate her inferences: What are some of the instances of separation? How might they be grouped? Do any of these separations change as the chapter progresses? So what? How do these changes affect my reading of the chapter? These questions also suggest that this writer was following the approach taken in class discussions: focus on an issue, then explore it through a close linear reading of the work.

In contrast to the more successful papers, the less successful ones did not focus on an issue that would take them beyond plot summary or that would lead them to integrate their interpretations. They seemed bound to "what is x?" questions that tied them to explication and reflected no sense of any dissonance. For example, one paper implicitly focused on the question, "What is the theme of Wordsworth's poem, 'Extempore Effusion upon the Death of James Hogg?'" His paper reads as a paraphrase of the poem, although he made the passing comment that the poem can be read "as a beautiful eulogy for the era of the romantic poet." This comment represents a missed opportunity since *how* the poem could be read this way might have made an interesting issue.

Another student, in a paper on Wordsworth's "Nutting," tried to consider both theme and technique, but she did not *relate* them effectively. Her difficulty in doing so may have resulted from her trying to answer a number of "what" questions about both theme and technique. Further, instead of focusing, say, on imagery, she commented on a number of aspects of technique: What is the tone? What sort of language is used? Is there much figurative language? These "what" and "how much" questions led the writer to what the professor called "pointing." By trying to cover so many topics, she ended up not investigating any one in depth and not relating them. Her concluding statement reflects these limitations: "This poem is very charming; its rich descriptions and smooth execution make it easy and interesting to read. . . . This shows how vivid, happy memories never really fade away with time." This conclusion restates the writer's general affective response and her interpretation of what the poem means; it does not integrate her observations about theme and technique.

Claims

The types of claims made in these papers are reported in Table 2. Table 3 reports on the frequency with which each type of claim was made. Together, these two

Table 2. Types of Claims Made in the Students' Literature Papers

I. Personal Reaction
   A. To the Content
      "Thus far in the story, Ned's description of the ship have done two things to me: fascinated me and angered me."
   B. To the Technique
      "This repetition is done, however, so subtly that I am not even aware of it until I look for it."
      "By reading the words 'brute' and 'wicked' and 'savage' and 'killer' and 'evil' so many times, I had a very good idea of what this ship and her crew were like."
   C. To the Author in General
      "After thoroughly reading this story several times, I find it almost impossible to believe that Conrad spoke no English until he was 21 years old."
   D. Expressing one's own confusion or other comment about the process of reading and trying to interpret the work.
      "It isn't really clear to me why he tells us as much as he does about seemingly insignificant characters, such as Mr. Stonor, who has nothing to do with the story."

II. Interpretation of Meaning
   A. Interpretive inference about the meaning of some part or all of the work.
      "Soon after, the boy looked around once again and saw how tranquil everything was; this seems to make him feel guilty for what he has done."
      "His fear and anger cause him to become disoriented; he is helpless to better the situation because deep within himself he is at the same time dealing with the fears that the child expresses vocally."
   B. Claim linked to some biographical detail about the author.
      "The fact that he wanted this poem in all collections of his work to be the final one seems to say that this is how he would like to be remembered."
   C. Claim linked to other works of this author.
      "There is, however, an important distinction to be made between Keats's habitual handling of physical indulgence and his handling of it in this poem. Here, he is writing about the *process* of feeling as opposed to merely describing his sensation."
      "To encounter such verse in Byron's work would surprise some readers; yet Byron, in a poem such as 'Darkness,' could be quite serious."
   D. Claim linked to a broader context, e.g., a literary genre, a social-cultural, religious, historical, or literary analogue.
      "The degree of decline resonates with the nearly total destruction of human beings in *Revelations,* where the mystically divine lamb releases the four Apocalyptic horsemen to ravage the earth (*Rev.* 6)."
      "Tess appears as a 'Wordsworthian child of nature' . . ."
   E. Claim linked to effect on readers. Different from I. Personal Reaction because the claim is generalized to "readers."
      "The second poet finds value in his existence because of its beautiful though momentary quality; it offers a temporary escape into a bright sunny world for him, as it does for us as readers."
      "Here a reader may think, 'Eveline, you've done enough for the family'."
   F. Claim linked to the author's intention.
      "He feels sorry for what he has done and wants his readers to learn from his mistakes; I think he has changed his mind and no longer believes that relaxing in the shelter of nature is such a waste of time."

(continued)

Table 2 *(Continued)*

III. Interpretation of technique, e.g., language, form, tone, literary-rhetorical devices used.
   A. General interpretive claim, e.g., identifying the presence of some technical aspect or the quantity of it.
      "I think the climax of the story is the death of Maggie, Ned's would-be sister-in-law."
      "In the poems, 'Crossing the Bar' and 'So We'll Go No More A Roving,' their styles, though different, are intertwined in that they use similar poetical devices such as line length and rhyme scheme."
   B. Claim linked to some biographical detail about the author or to the author's state of mind.
      "His handling of the physical realm can be direct because in it dwells Keats. But his understanding remains with his poetry in this realm and cannot yet transcend to the philosophical."
   C. Claim linked to other works of this author.
      "The fuzzy picture he paints is entirely out-of-character for Keats. But the reason for the confusion is simple: he is attempting to describe a realm of thought of which he is not a part." [II.B also]
   D. Claim linked with a broader context, e.g., a sociocultural or religious analogue. Focuses on technique.
      "Through the use of strong ironies, the sufferings take on the qualities of religious rites."
   E. Claim linked to effect on readers.
      "In the first poem, rather than relating the change from the observer's point of view, the poet allows us to watch the transformation take place before our very eyes."
      "The form that Wordsworth uses . . . is quite inconspicuous, thus allowing the reader to concentrate on the meaning and language of the poem, instead of paying close attention to its rhyme scheme."
   F. Claim linked to the author's intention.
      "Using this technique [switching the point of view of the narrator], Joyce allows the reader to see what Eveline cannot see and learn what Eveline does not learn."
   G. Claim linking technique to the meaning of the work.
      "The language of the poem is obviously that of an adult, which makes it quite evident that the author is looking back on a momentous event of his childhood."
      "In a way, this question he is pondering and the form of the poem itself are consistent: on the surface there is only an understanding of the physical; all else exists only in the form of unanswered questions."

IV. Evaluation
   A. Claim about the evocativeness or affective power of the work.
      The fervor of Ferguson's passions lends intense power to the story."
      "Joseph Conrad's 'The Brute' captivatingly tells of a ship that wreaks havoc and unmercifully 'kills' countless victims worldwide."
   B. Claim evaluating technique in this specific work.
      "By omission of the first stanza, Keat's poem is made far more meaningful, because the poem then follows a pattern of religious initiation and revelation, reflecting the theme in the structure itself."
      "The most important part of this story, the 'Apse Family' herself, is exquisitely described."
   C. Claim evaluating the author and the nature of the author's corpus (e.g., the nature of the author's vision or technique).
      "He will find that statement only when his philosophy and his poetry become one, and then, not in a vision, but in a picture as clear and tempting as only Keats could paint."

(continued)

Table 2   (*Continued*)

V. Comment on a Critical Approach
   A. Justification or Advocacy of a Critical Approach: Claim asserting that a particular crit-
      ical approach is useful or advocating that it is the best or necessary approach to
      take when studying a work.
      "This deviation [in point of view] serves as a major instrument by which the story can
      be interpreted and by which the story works."
   B. Claim referring to critics' interpretations or evaluations of the work or the author.
      "Critics often focus on the sexual imagery in 'Kubla Kahn'."
VI. Miscellaneous Claim: Too general to attach to a specific category, e.g., interpretive remark
      that is so broad or vague that it cannot be distinguished as either related to content or
      technique.
      "Tennyson and Byron appear to be poetically polarized."

tables reflect the nature of the interpretive inferences these students were making
in this class.

Not surprisingly, given that most of the issues were interpretive, so too were
most of the claims. As Tables 2 and 3 indicate, 89% of the claims were interpretive claims about the meaning of a work (II) and about technique (III). In
contrast, only 8% were evaluative claims (IV), and only 1% personal reaction
claims (all made by the same student).

This distribution of types of claims is consistent with the focus of class
discussions. All claims focused on the work, instead of, say, on published
scholarship on the work. For instance, the evaluative claims were evaluations of
the affective power or technique of the specific work, instead of evaluations of
the validity of scholars' interpretations.

Table 3 shows that the majority of the claims were of two types: II.A.
Interpretive inferences about the meaning of some part or all of the work (representing 55% of all claims) and III.G. Interpretive inferences linking technique to
the meaning of the work (representing 10% of all claims).

The claims analysis also reflects differences between the more successful and
the less successful papers. In discussing these differences, to illustrate the less
successful papers, I refer to papers written by two of the case study students,
Kerri and Sheila. Examples of the more successful papers are from papers by
four other students, including Sandy, the other case study student.

The more successful papers were distinguished from the less successful papers in three ways:

1. They made more claims that indicate relationships, e.g., II.E. "Meaning
   linked to effect on readers."
2. They were focused: the distribution of claims was consistent with the issue
   of the paper.
3. They answered not only the question "what," but also "why," "how," and
   "so what."

Table 3. Frequencies of Types of Claims in the Students' Literature Papers

Type of Claim	Number	Percentage
I. Personal Reaction		
A. To the content	2	
B. To the technique	1	
C. To the author in general	1	
D. Expressing own confusion	2	
Subtotal:	6	1
II. Interpretation of Meaning		
A. About the work alone	231	
B. Linked to some biographical detail	7	
C. Linked to the author's other work	6	
D. Linked to a broader context	34	
E. Linked to effect on readers	12	
F. Linked to author's intention	4	
Subtotal:	294	70
III. Interpretation of Technique		
A. General	11	
B. Linked to some biographical detail	1	
C. Linked to the author's other work	3	
D. Linked to a broader context	1	
E. Linked to effect on readers	15	
F. Linked to author's intention	6	
G. Technique linked to meaning	42	
Subtotal:	79	19
IV. Evaluation		
A. About the evocativeness of the work	3	
B. Of Technique in this specific work	27	
C. Of the author and the author's corpus	5	
Subtotal:	35	8
V. Comment on Critical Approach		
A. Justification of a critical approach	2	
B. Based on other critics' claims	2	
Subtotal:	4	0
VI. Miscellaneous: Too general to classify		
more precisely	5	1
Grand Total:	423	

1. In contrast to the less successful papers, the more successful papers, in general, made proportionately more claims that arise from looking at some relationship: i.e., Meaning or Technique in relation to some biographical detail about the author (II/III.B), to other works of the author (II/III.C), to a broader context (II/III.D), to effect on readers (II/III.E), or to the author's intention (II/III.F). (See Table 4.) Relationship claims of this sort moved the more successful papers from inferences about the meaning of the work consid ered in isolation to inferences that linked the work to another point of reference. For

Table 4. Percentages of Types of Relationship Claims in the Students' Literature Papers

	Types of Claims and Percentages		
Papers	II.B,C,D III.B,C,D	II.B,C,D,+E,F III.B,C,D,+E,F	II.B,C,D,E,F III.B,C,D,E,F+G
More Successful			
Sandy's First	17%	29%	24%
Second	12%	21%	31%
Lori's First	18%	32%	41%
Second	37%	37%	47%
Antonette's First	19%	34%	44%
Second	5%	56%	68%
Less Successful			
Kerri's First	8%	29%	46%
Second	3%	11%	18%
Sheila's First	4%	4%	24%
Second	0	7%	14%

instance, in her first paper, Sandy not only made claims about "what" the work was saying ("In 'Sleep and Poetry,' Keats asks that his life may follow the conviction of his soul to write poetry for as long as he is able"), she also made claims showing she was reading the work in relation to Keats' other works and his struggles as a poet:

> Keats is perhaps the most intensely physical poet [II.C Claim]. In "'Sleep and Poetry," he is questioning this method, however, believing in the existence of a deeper understanding of human circumstance that his poetry will never reach through dwelling on the physical [II.A Claim]. In a way, this question he is pondering and the form of the poem itself are consistent: . . . [III.G Claim].

As Table 4 indicates, the percentages of these claims varied depending on whether they required additional knowledge of the author, his or her other works, or a broader context (B, C, and D claims). With one exception, in the more successful papers, these types of claims about meaning (II. B, C, and D) or technique (III. B, C, and D) represented over 10% of the claims. In contrast, in the less successful papers of Kerri and Sheila, fewer than 10% were relationship claims. Since claims of this sort are based on the writer drawing on knowledge external to the work (e.g., knowledge of other works of this author), the absence of such claims in papers of less successful students may reflect their limited knowledge.

Limited background knowledge, however, should not limit students in making inferences about the effect of a work on readers, the author's intention, or the relation of technique to theme (II. E and F; III. E, F, and G). Looking at the percentage of relationship claims when claims relating theme to technique (III.

F) are included, it would seem that Kerri and Sheila did make this type of claim in their first papers (Table 4, Column 3). They did not make many such claims in their second papers, however. This low percentage is surprising since the issues they tried to focus on in both of their papers related technique to theme. One would expect, then, a high percentage of such claims in both of their papers. The difference may be explained by the fact that both Kerri and Sheila had a conference with the professor to review a rough draft of their first papers; neither conferred with the professor about her second paper. It may be that they needed the guidance of the professor to help them explore the work in a way that would lead them to make inferences about this relationship. Even given the higher percentage of relationship claims in their first papers, Kerri and Sheila did not as effectively focus these claims to develop consistently the stated issues of their papers; nor did they go beyond answering "what" to making inferences about "why" and "so what."

2. In the more successful papers, the types of claim statements and ratio of them were consistent with the issue of the papers. That is, they reflected a particular interpretive approach, consistently used. In the less successful papers it was not always so. For example, Sheila opened her second paper saying it would focus on how Lawrence uses "description" and "repetition of thematic words" to develop a particular theme. The ratio of meaning (thematic) to technique claims suggests she did not keep focused on this relation of technique to theme. That is, 86% of her claims were thematic ones, and only 10% were technical ones. In contrast, in Antonia's second paper—one of the more successful ones—that focused on Joyce's manipulation of point of view in "Eveline," 53% of the claims were thematic ones and 34% were technical ones.

The contrast between Kerri's first paper and Antonia's "Eveline" paper shows a second difference between the less and the more successful papers. Kerri's first paper on "Nutting," in which she discussed both theme and technique without a focused issue, did have a high percentage of technical claims (42%), but these claims did not reflect any focus or consistently applied interpretive approach. That is, they were general evaluative claims (IV.B: "This poem is very charming; its rich descriptions and smooth execution make it easy and interesting to read"), claims linking technique to content in obvious ways (III.G: "The language of the poem is obviously that of an adult, which makes it quite evident that the author is looking back on a momentous event in his childhood"), and claims about the effect on readers (III.E: "These phrases conjure up thoughts of discomfort and very unattractive scenery"). In the paper, Kerri did not relate these various claims in any way. In contrast, Antonia's technical claims reflected a consistently applied reader-response approach: That is, 4 of the 11 technical claims were about the effect on readers (III.E) and 3 were about the author's intent (III.F). Further, as the following sentences illustrate, they consistently related technique to theme to make a case for Antonia's reading of the story:

"The switch in narrative technique pulls the reader out of the story [III.E Claim]. . . . Using this technique, Joyce allows the reader to see what Eveline cannot see and learn what Eveline does not learn [III.F Claim]." The other successful papers displayed this consistent focus in the type of claim that predominated.

3. The more and less successful papers also differed in the nature of the specific claim statements made. In general, the writers of the more successful papers were answering questions that led them to make relationship claims and integrate those claims. First, the more effective claims not only answered the question "what," (i.e., made an inference about what something means), they also made an inference about "why." The less effective ones just answered "what" questions. This difference is illustrated in Table 2 by the claims included as II.A. "Interpretive inference about the meaning of some part or all of the work." Note that the first example makes a tentative inference about the effect a scene had on the narrator (made "him feel guilty"), but it does not make any inference as to why this happened. The second example not only points to feelings ("disoriented" and "helpless") but says "why." By answering this question, the writer made connections that helped form an interpretation of the story, here making connections between feeling and action. The writer making the first claim did not make such a connection, so she offers readers less insight into the nature of the narrator's actions or the reason he feels guilty.

Effective claims evaluating technique (IV.B) also seemed to answer "why" or "how" questions. For example, the first such claim included in Table 2 moves from the opening claim that the poem is "made far more meaningful," to say "how" it is. In doing so, the writer makes a connection between theme and structure. In contrast, the second claim opens with an evaluative judgment about the quality of the description ("exquisite") but does not go on to say how it is exquisite or how that relates to some point about the work. As a consequence, it never goes beyond stating an initial affective reaction to claiming what may have evoked this reaction. (See also the Personal Reaction Claims, all made by the same student.).

Other effective claim statements, particularly those making an inference about effects or intention, answer the question "so what." (Refer to Table 2, the first example of III.E. "Meaning claim linked to effect on readers," and the first example of III.F. "Technique claim linked to author's intention.") Both of these claims not only point to a technique, but also say "how" it affects our experience of reading the work. Less effective claims either just identify a technique ("There is not very much figurative language in this poem") or make an inference about effects at a basic level of understanding. For example, in Table 2, the second illustration of a III.E claim just says that the form doesn't distract us so we can concentrate on the "meaning" and "language." (See also the second illustration of I.B. "Personal reaction to technique.")

By not answering "why," "how," and "so what" questions, the less successful papers were less likely to develop a line of argument. The following excerpt from Sheila's paper on Lawrence's story "The Horse Dealer's Daughter" illustrates this limitation:

> Lawrence's repetition of certain words defines the atmosphere of the first part of the story. The three young Pervin men are feeling "helpless" and "restless." Their discussions are "futile" and "ineffectual." As Mabel enters the mucky waters of the pond, Lawrence repeatedly describes her as "the small black figure." The author extensively uses the word, "dead," to describe the afternoon and, more importantly, the water.
>
> Ferguson enters the dead, cold water of the pond to save Mabel's life. Through contact with the water they both experience regenerations of spirit.

In this excerpt, Sheila makes a number of claims, but they are not connected. The first paragraph begins with a claim and then lists illustrations of the claim. It does not answer questions that would help reader's (and perhaps Sheila herself) understand their significance: "So what" that the atmosphere is deathlike and hopeless? "How" does this atmosphere relate to the pond scene discussed in the next paragraph? "Why" is it that in this deathlike atmosphere, where water symbolizes death, that Ferguson and Mabel "experience regenerations of spirit"? Sheila named and illustrated, but she did not seem to ask "so what" or "why." Trying to answer such questions might have helped her integrate what she was reading and build a line of argument.

LEARNING: THREE CASE STUDIES

The three students I report on were chosen for the following reasons: all three were just beginning their English literature studies in college, so they are precisely the students for whom English 222 is intended. Also all three are representative of the class in perceiving "exploring and shaping one's own ideas" as a primary purpose for doing the papers. I believe this shared perception is attributable to the way the professor taught the course. Beyond that, they differ in their backgrounds and their interpretation of the task. Their papers and interviews show how these differences influenced their performance.

Sandy

Sandy was a fourth semester English and Linguistics major in the University Honors Program. Although she had taken no college literature courses prior to this one, she had had a strong literature program in high school, particularly in British Literature, and she felt confident about this background. She was also quite independent: "I never adjust my writing to teachers—ever—even if I know they're disagreeing with me or hate my style. I never have." In this course, when

I asked her to participate in the study, she had already earned an A on her first exam, and the professor judged her to be a superior student.

Perceptions of purposes and audience. Of the three students, Sandy's perception of purposes was most similar to the professor's. That is, she perceived the primary purpose to be "exploring and shaping your own ideas" (6 on scale of 1 to 6), with "convincing someone to agree with your point of view" as dominant as well (5). Given her confidence in her abilities, it is not surprising that she did not perceive "demonstrating knowledge" as a dominant purpose (3). When asked to rank possible audiences as primary, secondary, and not an audience at all, she ranked herself as the primary audience, with the professor as secondary, and other students as not at all an audience. When asked to characterize the interests her primary audience (herself) would have as a reader, she posed the question "Have I resolved the poem or story for myself?" This comment reflects what Britton et al. (1975, p. 26) see as central to an expressive intent during invention: "the need to get it right with the self."

Her perception of "issue" was similarly linked to an argumentative purpose, both for herself and her other readers. When asked to explain what she thought the professor meant by asking them to find an "interesting issue," she said "it seems like it should be an original idea that includes some unique interpretation, not just a spit-back, some reason you should be writing this paper." She went on to restate her persuasive aim: "I'm always trying to persuade because I always have a point. . . That's my whole purpose. I have to argue the case perfectly for myself." As her second paper shows (see Figure 2), the way she formulated an issue was consistent with the professor's conception of an effective issue: In this paper on *Tess*, she explored a relationship (i.e., the novel viewed in relation to society) and a contrast between what "seemed to be the perfect ending" and her perception of why it was not. In her paper, she also answers the question 'So what?'arguing that *Tess* is Hardy's social comment that "there is no escaping in death the tainting of society which could not be escaped in life."

This paper illustrates well how what begins as an expressive purpose can result in a paper that serves a transactional, here persuasive, purpose as well. All four professors who reviewed it felt that both of these functions were evident in the paper. Further, it seemed to model the exploratory process of the class: establish an issue, something that disturbs you (paragraphs 1–2), and make an argument of some sort (paragraph 3) by going back through a text to work out a resolution to the issue. Her professor commented that "it shows a process of trying out an interpretation and rejecting it, and coming to another. . . and that seems to me to indicate a mind at work on the problem." (See, for example, paragraph 11.) In Sandy's case, it is a mind at work that reaches some resolution and makes a convincing argument.

Did she learn to do this from the class? I suspect not. She appeared to have entered the course knowing "how to read like an English major" in the way this

1. It seemed the perfect ending. Tess would return herself to the natural world from which she had come, to which she had tried so desperately to cling during her lifetime, and from which society had ultimately succeeded in separating her. Her death should have completed the cycle. At Stonehenge, where the pagan people of an ancient world once made pure sacrifices to the sun, Tess would offer herself.

2. But something in the scene was wrong. Tess was lying on the wrong stone, on the Altar Stone, not the Stone of Sacrifice. And as she lay there, her faith did not belong to the sun—she worshipped Angel Clare. And with the dawn came men who took her away to die by their hands in a place that was far removed from nature. The sacrifice was not complete—the elements were wrong. Neither the offered Tess, nor the deified Clare adequately fulfilled their roles; the former was inescapably contaminated and the latter, completely unworthy. The rite could not procede.

3. In *Tess of the D'Urbervilles*, Hardy examines the power of society and convention to determine human destiny. The society of the novel is a complicated convergence of an old with a new realm, complicated because the old, degenerate era has not yet entirely lost its influence, although the new and corrupt is already powerful. In this world of repression, even Tess, Hardy's epitome of innocence and purity, cannot escape the contamination or the judgement of society. In fact, she is so devastated by it that she looks to death for salvation and the restoration of the innocence that had been stolen from her. Through the use of strong ironies, Hardy makes one point very clear in the scene at Stonehenge: there is no escaping in death the tainting of society which could not be escaped in life.

4. Tess appears as a Wordsworthian child of nature, but there are forces working on her which will not let her remain so.

     •   •   •   •   •   •   •   •   •   •

11. Finally, when the authorities come to take Tess, she is sleeping on the Alter Stone. It is not these men that wake her but the sun itself, "peering under her eyelids and waking her." At first, this detail seems confusing, . . . But in fact, this point testifies to the even greater power of society. . . .

12. After a life of undeserved condemnation Tess looked to death as salvation. But the corruption that her society forced on her and then condemned her for, prevented her finding any redemption in death. What should have been her sacrifice to the natural world that bore her and to the man she loved was never to be. She could not reclaim her purity in death which was stolen from her in life. Recalling that she is, even at the close of the story, Hardy's embodiment of virtue brings the painful realization that Hardy saw no purity surviving this society.

Figure 2.   Sandy's second paper on Hardy's *Tess of the D'Urbervilles.*

professor meant. Still, she felt she learned from the class: the readings and discussion were stimulating, and the papers gave her the freedom for independent learning, to explore and test out her ideas about works she chose to interpret. In fact, she perceived that the process of writing successive drafts provided the occasion for that thinking. As she explained, "I never have a clear idea of what I'm doing until my paper's done. I do start with a thesis. It always gets modified or sometimes it's completely changed, but I always start out with it. So writing the papers did serve a learning function as she tried to "resolve a work for herself."

Kerri

Kerri was an English major in her fourth semester. Like Sandy, she had taken no college literature course prior to this one, but unlike Sandy, she did not not have as strong a background in English and she was not confident of her abilities. In this class, she had received an F on the first exam and was discouraged by her performance in this course and her other literature course. She talked with the professor, who encouraged her not to feel intimidated by the others in the class, to keep trying, and to trust in her own reactions to what she was reading.

Perception of purposes and audiences. Like Sandy, Kerri perceived "exploring and shaping her own ideas" to be a primary purpose for writing the papers (rated 6). Unlike Sandy, she also perceived "demonstrating her knowledge" and "proving a point" as primary (both rated 6). Also in contrast to Sandy, Kerri perceived the primary audience to be the professor, with herself as secondary. In characterizing her perception of the professor's interests as a reader, she explained the professor would be interested in her "knowledge of the work" and "whether she recognized the style. . . that I know what's going on." These characteristics seem consistent with demonstrating in the sense of showing that she is competent at a basic level of understanding of the work. Given her lack of confidence, it is not surprising that she had this perception.

Interestingly, though, Kerri perceived "exploring her own ideas" as still a primary purpose as well. That this was so was evident in her decision to write on Wordsworth's "Nutting" for her first paper. She said she chose it not only because she liked it, but also because she didn't understand it, and, as she explained, "doing this really helped me look under the surface." As I will show, that purpose is evident in her second paper as well.

As Kerri's reason for choosing "Nutting" suggests, she perceived an "interesting issue" to be something that interested her and that she didn't understand. By the time she did the second paper, she had a second notion of what constitutes a "good" issue. She explained, "Looking at narrative technique is useful. It makes you look at something more closely to find repeated words, interesting endings, use of detail, etc." That is what she perceived she had done in deciding on the "issue" for her second paper. As she explained, "I had written down what she had gone over in class, different aspects we could take. I decided on narrative technique. . . . I hope I was successful in choosing the topic that I did because [Conrad's] descriptions really astounded me." These comments indicate that Kerri was trying to follow the professor's suggestion about an approach, but, unlike Sandy, she did not seem to have an aim for using this approach. She did not seem to ask the question that gives an argumentative edge to a paper: 'So what?' Further, she was not looking at any focused relationship, beyond "Conrad's descriptions astounded me."

This limited perception of issue is evident in her paper. (See Figure 3.) In the opening paragraph, she does not set up any apparent issue: She says she is going to "explore Conrad's use of descriptions" and that she will show "how they make this story powerful and involving." In her paper, however, she never goes beyond the obvious to explore these effects. Instead, most of the paper is a plot summary. As one of the professors who reviewed it stated, "she can admire and praise, but she can't say anything to us that is really moving or exciting the way Sandy did." Another comments, "It's descriptive . . . a kind of summary."

1. Joseph Conrad's "The Brute" captivatingly tells of a ship that wreaks havoc and unmercifully "kills" countless victims worldwide. Through the inattention of an officer named Wilmot, the destructive "Apse Family" finally meets her long-awaited—from the seamen's point of view—death by colliding with the coast. I will explore Conrad's use of descriptions and how they make this story powerful and involving.
   • • • • • • • • • •
6. After setting the scene in the bar's parlor by describing its inhabitants, Conrad allows Ned to take over the story. It isn't really clear to me why he tells us as much as he does about seemingly insignificant characters, such as Mr. Stoner, who has nothing to do with the story; I do, however, have clear impressions about their personalities and appearances, so Conrad is successful that way.
7. The most important part of the story, the "Apse Family" herself is exquisitely described. Abominable. Dangerous. Brute. Ugly. Wicked Beast. Savage. Evil-Minded. Sanguinary Female Dog. These are just some of the words applied to her, and they paint a sinister picture indeed.
12. Thus far in the story, Ned's descriptions of the ship have done two things to me: fascinated me and angered me. I would think that these two reactions are the ones Conrad hoped to achieve, and the repetitious words such as savage, wicked, dangerous, and brute certainly help depict the rage and frustration the ship's sailors must feel.
   • • • • • • • • • •
19. After thoroughly reading this story several times, I find it almost impossible to believe that Conrad spoke no English until he was 21 years old. . . . He has an amazing command of language; he repeats things over and over to make sure the reader gets every idea.
20. This repetition is done, however, so subtly that I am not even aware of it until I look for it. In a story of this type, this constant repetition is invaluable. By reading the words "brute" and "wicked" and "savage" and "killer" and "evil" so many times, I had a very good idea of what this ship and her crew were like. These words helped Conrad build my picture of and my emotions against the "Apse Family," and really understand that she is indeed "The Brute." I have to admit, though, I am still in the dark as to why Jermyn and Miss Blank are even in the story. Comic relief maybe?

Figure 3.   Kerri's second paper on Conrad's "The Brute."

The paper does, though, reflect a writer trying to figure out a story for herself, exploring her ideas, and admitting to her primary audience, her professor, what she doesn't understand. That is evident in paragraph 6 and the final paragraph where she writes that she can't figure out why Conrad gave such extended descriptions of Jermyn and Stonor. When I asked her about that, she said, "I just thought it was rather strange that he kept describing them so much and especially Mr. Stonor. . . . What are they doing there? I figured I was missing something . . . . I guess it's just being honest." So, in writing the paper, Kerri was honestly reflecting her questions about the story, and her inability to resolve the story for herself. As a consequence, neither this paper nor Kerri's first paper "proves a point" or "convinces." Kerri acknowledged this, indicating that although she perceived "proving a point" to be a purpose, she was unable to do it. Commenting on her first paper, she said, "it's more interesting if you just tried to persuade a little bit . . . [but] I didn't try to persuade anybody about anything . . . I think because I really didn't understand [the poem]. I just summarized the whole thing." She did the same in her second paper.

What did Kerri learn from the course about "reading like an English major"? She felt she "gained confidence" because, as she said, the professor "makes me feel less intimidated . . . . Prof. J gives us the chance to really explore anything that we got out of it." She contrasted Professor J with professors of "a lot of classes that I have up here. Like in my other lit. class, the prof. is like 'this is my opinion and don't tell me otherwise'." The writings gave her that opportunity. Instead of just parroting back what critics had said about a work, or what the professor had said, she was actively trying to interpret it for herself. She also felt she had a better idea of how to "understand" a poem" that is, "to look at everything carefully" and look for "how [things] are connected." As is apparent from the second paper, though, she had little sense of how to go beyond her initial sense of liking a work or not understanding it. Coming in without the background that Sandy had, Kerri probably needed more guidance as to *how* to go about formulating an issue and working out an interpretation to resolve it. Only then would she be able to make an argument of some sort and "get it right" with herself and other readers.

Sheila

Sheila was an English major in her fifth semester. She had taken one college literature course prior to this one. Like Sandy, she was in the University Honors Program and had done well in her literature courses in high school. She mentioned specifically doing well with the writing. She attributed this success in part to having learned "rules," what she called "tight structures," for writing: e.g., the formulaic introductory paragraph, with a catchy opening sentence. She was frustrated now because those rules seemed not to work so well: "The more I get into English classes—it is really frustrating. . . . I've never been forced before to break away from the mold. In a way, I'm scared to because I'm not sure what is considered right and what is not." This concern for getting it "right," as that is defined by a teacher, came up often in Sheila's interviews. It was reflected in her desire to get the "correct" interpretation of a work and in her reluctance to take risks. In this course, she had received a B on her first exam.

Perceptions of purposes and audience. Like Sandy and Kerri, Sheila ranked "exploring and shaping one's own ideas" as a primary purpose (rated 6). Also like Kerri, she perceived "demonstrating her knowledge" as primary (6), but, unlike either Kerri or Sandy, she perceived neither "proving a point" or "convincing someone" as dominant (both rated 4). Further, as to audiences, like Kerri, she perceived the professor as primary, but unlike Kerri, she perceived of other students as secondary, with herself not an audience at all. That she did not perceive of herself as an audience is one indication of her very limited sense of the writing serving an exploratory purpose. Characterizing the professor's interests as a reader, she focused primarily on formal features of text: "solid standard English, logical organization, and substantiated generalizations." Given her concern about her writing, it is not surprising that her primary purpose for doing the papers was improving her language skills: "For me, the writing is such a battle, the fact that I said everything with the fewest words as possible and with the crispest words as possible was more important to me than the correct interpretation."

She perceived of the issue as follows: "She wanted us to search actively through the poems to come up with something different and something we hadn't discussed in class. She wanted us to take the challenge and to direct ourselves in our own way." For Sheila, this was particularly difficult, because she still was concerned with doing what the teacher wanted and she didn't have much of an idea as to how to formulate an issue for herself. She said she was unclear what Prof. J wanted for the first paper. Going back over what the professor had said in class, she reduced the task to a formula: "comment on theme, voice, and rhyme." She then had difficulty writing the paper because she said she realized "rhyme and voice weren't integral to the point I was trying to make." She still tried to include them, however. Because of her difficulties, she took a draft of her paper to Prof. J who, as Sheila said, "was able to show me what I was aiming for" and "help me pull out the parts of my paper that were really important."

Writing the second paper, she still felt frustrated by the openness of the assignment: "I should have spent more time with Dr. J. working on this paper's topic. It was frustrating not to be given more direction, even though she did give us five general things. They were so general—write about the themes—so I had a lot of trouble focusing in." She said she finally decided to write on the Lawrence story based on "things we had discussed in class and questions I had jotted down. As I said, I find symbolism very interesting and to see the water as a

1. In "The Horse Dealer's Daughter," by D.H. Lawrence, a dead, gray pond provides regenerative salvation for Dr. Ferguson and Mabel. Though previously quite inhibited, their trial by water excites their passions. Through selective description of certain significant traits and repetition of thematic words, Lawrence achieves a delicate balance of realistically passionate emotions between Dr. Ferguson and Mabel.

2. At the beginning of the story, Mabel is introduced as the oppressed sister of three young men who treat her rudely. . . .

3. In much the same desolate way, Dr. Ferguson has a disconsolate outlook on life. . . .

4. Before Ferguson saves Mabel, there is very little interaction between them. . . .

5. Lawrence's repetition of certain words defines the atmosphere of the first part of the story. The three young Pervin men are feeling "helpless," "hopeless," and "restless." Their discussions are "futile" and ineffectual." As Mabel enters the mucky waters of the pond, Lawrence repeatedly describes her as "the small black figure." The day is cold, gray, damp. The author extensively uses the word, "dead," to describe the afternoon and, more importantly, the water.

6. Ferguson enters the dead, cold water of the pond to save Mabel's life. Through contact with the water they both experience regeneration of spirit. They experience a sexual awakening. The water represents death. It tries unsuccessfully to take them. As Ferguson enters the water to save Mabel, "the water clasped dead cold round his legs." Nevertheless, he overcomes the forces and saves her. [QUOTE] Having conquered death, he and Mabel will now live more passionately.

7. After this regeneration it is most important to look at the relationship between Ferguson and Mabel. Their emotions vascillate realistically from love, passion, and trust to fear, tension, and distrust. . . . The story ends with their irrational, conflicting, passionate emotions intertwining. They are so insecure, yet so fervent, in their new feelings. [quote]

8. Though nothing is resolved at the end of the story, we are satisfied in seeing the regeneration of spirit and subsequent heated passion of lovers, in Dr. Ferguson and Mabel. Their emotions at the end are a striking contrast against their alienated, death-like attitudes at the beginning. Through a close brush with death in a murky pond, Dr. Ferguson and Mabel gain a strong fervor for life.

Figure 4.   Sheila's second paper on "The Horse Dealer's Daughter."

symbol, that really interested me." So, in this case, she decided on the "topic" based on what interested her. Further, unlike Sandy and Kerri, she chose a work that had been discussed in class.

When reviewing this paper (see Figure 4), one of the professors commented that "It's too limited a topic." As another explained, "it tells what happens; it has very little sense of why these things are happening."

In the paper, Sheila presents a limited explanation of the way descriptions are used in characterizations, then a summary of the "water" scene. Her interpretive comments are limited to restatements of points made in class discussions. Further, she seemed to feel a need to show that she could "solve" the story, so she tried to tie up her interpretation too neatly. What she did not focus on was a potential angle that she mentioned in her interview comments: When asked about her choice of the word "realistically" in paragraph 6, she commented, "I mean, it's a little strange when this girl walks into the pond without any reason or excuse. I think that's really strange, but yet all their feelings are very real and that's why I emphasized that." Also, commenting on the opening phrase of the final paragraph, she explained, "This story kind of hangs—leaves one hanging. There's not that much satisfaction in having reached the resolution." In these comments she mentioned two things that disturbed her. Instead of pursuing either, she ended her paper claiming, "We are satisfied. . . " Like Kerri, she did not seem to pick up on or know how to resolve what seemed "disturbing" or "strange" to her in a work.

What did Sheila learn from the course about "reading like an English major"? She said that this professor helped her "to see what questions one should ask" and "what to look for." She also indicated that this course and the other literature she had taken that semester had increased her interest in reading literature. Still, her papers reflect her continuing reluctance to take risks and begin with what strikes *her* as strange or unsettling. So, while she perceived exploring her own ideas as a function of writing the papers, it is questionable to what degree she used them as an occasion for trying to resolve her own questions and work out her own interpretations. Still, the openness of the assignment—even though it frustrated her—made it difficult for her to rely on her old formulas, and she did feel that the professor wanted them, as she said, "to take the challenge and direct ourselves in our own way."

CONCLUSION

In general, this study illustrates how the functions writing serves for learning for individual students are shaped by the way we present assignments, the role we project, our manner of conducting class, and individual students' backgrounds and intentions. It also warrants the following more specific conclusions.

The way we conduct our classes influences not only students' perceptions of the purposes of a writing assignment, but also the interpretive strategies they are learning in our courses. In this course, one of the professor's aims was for students to "learn to read like English majors." She was well aware that means many ways of reading, not just one. What she was not so conscious of was the particular approach she was teaching in that class and the way it was embodied in her manner of conducting class. Professor J. acknowledged this point after reading a draft of this chapter. As she said, this study "shows how much is *implicit* in the classroom, how everything we do *has* a method and involves a *choice* of approaches. Thus, although I don't define my course as exhibiting a certain approach, it does have one, and it does exclude others."

These findings should give us cause to step back to consider the approach we value and how it is reflected in our manner of teaching. It is important that we ask, for instance, what way of interpreting literature or interpreting history am I teaching? One way to answer this question is to examine our students' writings. As I have demonstrated in this study, they are often mirrors of our teaching.

As members of a department educating "majors" in our discipline, it is equally important that we as a group consider the interpretive approaches implicit in our curriculum. Through that curriculum, we are teaching students what Kintgen and Holland term the "communal tools" of our discipline, "tools" that "both enlarge and limit the way we can interact with reality" (1984, p. 491; see also Graff, 1985). In doing so, we are influencing the way students will view texts and how they will read them, not only during school, but also after graduation—whether they choose to become literary scholars or not.

One of the ways students learn these interpretive approaches is by writing. Despite the difficulties Kerri and Sheila had, doing the writings gave them the opportunity to try to use the approach of class discussions in their own independent inquiries, trying to decide on an issue and use a particular technique.

This study also shows how writing can serve multiple functions for learning. Most importantly, it shows how one teacher, by letting students choose their own issues for papers and by her open-minded attitude and exploratory approach in class, created an environment conducive to the beginning of any independent inquiry—what Britton et al. (1975) identify as the expressive intent to explore one's own ideas.

Whether students will be able to carry that inquiry forward, even to their own satisfaction, as Sandy did, depends on their knowing how to *use* some method of inquiry. Her interviews and writing also show that her thinking was directed by both exploratory and persuasive intentions. The case studies of Kerri and Sheila illustrate the problems many students have: Kerri, willing and open to learn, but with little idea of *how* to go about the process; Sheila, having done well when given structured guidelines, but with little confidence in how to go about independent inquiry. Their difficulties are similar to those Graff (1985) identifies in his literature students: some lack interpretive strategies while others have mastered and become "captive" to a particular strategy that they use as a formula for interpretation. The difficulties these students have underscore the importance of our teaching them ways of beginning that inquiry process and carrying it forward. Explaining the assignment and demonstrating a method *implicitly* are perhaps not sufficient. In this class, Kerri and Sheila perhaps needed more explicit explanations and more *individual* guidance from the professor early in the process of each writing, advice that would have helped them identify and work from their own sense of what was "strange" or "disturbing." They also need the experience they will gain from a number of literature courses.

The difficulties Kerri and Sheila had should not overshadow what this study shows was valuable for them and other students about this professor's teaching and the writing assignments. By participating in class and doing the papers, students were *actively* involved in trying to make sense for themselves of their reading. I would think that should be an aim for any course. While I am not advocating this professor's approach as the only way to achieve this end, I am advocating that through studies such as this and through our own self-reflection we examine the approaches we are using, how they influence the functions writing will serve for learning in our courses, and how our students respond to our teaching.

REFERENCES

Applebee, A. (1984). *Contexts for learning to write: Studies of secondary school instruction*. Norwood, NJ: Ablex Publishing Corp.

Aristotle (1954). *Rhetoric*. In *The rhetoric and poetics of Aristotle* (W. Rhys Roberts, Ed. and Trans.) New York: Modern Library.

Bazerman, C. (1982, December). *Discourse paths of different disciplines*. Paper presented at the annual meeting of the Modern Language Association, Los Angeles.

Bizzell, P. (1982). Cognition, convention, and certainty: What we need to know about writing. *PRE/TEXT, 31* (3), 213–243.

Britton, J., Burgess, T., Martin, N., McLeod, A., & Rosen, A. (1975). *The development of writing abilities (11–18)*. New York: Macmillan Education Ltd.

Denzin, N. (1970). *The research act*. Chicago, IL: Aldine.

Doheny-Farina, S., & Odell, L. (1985). Ethnographic research on writing: Assumptions and methodology. In L. Odell & D. Goswami (Eds.), *Writing in nonacademic settings*. New York: Guilford.

Dyson, A. H. (1984). Emergent writers' interpretations of school literacy tasks. *Research in the Teaching of English, 18* (3), 233–64.

Faigley, L., & Hansen, K. (1985). Learning to write in the social sciences. *College Composition and Communication, 36* (2), 140–49.

Florio, S., & Clark, C. (1982). The functions of writing in an elementary classroom. *Research in the Teaching of English, 16* (2), 115–30.

Freisinger, R. (1982). Cross-disciplinary writing programs: Beginnings. In T. Fulwiler & A. Young (Eds.). *Language connections: Writing and reading across the curriculum*. Urbana, IL: National Council of Teachers of English.

Fulwiler, T. (1982). Writing: An act of cognition. In C. W. Griffin (Ed.). *Teaching writing in all disciplines*. San Francisco, CA: Jossey-Bass, Inc.

Graff, G. (1985). The university and the prevention of culture. In G. Graff & R. Gibbons (Eds.). *Criticism in the university*. Evanston, IL: Northwestern University Press.

Herrington, A. J. (1985). Writing in academic settings: A study of the contexts for writing in two college chemical engineering courses. *Research in the Teaching of English, 19* (4), 331–59.

Kintgen, E. R., & Holland, N. N. (1984). Carlos reads a poem. *College English, 46*, (5), 478–91.

Knoblauch, C. H., & Brannon, L. (1983). Writing as learning through the curriculum. *College English, 45.* (5), 465–74.

Maimon, E. (1983). Maps and genres: Exploring connections in the arts and sciences. In W. B. Horner (Ed.), *Composition and literature: Bridging the gap.* Chicago, IL: University of Chicago Press.

Mosenthal, P. (1983). On defining writing and classroom writing competence. In P. Mosenthal, L. Tamor, & S. Walmsley (Eds.). *Research on writing: Principles and methods.* New York: Longman.

Odell, L., & Goswami, D. (1982). Writing in a non-academic setting. *Research in the Teaching of English, 16* (3), 201–24.

Odell, L., Goswami, D., & Herrington, A. (1983). The discourse-based interview: A procedure for exploring the tacit knowledge of writers in nonacademic settings. In P. Mosenthal, L. Tamor, & S. Walmsley (Eds.). *Research on writing: Principles and methods.* New York: Longman.

Purves, A., & Rippere, V. (1968). *Elements of writing about a literary work: A study of response to literature* (Research Report No. 9). Champaign, IL: National Council of Teachers of English.

Schatzman, L., & Strauss, A. (1973). *Field research: Strategies for a natural sociology.* Englewood Cliffs, NJ: Prentice-Hall.

Toulmin, S. (1972). *Human understanding.* Princeton, NJ: University of Princeton Press.

Toulmin, S., Rieke, R., & Janik, A. (1979). *An introduction to reasoning.* New York: Macmillan.

5 Rhetoric and Epistemology in the Social Sciences: A Contrast of Two Representative Texts

Kristine Hansen

Brigham Young University

This chapter compares written texts from two disciplines in the social sciences, sociology and social anthropology. The authors studied a similar subject—modern American black families living in poverty—but the texts are quite different rhetorical products because, as I will argue, the rhetorical conventions of each text reflect some of the epistemological assumptions of the dominant research model in its author's discipline. Hence, to analyze the rhetorical product is to learn something of how each discipline ostensibly conceives of the nature and origin of knowledge, and thus of how the disciplines define themselves. More importantly, to scrutinize the texts in this way is to describe some of the rhetorical knowledge practitioners of these disciplines must have.

The chapter is divided into three major parts. In the first part, I compare new attitudes about language and rhetoric in the social sciences with more traditional attitudes. In the second part, I provide brief histories of the authors of the two texts, their rhetorical situations, and the genres they use to report their research. In the third part, I contrast the rhetoric of the two texts, using the classical categories of invention, arrangement, style, and types of argumentative appeals, adding Stephen Toulmin's method of analyzing arguments to the discussion of appeal to logic.

SOCIAL SCIENCE WRITING AS RHETORIC

In the past, study and criticism of social scientists' writing has focused mainly on surface features, especially diction and syntax, and the same focus is still common today. One well-known example of such criticism is Samuel Williamson's 1947 article, "How to Write Like a Social Scientist," which gives six "rules" for writing wordy, polysyllabic, pretentious prose. Williamson implies that a good dose of, say, Strunk and White, is what social scientists need to learn to write well. His advice is well meant, and, as far as it goes, it is something many social scientists agree with. As recently as 1983, John Harley, editor of the *McGill Journal of Education*, took behavioral scientists to task for syntactic ambiguity, jargon, "perhapsism," and conglomerations of nouns, among other things. Sociologists Selvin and Wilson in 1984 published two articles for their colleagues in *The Sociological Quarterly*, giving them "A Limited Glossary of Stumblebum Usage" and advice called "On Sharpening Sociologists' Prose." In the latter article, they ask, "What happened in required freshman courses in composition? As far as we can see, they have had no effect on sociologists exposed to them" (p. 205). Similar voices in other social science disciplines have raised the same sort of cry, one that provokes questions I hope this chapter will help answer: Is a required freshman course in composition sufficient training? Is teaching a future or present social scientist to write well merely a matter of teaching a clear prose style?

Rhetoricians would no doubt agree that style is an important part of what any writer in any discipline should learn, but that to stop there is to conceive the issue too narrowly. Both social scientists and English teachers would profit from perceiving disciplinary discourse as not merely *writing* but *rhetoric*, because this view clarifies that such writing is essentially a sort of argumentation. Style is integral to the argument, but so are other matters that have not been focused on sufficiently in past discussions of social science writing.

One critic who did see beyond the surface of social science discourse is Richard Weaver (1985), whose 1953 book *The Ethics of Rhetoric* includes a provocative chapter entitled "The Rhetoric of Social Science." In it he chides social scientists for not having learned "the principles of sound rhetorical exposition" (p. 187), but his criticism is based on a theory of language that is no longer tenable. Social scientists' fundamental problem, he concludes, stems from their ignoring the distinction between *positive* and *dialectical* terms. To illustrate his point, Weaver compares a definition from biology, that of the genus *Felis*, with a definition from sociology, that of *slum*. The first is what he calls a positive term (he might as well have said "positivistic") because the properties that define the genus—"mammal," "vertebrate," and "quadruped"—have an empirical ontological basis. "The genus *Felis* has a reality in the form of compresent positive attributes which 'slum' cannot have" (p. 191). *Slum* is for Weaver a dialectical term: it is nonempirical; it reflects judgment of value; it is defined by its negative, not by positive attributes; it depends on something more than the external world for its significance. The properties a social scientist might use to define *slum* exist only in logical connection, says Weaver, not as empirical positive attributes. They have a different ontological basis from the properties that define *Felis*.

Because the natural scientist deals in positive terms, he or she is able to use "a rhetoric of positive terms . . . a rhetoric of simple description which requires only powers of accurate observation and reporting" (p. 188). The social scientist,

Weaver believes, has a harder task, because he or she deals in dialectical terms and therefore in a different sort of rhetoric. Like Plato in the *Phaedrus*, Weaver maintains that dialectic—the method of investigation whose object is the establishment of truth about doubtful propositions—must precede rhetoric. Too often, Weaver claims, the social scientist is "a dialectician without a dialectical basis," using a dialectical term as if it were a positive term. Such a use makes the social scientist guilty of equivocation; for, since a dialectical term expresses one's commitment to the value represented by that term, the social scientist may be guilty of passing off what is only "morally or imaginatively true" as if it were "objectively true" (p. 189). Hence, "social science writing . . . fails to convince us that it deals clearly with realities" (p. 187), because the social scientist cannot "use his terms with the simple directness of the natural scientist pointing to physical factors" (p. 189).

I have presented Weaver's comments at some length, since they represent a way of thinking about language and writing in the natural and social sciences that still prevails today. Our society commonly grants that the natural sciences are somehow more "real," "hard," "objective," and "value-free" than the social sciences, which are thought to be "soft," "subjective," and "value-laden." The discourse of the physical and natural sciences has commonly been described as decidedly expository, informative, or referential, with only a slight nod toward the possibility that it is also persuasive (see, for example, Bitzer, 1968). The discourse of the social sciences, in contrast, has been regarded as aspiring toward the ideal represented by the discourse of natural science, but falling short, because it doesn't deal with the same order of phenomena. But neither kind of discourse has been seriously regarded as rhetorical until recently.[1]

Increasingly now, philosophers, rhetoricians, historians and sociologists of science, and scientists themselves are admitting that scientific discourse of any kind should come under the name of rhetoric. The philosopher and rhetorician Chaim Perelman (Perelman & Olbrechts-Tyteca, 1969) avers, "The rhetorical dimension is unavoidable in every philosophical argument, in every scientific discussion which is not restricted to mere calculation but seeks to justify its elaboration or its application, and in every consideration on the principles of any discipline whatever" (p. 119). Economist Donald McCloskey (1984) would add that even calculations are rhetorical in nature, claiming that "statistics . . . are figures of speech in numerical dress" (p. 98). The mathematicians Ruben Hersh and Philip Davis agree that "even the best and purest of mathematics is in some respects rhetorical," since mathematicians seldom give complete proofs, relying instead "enthymematically on appeals to shared but unspoken premises, and on

---

[1] In fairness to Weaver, I note that his 1963 article, "Language is Sermonic," (reprinted in Weaver, 1970) states his belief that "rhetoric is cognate with language" (p. 221) and that even the seemingly most objective expressions "can be seen as enclosed in a rhetorical intention" (p. 222). But the article also discounts the scientist's skill in and consciousness about the art of rhetoric.

appeals to their own authority" (reported by Simons, 1985, p. 54). The political scientist John S. Nelson (1983) states bluntly that "all speech (oral or written) is rhetorical" and that "dialectic and logic are rhetorically created and sustained; in other words, they are rhetorical constructs" (p. 175). The psychologist Walter B. Weimer (1977) also includes logic and dialectic in rhetoric, saying they are "comparatively restrictive facets . . . which have applicability to limited domains compared to the full range of rhetorical transactions" (p. 1). Weimer claims that the belief in value-free science is untenable, since it is impossible to separate knowing and doing from valuing. "Knowing, doing, and valuing can and must be reunited," he says, and "rhetoric is the domain in which that unification must occur" (p. 13).

If this is so, how are we to define rhetoric, and how are we to define *science?* I will use Barry Brummett's (1976) definition: Rhetoric is "the advocacy of realities" (p. 31). The plural ending of that last word may be puzzling, but it will, I trust, become clearer. Let us return to Weaver's points that the attributes that define the genus *Felis*—"mammal," "quadruped," and "vertebrate"—are positive, empirical, and real, and that to write natural science discourse "requires only powers of accurate observation and reporting." This position is not as solid as it first appears, because as Weimer points out, all description occurs within a pragmatic context and in relationship to a theory, which organizes "observations or data into meaningful patterns. Theories argue for a particular pattern or way of seeing reality" (p. 5). Northrop (1948, p. 317) has stated that "the only way to get pure facts independent of all concepts and theory, is merely to look for them and forthwith remain perpetually dumb," implying that the mere act of expressing an observation in language commits one to a theory or conceptual viewpoint. But Weimer goes a step further and shows that the interpretive framework influences not only the reporting but the very perception of facts. He notes that the sixteenth-century astronomers Kepler and Tycho Brahe were both equipped with eyes, yet "they perceived quite different 'facts' as they watched the sun rise" (1977, p. 5). Toulmin (1972, p. 246) agrees: "Nature has no language in which she can speak to us on her own behalf, and it is up to us . . . to frame concepts in which we can 'make something' out of our experience of Nature."

Interestingly, Weaver (1985, p. 193) admits the same point when he says, "Experience does not tell us what we are experiencing." He makes this statement in order to castigate social scientists for hedging about the meaning of their data, but it can also be applied to such "positive" things as mammals, vertebrates, or quadrupeds as well. Perceiving animals as such is not merely a matter of looking at them. The concepts those words represent are not self-evident, not branded on the animal, as it were. Toulmin (1972) has shown that all human thought has a social or collective dimension; although we each think our own thoughts, "our concepts we share with our fellow men," and "the language in which our beliefs are articulated is public property" (p. 35). Our concepts and language "reflect forms of life and thought, understanding and expression current in our society," and they are "demonstrably products of cultural history" (p. 38). Thus, a term like *mammal* is a word that we share for a concept that we also share because of our common culture and history.

Both Toulmin and Weimer stress that the content of scientific disciplines is not passed on by means of Platonist dialectic or logical deduction, but by some means of initiation into the discipline. Toulmin calls it "enculturation" into "the repertory of intellectual techniques, procedures, skills, and methods of representation, which are employed in 'giving explanations' of events and phenomena within the scope of the science concerned" (p. 159). Weimer claims that "scientific articles and research training given to novices *enjoin* their audiences to behave a certain way. . . . Science very literally is a 'cookbook' endeavor—it is a matter of recipes for conceiving, perceiving, and doing" (p. 12). John Ziman concurs, declaring that science is a practical art, learned not out of books but through imitation and experience. Moreover, Ziman says, the scientific enterprise is "corporate"; it is a social activity, and young scientists do not study formal logic or metaphysics in order to understand how to do research, but instead are trained by apprenticeship to more experienced scholars. They learn to play a role in a system of social relationships "by which knowledge is acquired, sifted and eventually made public property" (p. 10).

In their book *The Social Construction of Reality* (1966) Berger and Luckmann explain more fully how social institutions—which would include academic disciplines—are passed on. They argue that what is experienced as objective reality is a product of humans whose actions in a given situation become so habitual and typical that the actions are experienced as "existing over and beyond the individuals who 'happen to' embody them at the moment." The actions become an institution, and they are experienced as "possessing a reality of their own, a reality that confronts the individual as an external and coercive fact" (p. 55). Berger and Luckmann say that this socially constructed reality is "analagous to the reality of the natural world." They continue:

In the early phases of socialization the child is quite incapable of distinguishing between the objectivity of natural phenomena and the objectivity of the social formations. To take the most important item of socialization, language appears to the child as inherent in the nature of things, and he cannot grasp the notion of its conventionality. A thing *is* what it is called, and it could not be called anything else. (p. 56)

The language of a social institution such as scientific study might be accepted in much the same way by the novice being socialized into the institution, since language is the chief means of mediating knowledge about the institution. The world is objectified by language, say Berger and Luckman; language "orders it into objects to be apprehended as reality" (p. 62). The taken-for-granted nature of such language contributes to the taken-for-granted nature of knowledge, so that "any radical deviance from the institutional order appears as a departure from reality" (p. 62).

Thus, to answer Weaver, our social world has objectified as part of the institution of taxonomic biology certain perceptions about horses: that they are quadrupeds, vertebrates, and mammals. Everyone knows they are, and so of course they are. To disagree with those perceptions is to fly in the face of reality —the reality of socially constructed knowledge, that is. The attributes of the genus *Felis* are positive only in the sense that they represent socially mediated perceptions and socially constructed knowledge, and in the sense that there is unlikely to be argument over the reality of those perceptions or the factualness of the knowledge. But in the same sense, the term *slum* can be just as positive as *mammal*—though perhaps *slum* might be argued over sooner, because its reality is agreed upon by a smaller community or because it has a less entrenched history.

Hence, the social sciences do not differ from the natural sciences (or any other discipline) in the nature of the language used, since words are the shared stock of a social group and they objectify a socially constructed world, ordering it into objects to be apprehended as reality. Since each discipline concerns itself with different aspects of the overall reality we humans find ourselves in, it is fair to say that there are a number of smaller "realities," as many as there are social groups who share an understanding of particular phenomena. Within each of these communities, rhetoric is the medium for constructing and effecting change in the shared body of knowledge of the community. In other words, rhetoric advocates these communities' realities.

When practitioners of any discipline advance a claim of knowledge, they use the rhetorical conventions of their discipline to make their case. As Bazerman (1983), Gilbert and Mulkay (1984),and Myers (1985) have shown for the physical sciences, any new claim that is advanced has to steer a careful course through a highly politicized social context before it gains the status of knowledge; therefore, the maker of the claim must pay careful attention to the audience and the text's organization, language, emphasis, and even references—rhetorical matters all—in order to gain a hearing for the claim. Over time, a discipline develops regularized, sometimes explicitly codified, ways of presenting arguments. These ways amount to rhetorical strategies for persuading an audience within the discipline to accept the claims of the arguer. Moreover, they reflect the assumptions of the discipline about what can be known, how it can be known, and how certainly it can be known; in other words, they reflect the discipline's epistemology.

In the next section, I show what epistemological assumptions have shaped the genres used for reporting research in social anthropology and sociology, and, in turn, how the genres shape the creation and presentation of knowledge.

THE TEXTS AND THEIR GENRES

The two texts to be analyzed here are parts of *All Our Kin: Strategies for Survival in a Black Community* (1974) by Carol B. Stack, a book that is a revision of her doctoral dissertation earned in anthropology at the University of Illinois-Urbana in 1972; and "Marital Status, Household Structure, and Life Satisfaction of Black Women" (1983), an article by Richard E. Ball, a professor in the Department of Sociology, Psychology, and Geography at Ferris State College in Michigan, who earned his Ph.D. in sociology at the University of Florida in 1980. Judging from the abstract of Ball's dissertation, it appears that the 1983 article is essentially a condensation of some of his dissertation findings. Ball examined the relationships between marital status, household structure, and life satisfaction in a sample of 373 black women in Florida who responded to a 317-question interview administered between 1970 and 1973. Stack analyzed black family and kinship organization as an adaptive response to chronic poverty in a midwestern ghetto she calls "The Flats," where she observed, interacted with, and sometimes lived with the members of fifteen extended kin networks for about 3 years in 1968–1970.

The two researchers wrote for different audiences: Ball wrote primarily for his fellow sociologists and all interested others who read the journal *Social Problems*. Stack wrote primarily for fellow anthropologists; but, as I will explain in a later section, the conclusion of her book implies that public policy makers may be a secondary audience, and Harper and Row's apparent strategies for marketing the book imply that students and interested general readers are targeted as well. This difference in audiences obviously has some implications for the discussion of rhetorical matters that will follow, but the fact that *All Our Kin* may have been written with a secondary, nonspecialist audience in mind does not alter the epistemological assumptions that informed the original data gathering.

The two researchers also did not investigate exactly the same things, but they share a common focus on family and household organization among predominantly disadvantaged American blacks, and that is the reason I have selected these particular texts. Because the two authors studied similar phenomena, the contrasts between the two different disciplines' rhetoric and epistemology will be more meaningful. This assertion requires an immediate qualification, however; not every anthropologist would approach the task of observing and writing about black families exactly as Stack has done, nor would every sociologist do as Ball has. In fact, the discipline of sociology also recognizes Stack's methodology; her book has been highly praised by sociologists and is sometimes used in courses they teach. More accurately, I am contrasting here not two disciplines, but two main kinds of social science research—qualitative and quantitative. Yet, insofar as the two modes of research and the resultant reports typify the mainstream of the disciplines their authors belong to, this chapter contrasts two disciplines' assumptions about the origin and nature of knowledge. The following brief history of the genres used for writing up research in anthropology and sociology will show that these assumptions are, in the main, quite different.

The Ethnography Genre

All Our Kin is an ethnography, or a full account of field work carried out by a cultural or social anthropologist, written with the intent to describe or interpret another culture or social group among whom the author has lived. The ethnography genre virtually defines the discipline of social anthropology. According to Marcus and Cushman (1982), it has a history in Anglo-American anthropology reaching back over 60 years to the pioneering anthropologist Malinowski and has its roots in the narratives of missionaries, colonists, and travelers who spent time among the people of other cultures. Sanday (1979) locates the beginning of a paradigm for American anthropological ethnography with Boas' study of the Eskimos.

Marcus and Cushman (1982) have reviewed over 100 ethnographies in order to contrast the genre conventions of a 60-year period they call *ethnographic realism* with those in experimental ethnographies that have appeared in approximately the last 15 years. They identify nine conventions for realist ethnographies, including the following: (a) an obligatory structure or table of contents covering geography, kinship, economics, politics, and religion; (b) marked absence of the narrator as a first-person presence in the text, so that the narrative is told from the point of view of an omniscient narrator; (c) "common denominator" people, or composite portraits of individuals to represent the typical person of the culture studied; (d) various ways of marking the field work experience without foregrounding it; (e) a focus on everyday life situations; (f) representation of the native point of view as if this were a relatively unproblematic task; (g) "stylistic extrapolation of particular data" into statements of typicality; (h) embellishment by jargon; and (i) exegesis of native concepts and language. The aim of ethnographic realism, Marcus and Cushman claim, is to "represent the reality of a whole world or form of life" (p. 29) much in the way a Dickens novel evokes a social and cultural totality by its abundance of description. The realist ethnographer tries to give his or her text this pervasive sense of concrete reality, they say, in order to present claims as certain objective knowledge.

In contrast, the recent experimental ethnographies are marked by a concern with how the interpreter affects the interpretations. Marcus and Cushman point to the influence of Gadamer, who conceived of the interpretive act "as a process of translation in a continuing dialogue between the interpreter and the interpreted," an act that "depends on the *explicit* examination of one's bias and preunderstandings as a basic, positive step of analysis" (p. 38). The central problem this hermeneutic concern sets for the ethnographer is how to establish authority in the text. Marcus and Cushman focus on three ways the ethnographer establishes authority. The first is to create a narrative presence by calculated intrusion in the form of first-person incidents and by self-reflection on one's purpose, particularly at the beginning of the text. One of the most common devices is for the ethnographer to situate himself or herself on a historical continuum with prior investigators and orient the current ethnography to problems or lacunae in their texts. The second way the ethnographer gains authority is by envisioning a new textual organization, letting the writing project seem to explore its own, rather than disciplinary, goals. Of the different ways of organizing subject matter, one is "picking apart a unit"; an example Marcus and Cushman give of this textual organization is Stack's ethnography. The third device for establishing authority is very closely linked to the second; it is to take a novel stance for selecting data for interpretation. The ethnographer may suggest that he or she is like a child or apprentice learning the rules of behavior from the master actors, or is like a translator decoding cultural performances. Data can be represented as interactions, principally dialogues, between the ethnographer and the informants or as isolates elicited by the ethnographer from interactions. The implication of these three changes in ethnographic writing for the changing epistemological basis of the discipline is spelled out by Marcus and Cushman:

> A basic "message" of much of the hermeneutic and interpretive spirit in current ethnographic experiments is that meanings are contingent upon ever changing contexts of interaction, that they are impossible to express as determinant knowledge, nailed down, so to speak, and that both ethnographers and their readers must possess a high tolerance for unending ambiguity as an aspect of understanding in place of a satisfying explanation of a fixed object of analysis. (p. 45)

As I will describe later, Stack establishes her authority in precisely the hermeneutic ways characteristic of the experimental ethnographies, as these are described by Marcus and Cushman. However, it is also clear that Stack's ethnography is not radically experimental, because it exhibits several of the characteristics of realist ethnography as well. Most obviously, it focuses on everyday life situations; it also attempts to represent the native point of view, though Stack does this frequently by letting residents of The Flats speak in their own voices by recreating dialogues she heard. Stack's use of native informants to verify her interpretations of events also puts her work in the realist tradition, as do her extrapolations of particular data into statements of typicality, and her analyses of native concepts and language. Thus, if Marcus and Cushman's "realist" and "experimental" categories represent the two ends of a continuum, Stack's ethnography would probably be located closer to the realist end than to the experimental end, especially since her work was completed in 1972, about the same time experimental ethnographies began to appear. However, her work is experimental in that it does not assume a privileged, omniscient point of view.

Sanday (1979) provides another perspective on the ethnography genre, differ-

ent from Marcus and Cushman's but also pertinent for understanding Stack's use
of the genre. Sanday names three styles of ethnography—the holistic, the semiotic, and the behavioristic—along with subdivisions of these and prominent writers of the three styles. Although she does not name Stack's ethnography as
representative of a particular style, it would, I believe, be considered semiotic, a
broad label Sanday uses to encompass the diverse styles of both Clifford Geertz
and Ward Goodenough. Stack's aim in her ethnography seems to follow from
Goodenough's definition of culture—that it is "a system of standards for perceiving, believing, evaluating, and acting" (Sanday, p. 534). According to
Sanday, a cultural description based on this definition attempts to give the rules
one must follow in order to act appropriately in a given cultural scene and to
anticipate the actions of others. As I will show, Stack's own statements verify
that this is indeed her aim; moreover, she cites Goodenough liberally in her text
and there is a prominent endorsement of her work by Goodenough on the back
cover of the paperback edition of *All Our Kin*, suggesting that the two of them
agree on what cultural description is.

In summary, the ethnography genre in anthropology is currently undergoing
changes that reflect changing epistemological assumptions in the discipline. The
conventional realist ethnography presented knowledge of a culture as objective
and certain understanding of relatively fixed categories. The role of the investigator was not at all prominent in the presentation of this knowledge, but more
like the role of an omniscient narrator. In contrast, many recent ethnographies
emphasize that understanding of a culture must proceed not from the imposition
of predetermined categories, but from attempting to perceive the culture as an
insider does. From this new perspective, knowledge of social phenomena is very
much a result of the researcher's interaction with what is to be known, and also a
result of who the researcher is, since she inevitably brings her own past to the
task of observation. The rhetoric of Stack's text implies that facts are not merely
observed and then unequivocally represented in transparent language, but rather
that knowledge is constructed out of the processes of interaction and presented in
language that is committed to telling the truth a certain way.

The Quantitative Research Report Genre

The genre of "Marital Status, Household Structure, and Life Satisfaction of
Black Women" is the report of an empirical study that tests a specific hypothesis
quantitatively, a genre that is not unique to sociology, because it is based on
epistemological assumptions borrowed from the physical sciences. According to
Oberschall (1972), sociologists consciously emulated the well established physicists and biologists, as well as the relative newcomers in the academy, the
psychologists, in their bid to become established in American universities over

80 years ago. Franklin H. Giddings, one of the pioneers in American sociology at Columbia University, called in 1901 for

> men not afraid to work, who will get busy with the adding machine and the logarithms, and give us exact studies, such as we get in the psychological laboratories, not to speak of the biological and physical laboratories. *Sociology can be an exact, quantitative science*, if we get *industrious* men interested in it. (quoted in Oberschall, 1972, p. 227; emphasis in original)

Though Giddings himself did not become proficient in modern statistics, his students William Ogburn and Stuart Chapin learned statistical methods at Columbia from Henry L. Moore, himself a student of Galton, Pearson, and Edgeworth, some of the founders of modern inferential statistics. Ogburn and Chapin were instrumental in the transformation of American sociology from a loosely tied group of theorizers, social reformers, and muckrakers into an academic discipline that boasted a scientific methodology. They published extensively on research methodology, and throughout the 1910s and 20s the journals and professional meetings devoted more space and time to quantitative research. When John Gillin became president of the American Sociological Society in 1926, he saw the new methodology as a way of getting rid of what he considered the less scholarly members of the profession. He noted that "the application of the scientific method and the increased emphasis on objective data have been acting as selective agents in consigning these enemies of sociology to a deserved innocuous desuetude" (Oberschall, p. 242).

Oberschall further relates that Ogburn, in his 1929 presidential address, predicted that sociology would grow into a science "by the accumulation of bits and pieces of knowledge" meticulously verified by quantitative techniques, and that nearly all future sociologists would be statisticians. Ogburn also predicted that it would become necessary to "crush out emotion and to discipline the mind so strongly that the fanciful pleasures of intellectuality will have to be eschewed in the verification process," and to "taboo ethics and values (except in choosing problems)" (p. 243). Writing 43 years after Ogburn, Oberschall notes that "it is primarily the orientation expressed by Ogburn that has become institutionalized within American sociology as our professional ideology" (p. 244).

This view of the sociological enterprise is based on a positivist epistemology, according to the sociologist Richard H. Brown (1977). He names Descartes and Bacon as the ultimate sources of this epistemology, because, even though Descartes inspired a logical-deductive tradition and Bacon, an empirical and inductive one, both believed observations could be totally objective, or independent of the observer and methods of observation, and both believed general laws could be stated that expressed necessary, causal relations between functions or variables. When these beliefs are applied in the social sciences, Brown concludes, people must be "redefined as objects" (p. 80), and abstract concepts must be "translated into discrete units of data" (p. 81) by means of operationalism, i.e., defining a concept in such a way that it is observable and measurable.

Brummett (1976) points out that this kind of social science research is based on the methodological approaches of reduction and control. Reduction is required because "systems and people don't appear to behave causally and determinately"; however, "selected focus upon certain parts of systems and people will reveal subjects that *do* seem to to act causally" (pp. 23–24). Reduction leads to control because it allows the investigator to exclude from observation whatever variables are deemed irrelevant; therefore, control yields predictability, a must if some sort of determinate law is to be discovered. As Brown (1977) notes, however, "the idea of causality has been qualified by theories of probability" (p. 82); social scientists who do this kind of research generally do not claim to have discovered causal relationships, but patterns of covariance.

The genre that sociologists borrowed to report findings gathered by this methodology typically contains some or all of the following parts: statement of the problem, review of the the literature, statement of the hypothesis, description of the research design, description of the measurement techniques, statement of the results, interpretation of the results, and summary of the conclusions. Frequently, such a report contains four standard headings: *Introduction*, which contains the problem, the review of literature, and the hypothesis; *Method*, which contains the description of the research design and measurement techniques; *Results*, which contains findings exclusive of interpretation; and *Discussion*, which draws inferences from and suggests reasons for the findings. It is not the only genre used by sociologists, but it is the one used by Ball to report a controlled survey of selected variables in a randomly selected population. According to Thorns (1976), Ball's method of "sampling allied to the questionnaire or formal interview became the dominant mode of research" between the 1940s and early 1960s (p. 14), suggesting that this genre was also the dominant mode of reporting research in that same period. Morrison and Henkel (1969) found that half the articles appearing in the major journal the *American Sociological Review* between 1958 and 1967 employed tests of statistical significance, suggesting further the widespread use of the genre developed for quantitative research designs.

The positivist assumptions underlying sociology's quantitative research methodology have been and are still being questioned, both inside and outside the discipline (see, for example, MacIver, 1930; Lynd, 1940; Thorns, 1976; Lally, 1976; Brown, 1977 and 1983; Toulmin & Leary, 1985). Still, the methodology and the genre used to report findings from it have persisted in sociology for over 60 years and are likely to be around for some years yet, simply because institutions change very slowly. Hence, the rhetorical analysis to be presented next should have some enduring use for both sociologists and rhetoricians interested in the problems of disciplinary writing.

CONTRAST OF THE TWO TEXTS

In this section I contrast Ball's research report with Stack's ethnography in order to show how epistemological assumptions of the two authors' disciplines inform practically every aspect of their rhetoric. I have chosen to analyze their rhetorical products according to the classical categories of invention, arrangement, style, and types of appeals, because these are well-known concepts that offer a systematic and comprehensive method for exposing the epistemology underlying the rhetoric, insofar as epistemology can be inferred from the rhetorical product alone. I acknowledge that my analysis is only partial, since it does not include an account of the processes the authors went through to produce their texts; but I believe the texts contain enough direct and indirect representations of their authors' research and thought processes to allow many valid inferences to be drawn.

Invention and Arrangement

I discuss arrangement together with invention since to separate them would be artificial and entail needless repetition. Obviously, arrangement is closely related to genre, but I distinguish the two by defining arrangement as a particular use of the more abstract genre conventions. Perhaps not so obviously, arrangement is also closely related to invention; in fact, in the case of the sociology article, arrangement can be considered a heuristic for invention, since the genre is so standardized that it readily suggests how to do and write up research. However, in the case of the ethnography, as Marcus and Cushman point out, the form the writer imposes on his or her material is an index of how he or she perceives the story the culture has to tell; in other words, invention and arrangement are interdeterminate. Arrangement and invention in either case are the result of the researcher's application of method.

The difference in methods of research accounts for the strikingly different overall arrangements of the two texts. Briefly described, the sociology text is 10 pages long, including two pages of tables, 1 2/3 pages of reference, and a six-sentence abstract preceding the article itself. The anthropology text, in contrast, is a book with 129 pages of text proper; 15 pages of introductory matter; two appendices (one a survey of Aid to Families with Dependent Children case histories, the other an outline of interview topics) totaling 22 pages; five pages of notes, eight pages of bibliography; and a seven-page index.

This mismatch in length might at first appear problematic, but the length difference is in itself indicative of certain assumptions the two disciplines make about the acquisition of knowledge. Anthropologists generally use what is called the *naturalistic method* of participant observation. They assume that another culture can be described and interpreted only after the ethnographer has lived among the informants for at least a year (see Sanday, 1979, p. 527), not only learning about their lives but actually living as they do. As Stack herself describes it, the aim of the method is

> to learn how to move appropriately inside the private world of those observed. The researcher must take time and patience and practice, attempting to reduce the distance between the model outsiders used to explain social order and the explanations employed by those studied. . . . [The method attempts to] bring the observer to an intimate point of contact in the study whereby he becomes both an actor and a subject whose learned definitions can themselves be analyzed. (pp. xiv–xv)

Usually, the anthropologist will enlist the aid of informants, people in the target culture who can answer the ethnographer's questions and serve as sounding boards for his or her interpretations. The ethnographer takes copious field notes during the observation period and may spend a year or more writing the ethnography after leaving the group studied. Quite naturally, the resulting text is rather long. Of course, anthropologists may write short articles as well, but the ethnography is the typical medium for presenting comprehensive field work.

As noted earlier, sociologists do not limit themselves to the quantitative research report genre, but it is one of the most frequently used formats, and it is generally short because the quantitative research design usually requires that many variables be held constant in the population studied while only a limited number of variables are manipulated or otherwise studied. The researcher begins the study with specific hypotheses or questions that the research design is supposed to elicit answers to. Numerous books and academic courses exist to help with the designing of such research, and abstract paradigms may be selected that could apply in any number of situations for studying a certain number of variables in a certain way. Thus, the limited focus on a few variables and the precise design for narrowly specified results commonly produce relatively short reports of quantitative research. Moreover, since the methods rely on statistical tests, many data can be codified as numbers and presented in more compressed form— often in tables—than the more frequently discursive data of social anthropology. Though it is relatively short, Ball's article is the end result of the collection and analysis of a great deal of data. Moreover, the genre Ball uses has been around so long and is so well understood that, undoubtedly, much is left unsaid, because there is some tacit understanding between reader and writer. Stack's ethnography, however, represents a changing genre that tries, in Marcus and Cushman's words, to "balance both *reflection on* understanding and *an* understanding" (p. 26) of the culture in the same text. There is undoubtedly more explaining to do for the reader who is experiencing Stack's text as a new kind of ethnography.

Both Ball and Stack begin by justifying their own research in the context of previous research. Analyzing this previous research was undoubtedly a major step in each researcher's invention of a topic to investigate. But the interesting difference between the two studies is their textual representation of invention of research questions. Ball presents a sort of narrative that conceals his own role as the discoverer of new questions to ask, making the previous literature seem to yield the questions and variables he wanted to study. In contrast, Stack gives reasons for her decision to do her study and presents a direct personal narrative of the process she went through to enter The Flats and meet people who could help her understand their lives much as they do. Each researcher thus represents invention in a way consistent with their genres' epistemological bases: Ball removes himself from the picture altogether, since knowledge is objective, according to the positivist epistemology. Stack, however, presents herself very much as the knower interacting with what is to be known, according to the hermeneutic epistemology.

In arrangement, Ball's report is clearly based on the four-part format described earlier. There is no initial heading called *Introduction*, but there are 10 paragraphs which may be considered the introduction. Ball uses the first five paragraphs to cite research conclusions that black families and households are essentially different from white families in the U.S.—they are poorer, they function differently, their women have different attitudes toward marriage and children, and they have a variety of structures beyond the traditional nuclear one. He begins by simply citing statistics about the poverty of black families and the number of poor black families headed by women. He connects those statistics to claims that black family structure and functioning are to blame for income disparity, but refutes those claims with four studies that show black families are essentially different from white families. "Thus," he concludes, "there is a strong argument for comparing black families among themselves on variables such as income and structure, rather than comparing them with white families" (p. 400). The impersonal "there is" shifts the responsibility for limiting the study to only blacks from himself onto the literature, as if the argument had just been waiting to be found. In effect, he has presented a narrative of the thought processes he may have gone through to invent his research questions, but he disclaims the responsibility by making the narrative completely impersonal, so that the body of existing research, and not he, seems to be the source of the research focus.

Similarly, in the next three paragraphs Ball makes the previous research seem to yield the dependent variable *life satisfaction*, and the independent variables *marital status* and *household structure*, rather than presenting them as his own choices of factors to study. The sixth paragraph then states the research questions as follows:

This paper explores the relationship between marital status and the life satisfaction of black women. It also examines the relationship between family extension and augmentation and the life satisfaction of black women who are without husbands. Does sharing the household with adult relatives or friends help compensate for the lack of the husband/father in the home? In addition, what is the relationship between raising children and life satisfaction for these women? (p. 401)

In stating these questions, Ball uses an important stylistic device to be discussed in more detail later. He attributes agency to things by saying "this paper explores" and "it also examines," thus distancing himself from his research. He has presented the invention of his research questions and variables as if they were outgrowths of texts, not of his own actions and decisions; now he makes his own text, and not himself, the agent that examines and explores.

Given that positivist sociology patterned itself after the physical sciences, it is not surprising that Gilbert and Mulkay (1984) have noted a similar technique in biochemists' written accounts of research. They compared what each biochemist wrote with what he said in semi-structured interviews about his research. They found that written biochemistry reports don't give any sense of the author as an agent who made decisions and carried out procedures to get the published results. Yet when the biochemists spoke informally about their research, they clearly did not discount their own role as agents who were influenced by other biochemists, who made decisions and contrived their experiments to test their hunches. So, although the content of their written reports clearly depended on their beliefs, judgments, and actions, the reports were nearly always written so that, not the author, but the physical world "seem[ed] regularly to speak and sometimes to act for itself." The written discourse was nearly always organized in a way that "denies its character as an interpretative product and denies that its author's actions are relevant to its contents" (p. 56). This use of language as a "windowpane" on the world has also been noted by Gusfield (1976) in a study of research papers on drinking drivers. In Ball's report, it is not the physical world but other texts that seem to speak and yield the problems to be investigated. Ball's actions as interpreter of those texts is masked by his impersonal style, and his invention of research questions thus appears to be a function of the arrangement of the summarized literature.

In contrast, in the ethnography Stack freely claims final responsibility for invention and arrangement. The first sentence of the Introduction says that her preface "anticipates curiosity about how a young white woman could conduct a study of black family life, and provides a basis for evaluating the reliability and quality of the data obtained" (p. ix). Though this sentence is phrased impersonally, what follows is not. Stack explains that she was advised by her colleagues to enter the black community by first making contact with the established power structure of ministers, teachers, social workers, and other professionals. She rejected this advice because two other white social scientists had gained their entrance into the same black community in just that way in the mid-sixties, and they had come into contact only with people and families "chosen by the black establishment to represent the community: churchgoers, families on good terms with their social workers, and those men and women who had obtained legal marriages" (p. x). Stack implies that such people were not very representative of the whole community, and that the previous researchers came to be identified with the black leaders, who derived their status from their relationship to the white community and were regarded by many in The Flats as " 'uppity' individuals who 'thought they were too good to sit down on an old couch' " (p. x). Thus, Stack hints, the reliability of the two previous investigations is doubtful, and she relates how she chose to find her own way into The Flats.

She did, she explains, by meeting a young woman who had grown up on welfare in The Flats and who agreed to introduce Stack to two unrelated families. These people introduced her to others, and in time she knew over 300 Flats residents. By circumventing the power structure in this way and getting to know people on her own, Stack implies that her own research will be more authentic, or at least that it will address lacunae in the research of the previous investigators. This, as Marcus and Cushman note, is one of the ways experimental ethnographies establish the authority of the writer. Her account not only establishes her authority but suggests that her invention and arrangement of her material will present a more representative and realistic picture of life in The Flats than previous research has provided. As she continues, Stack explains how she dealt with the tasks of invention and arrangement by actually sharing the responsibility for them. She writes:

> In time I knew enough people well who were closely related so that after any family scene, gathering, or fight, I could put together interpretations of the events from the viewpoints of different individuals. . . . In addition to taking multiple observations of each event myself, I eventually asked others to assist me in the study. I found three Flats residents (two women and a man) who participated as part-time and casual assistants in the project. I selected individuals from the families I knew, who were interested in the study, and who were imaginative and critical thinkers. . . . Together we worked out questions on various topics to ask the families studied. . . .
>
> We selected questions in the general areas of social and domestic relations, kinship and residence, and child-keeping; these questions provided a starting point for long discussions on a single issue. . . . The theoretical perspectives that helped me to order the data I gathered can be divided into three central concerns: how people are recruited to kin networks; the relationship between household composition and residence patterns; and the relationship between reciprocity and poverty. (pp. xi–xii)

This quotation reveals that Stack claims ultimate responsibility for the focus and arrangement of her research, but she makes clear that they were worked out in exchanges with others—insiders in the culture—who could confirm that her thoughts and observations were accurate and meaningful. This is not to suggest, however, that Stack was a tabula rasa. The phrasing of the investigative categories—"kin networks," "household composition and residence patterns," "reciprocity"—indicate that, as a trained anthropologist, she brought to the study already defined concepts that must have helped her perceive and organize data as well.

Ball's and Stack's differing representations of the process of inventing research questions imply different epistemological assumptions. Ball's review of literature implies that knowledge about sociological reality is to be put together like a jigsaw puzzle—bit by bit, just as Ogburn described the sociological enterprise in 1929. The missing pieces of the puzzle are defined by the pieces already there. If one looks carefully at what is known, what is not yet known reveals its possible shape, so that one can hypothesize about the nature of the missing knowledge, then go and find it. The puzzle, not the puzzle-solver, is important in this metaphor for knowledge, so the role of the investigator is downplayed in the rhetoric. In contrast, Stack's text implies that acquiring knowledge about a cultural reality is more like learning the rules of an intricate game that others can play and can coach someone else to play. One first observes and questions others playing the game, then enters into it to try out one's own understanding of the rules and to learn more as the game progresses. The game is important in this metaphor, but so is the game-player, so the role of the investigator is foregrounded in the rhetoric.

With their respective focuses established, both authors faced additional problems of invention and arrangement after writing their introductions. In Ball's text, however, the problems seem considerably smaller. Once he has made the previous literature seem to invent his research questions and expose his variables, he merely has to apply the appropriate methodological procedures and the next two sections of his text more or less invent themselves. Obviously, Ball has made decisions about arrangement, but here the highly codified genre conventions help, because the *Method* section of a report typically includes a description of subjects, instruments or apparatus, and procedure.

Ball begins by noting that the data for the study were collected from 1970 to 1973, 10 or more years before his study was published. (It is not clear that he or his associates actually collected the data; sometimes sociologists do not administer their own surveys, but may arrange to have questions included on other people's surveys, or they may examine older survey data from new perspectives.) Next, Ball gives a description of the subjects. He reports, again impersonally, that the population studied was a group of 373 black women in four counties in central Florida, and that statistical techniques were used to ensure that the women were representative of the larger population. Next he describes the materials and the procedure. The women were administered a 317-question interview to obtain data about their "past and present physical and emotional states" (p. 402). Much of the "Method" section essentially describes the procedure by which the concepts that comprised the dependent variable—*life satisfaction*—and the independent variables—*marital status* and *household structure*—were made operational, that is, defined in such a way that they were observable and measurable. *Life satisfaction* was defined as a number between 0 and 10, corresponding to respondents' ranking of their lives on the Cantril Self-Anchoring Striving Scale, a part of the 317-question interview. *Marital status* was defined as a classification in one of five standard categories: married, widowed, single, separated, and divorced. For *household structure*, a six-category typology was developed to indicate the presence or absence of a husband, minor child, or adult friend or relative in the respondent's household.

Ball digresses at this point to explain that other household structure typologies developed by previous researchers were rejected since they contained "numerous categories, rendering them unusable for analytical (as opposed to descriptive) purposes" (p. 402). This explanation is significant, since it distinguishes analysis from description, implying that the former depends on few categories. This differentiation is true if statistical techniques of analysis are to be applied. If there are too many categories in an analysis of variance, a common statistical test, any apparent variance between categories will be so small that it is statistically insignificant, and no reliable conclusions can be drawn. If no conclusions can be drawn, no article can be published; hence, quantitative researchers try to design studies so that they can confidently state that variance or the lack of variance between categories is significant. Research design thus appears to be an important component of rhetorical strategy in quantitative research. Table 1 presents the number and percent of respondents in the six family/household structure categories used in Ball's design. As I will discuss later, Stack also investigated family and household composition, and a comparison of this table with Stack's graphs and records representing domestic networks will provide an enlightening perspective on the different epistemological assumptions of the two methods.

Table 1, as well as the four other tables in Ball's report, clearly illustrates

Table 1. Family/Household Structure Typology

Number and Percent of Respondents		Family/Household Structure Category	Husband	Minor Child	Adult Friend or Relative (Including Adult Child)
N	%				
52	13.9	Conjugal	Yes	No	Yes/No
103	27.6	Complete	Yes	Yes	Yes/No
83	22.3	Attenuated	No	Yes	No
23	6.2	Attenuated Extended or Augmented	No	Yes	Yes
62	16.6	Alone	No	No	No
41	11.0	Adult Extended or Augmented	No	No	Yes
9	2.4	Not Available			
373	100.0				

Brown's (1977) assessment of what the positivist epistemology requires when it is applied in a social science discipline: People and abstract concepts are re-defined as objects or numbers so that they can be translated into discrete units of data. Here, the concept of family and home life has been reduced to six controll-able categories based on the number and relationships of persons present in a household. Such abstraction further increases the distance between the investiga-tor and what he is investigating by making facts appear totally external to the observer, hence objective.

Ball further uses the "Method" section to describe how five control vari-ables—*welfare ratio, education, age, social participation,* and *health*—were made operational. These five variables were "included as controls for the multi-variate analysis" (p. 403) since previous research indicates that they "have a strong impact on subjective well-being" (p. 401). Thus, they give Ball a way of telling how the new variables of *marital status* and *household structure* compare to these older ones in their contribution to life satisfaction. *Welfare ratio* was determined by dividing the family's federally determined poverty level into to-tal family income. A welfare ratio of less than 1.0 indicated poverty. (Welfare ratio data was available only for 269 subjects, and only 133 of them were poor; thus, Ball's research, unlike Stack's, is not focused only on poor blacks.) *Educa-tion* was divided into seven categories, none through college graduate. *Age* was age at last birthday; *social participation* was a ranking on a scale of 0 to 14; and *health* was a self-evaluated ranking on a scale of 1 to 5.

Ball's method, then, is to turn the concepts which the variables represent into numbers that anyone else could derive given the same data and the same for-mulas, scales, or categories that Ball used. Once the variables are expressed as numbers, the final step in the method is to perform statistical analyses on them to determine if there are significant relationships between the variables. *Significant*, as it is usually understood by those who deal in statistics, means that what is true of the sample can confidently be inferred also to be true of the larger population the sample represents, as long as the sample was chosen randomly. There are varying levels in the measures of significance, with .05 generally being the minimal value accepted. The level of significance is expressed as a probability value, p; so, for example, if $p < .05$, the researcher is reasonably confident that the results are significant. This and other concepts from statistics are seldom explained in a quantitative research report; in Toulmin's (Toulmin, Rieke, & Janik, 1984) terms, the principles of statistics comprise the implicit warrants and backing for claims made, and any knowledgeable reader will be able to judge the validity or strength of the claims made. Ball, writing for other sociologists, offers only this terse statement about his own use of statistics:

> Analysis of variance was used to examine bivariate relationships [relationships between two variables]. Multiple correlation and regression were used for the multivariate analysis [relationships among more than two variables]. Pairwise dele-

tion was used for missing data. Being categorical, marital status and fam-
ily/household structure were used as dummy variables. Due to the paucity of prior
research on the life satisfaction levels of blacks, hypothesis tests did not predict
direction. (p. 405)

It is beyond the scope of this chapter to explain these statistical procedures; I
have included Ball's statement in order to illustrate what a writer of this kind of
sociology report must know in order to present a credible argument that will win
the assent of peers. Such knowledge belongs to the rhetorical knowledge a
practitioner of this method must have, since his argument depends a great deal on
the correct selection and application of statistical tests.

The application of the statistical analyses to the data invents practically all that
is needed for the next section of Ball's report, "Research Findings." Ball presents his findings in three tables and seven brief paragraphs. From the bivariate
analysis he found that "widows showed the highest mean level of satisfaction
(6.84 of a possible 10.0), followed by the divorced (6.75), the married (6.28),
the separated (5.30), and the single (4.98)" (p. 405). The difference between the
means was significant at the .001 level of probability. From the bivariate analysis
he also found that family/household structure was not significantly related to life
satisfaction, but several of the control variables were: welfare ratio, age, social
participation and health. However, from the multivariate analyses he found that
"no marital status category shows statistically significant variance in satisfaction
from the married" category (p. 405), and "the family/household structure
categories are not statistically significant in relation to life satisfaction" (p. 406).
Oddly enough, these multivariate findings, though statistically non-significant,
are meaningful, since Ball in the introduction argued that black families are not
like white families. For whites, marriage and complete households are related to
happiness; yet Ball found that for blacks they are not, which supports his fundamental thesis that black families need to be studied by themselves. The multivariate analyses, like the bivariate, show significant relationships between life satisfaction and age, social participation, and health. These are the principal findings
yielded by Ball's method of collecting and analyzing data.

Stack's method, in contrast, does not lead so neatly to conclusions. There is
no section in her ethnography labelled *Method*; in fact, her eight chapter titles are
of her own composing and reflect the focuses she describes in the introduction.
Each chapter contains information about method or information that makes inference of method possible, but chapter one, "The Flats," and chapter two,
"Black Urban Poor," explain the most. In a way, her first chapter is analogous
to Ball's "Method" section, since it too describes subjects and procedure,
though the subjects are presented as real people, not as a number of randomly
selected respondents, and the procedure is not made subject to quantitative
operations. But in other ways, Stack's first chapter is more like the opening
chapter of a novel or the beginning of a magazine feature article. The first

subheading of chapter one is entitled "The Setting," and it gives four pages of geographic and demographic information about The Flats as well as data about housing, health care, and relations with the police.

In the next section of chapter one, "The Research Scene," Stack introduces some of the main characters as she explains how she met the families of Viola and Leo Jackson and of Magnolia and Calvin Waters (names which are fictive, in accordance with ethnographic norms) and won their confidence by entering as naturally as possible into their family life—talking, eating, working, and even staying overnight with them. Stack reveals, for example, that she was 6 months pregnant the first time she met the whole Jackson family, and this gave her an instant way to communicate with their daughter Verna, who was also pregnant. Then Stack describes how Leo Jackson once mistook her for Verna in a dark room and how his resultant laughter when he discovered his mistake eased their communication with each other. Similar anecdotes show how Stack gained the confidence of the people so that she could observe their lives as intimately as possible. In contrast to Ball's method, which heightens the distance between investigator and investigated by means of abstraction, Stack's method emphasizes the involvement of the investigator with the investigated.

In chapter 1 , Stack offers the following summary of how her method led to what became the main focus of the book:

> My first year in The Flats was a period of intense observation and questioning of the familiar standard interpretations of black family life. I focused initially on the Jacksons' migration and the urban adjustment of ninety-six of their kin who had left rural Arkansas during the past fifty years and are now living in Chicago, St. Louis, or in The Flats. I began to notice a pattern of cooperation and mutual aid among kin during the migration North and formed a hypothesis that domestic functions are carried out for urban Blacks by clusters of kin who do not necessarily live together, and that the basis of these units is the domestic cooperation of close adult females and the exchange of goods and services between male and female kin. . . . This was the starting point for my study of the strategies of coping with poverty. (p. 9)

In a section entitled "My Home Base," chapter one also describes Stack's meeting with Ruby Banks, Magnolia Waters' oldest daughter. Ruby became one of Stack's principal informants and guides to the culture. It was she who advised Stack that "in order to interpret any single event I would have to talk with many people. I took her advice and it turned out to be wise" (p. 14). Ruby also insisted that Stack try out some of the life ways of the black urban poor, since Stack's expressed aim was not merely to observe, but to participate as well. Stack says, "For example, she insisted that I ask my friends to take care of Kevin [Stack's son] or to loan me money" as a way of testing those friends' loyalty to Stack, in the same way Ruby tested the loyalty of her own friends (p. 14). Stack claims that "meeting Ruby and gaining an entree into social relationships in The Flats through her made much of this study possible. Ruby had a quick, affirmative way of letting others know my presence was acceptable to her, and that it 'damn well better be acceptable to them'" (pp. 15–16). These and other anecdotes give important insights into Stack's method of investigation, a method she presents in some detail, in contrast to Ball's brevity.

Chapter 2, "Black Urban Poor," is analogous to Ball's introductory review of previous research. In this chapter, the first half of which is boldly entitled "Stereotypes Versus Reality," Stack points out the biased assumptions and methods of many previous studies of black families. For example, like Ball, she criticizes studies comparing black families to white families. She criticizes the "culture of poverty" notion, which holds that "raising the income of the poor would not change their life styles or values, but merely funnel greater sums of money into bottomless, self-destructing pits" (p. 23). She criticizes racist thinking and stereotypes that have shaped previous studies and concludes: "All of these assumptions are challenged in the present book" (p. 24). As she did in the Introduction, Stack shows a need for the kind of study she has done, because "few attempts have been made to view black families as they actually are, recognizing the interpretations black people have of their own cultural patterns" (p. 22), and because previous researchers have not asked before "what role the ties of kinship or friendship play in the black community, who socializes the children born in the ghetto . . . or what may be the adaptive functions of sexual unions and multiple household kin networks" (p. 24). Interestingly, this half of Chapter 2 is, like Ball's review of literature, written in an impersonal style. The strong declaration, "All of these assumptions are challenged in the present book," is even cast in passive voice. Yet, on the whole, this review is much more vigorous, even impassionated, in its assessment of weaknesses or deficiencies in previous research, and, as reader, I sense a strong authorial voice. Also, coming after Stack's earlier disclosure of how she selected research questions, this review does not appear as the sole grounds for her invention of research questions, but rather as evidence that her research focuses will indeed contribute needed corrections and additions to the existing knowledge.

In the second half of Chapter 2, which is headed "An Anthropological Approach," Stack again speaks personally, repeating some of the things already explained in Chapter 1, such as her decision to focus on adaptive strategies for coping with poverty and to participate in the exchanges of children (temporarily) and goods common in The Flats. But it is here that she states a definition that guides the organization and interpretation of data in all the subsequent chapters:

> Ultimately I defined "family" as the smallest, organized, durable network of kin and non-kin who interact daily, providing domestic needs of children and assuring their survival. The family network is diffused over several kin-based households, and fluctuations in household composition do not significantly affect cooperative familial arrangements. . . . An arbitrary imposition of widely accepted definitions of the family, the nuclear family, or the matrifocal family blocks the way to

understanding how people in The Flats describe and order the world in which they live. (p. 31)

Using this definition, then, Stack proceeds to describe family life in The Flats. Unlike the standard headings in Ball's article, her chapter titles epitomize the anthropologist's combination of analysis and narrative, of observation and participation, for each title expresses a cultural phenomenon both in the learned language of her discipline and in the everyday language of the culture. Chapter 3 is entitled "Swapping: 'What Goes Round Comes Round,' " and it explains how the members of families in The Flats participate in a daily exchange of goods and services that their survival literally depends on. Chapter 4 is called "Personal Kindreds: 'All Our Kin,' " and explains The Flats residents' understanding of motherhood, fatherhood, and friendship. Chapter 5 is headed "Child-Keeping: 'Gimme a Little Sugar' "; it presents data from Aid to Families with Dependent Children about who actually raises dependent children and also vignettes of scenes Stack observed in which there were conflicts over rights to children. Chapter 7 is entitled "Women and Men: 'I'm Not in Love with No Man Really,' " and focuses on mothers and fathers, fathers and children, men and mothers.

I will focus on Chapter 6, "Domestic Networks: 'Those You Count On,' " in order to illustrate how Stack's method compares with Ball's in the kind of data it yields about the structure of black families and households. In this chapter, Stack presents her observations of the "kin-structured domestic network" of Calvin and Magnolia Waters over a 4-month period between April and July 1969. As she stated in Chapter 2, Stack found that "domestic organization is diffused over many kin-based households which themselves have elastic boundaries" (p. 93). In other words, the significant unit of study is not the individual household or nuclear family, but the domestic network involving several households and the extended family of real kin or friends who are claimed as kin. Stack describes the members of the Waters domestic network for three pages, detailing the complex and shifting interrelationships of the various households in the domestic network. One paragraph will adequately represent the nature of the description:

> Magnolia's oldest sister, Augusta, is childless and has not been married. Augusta has maintained long-term "housekeeping" partnerships with four different men over the past twenty years, and each of them has helped her raise her sisters' children. These men have maintained close, affectional ties with the family over the years. Magnolia's youngest sister, Carrie, married Lazar, twenty-five years her senior, when she was just fifteen. They stayed together for about five years. After they separated Carrie married Kermit, separated from him, and became an alcoholic. She lives with different men from time to time, but in between men, or when things are at loose ends, she stays with Lazar, who has become a participating member of the family. Lazar usually resides near Augusta and Augusta's "old

man," and Augusta generally prepares Lazar's meals. Ever since Carrie became ill, Augusta has been raising Carrie's son. (p. 95)

After three pages of this sort of description of the domestic network—like a soap opera in its complexity—Stack depicts the network visually as well, first as a map showing the spatial relations between the different households involved in the network, then as a graph showing the nature of the bonds linking the members of the network to each other. (See Charts C and D.)

The verbal descriptions and the charts, however, are also supplemented by a sort of outline diary Stack kept on how domestic arrangements in the households changed from April to June 1969. Of the seven households she kept records for, only two remained unchanged by someone moving in or out during this brief 3-month period. Thus, using four different modes of presentation, Stack impresses on her readers the complexity of the domestic kin network's structure and function in a black urban ghetto.

Stack's method makes clear that these families and households are quite fluid in their composition, and they are this way so that economic and personal resources can be reallocated wherever the need is greatest. Recall that Ball's method, in contrast, was to fix the composition of a household or family as it was at one moment of observation, by classifying each respondent in one of six categories at the time she was interviewed. This fixed datum was then made into a number to be related to another number representing life satisfaction, so that a statistical analysis could be performed to test whether there was a significant correlation between family/household composition and life satisfaction. This contrast between Ball's abstract representation of 373 black households and Stack's particularized representation of a few kin networks epitomizes the different epistemologies informing the two research methods. In Ball's method, as R. H. Brown (1983) described, people are treated as objects to be counted and categorized; concepts such as *family* and *household* are made into discrete units of data; and relationships are apparently immutable, since there is no suggestion that family and household structure might change and no indication of what meaning the research findings would have if such changes did occur. In Stack's method, people are treated as people, with names, addresses, and complex emotions and motives; concepts such as *family* and *household* are treated as capable of definition and graphic representation, but they are not carved up into fixed, discrete categories, because family and household relationships apparently change constantly. Obviously, it is not correct to suggest that Stack's findings about the fluidity of black families and households invalidate Ball's findings, especially since the two researchers studied black people from different geographical regions. Still, if rhetoric is the advocacy of realities, it is interesting to contemplate the kind of reality that Ball's text advocates. It offers, as it were, an aerial photo of black families and households. Stack's offers something more

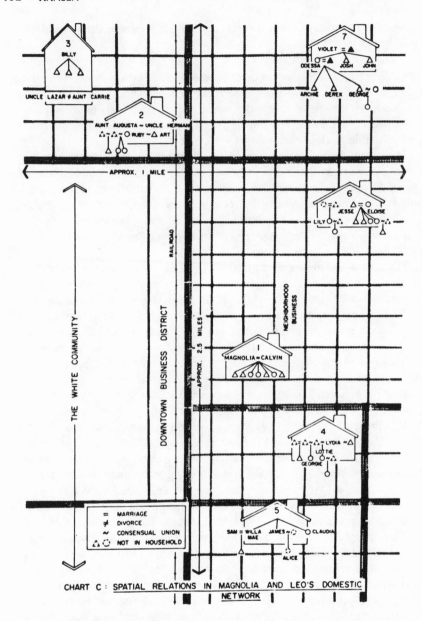

CHART C : SPATIAL RELATIONS IN MAGNOLIA AND LEO'S DOMESTIC NETWORK

like a videotape from a hand-held movie camera. Her text advocates a dynamic reality; Ball's, a static one.

Thus far, I have shown how the application of method is a means of invention for both authors because it produces data. In Ball's text, this data is arranged in a highly codified format, requiring little inventiveness on his part in arrangement.

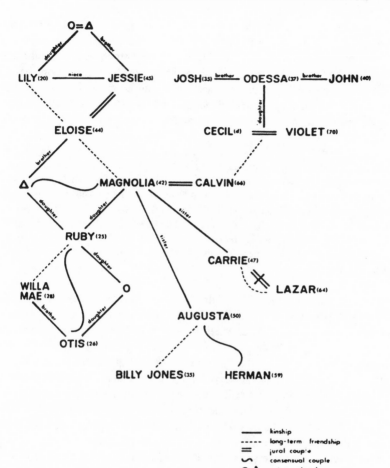

CHART D : KIN-STRUCTURED DOMESTIC NETWORK

Stack, in contrast, had to invent her own organization based on her perception of the important things the culture told about itself as she became an insider in it. After presenting the results of their observations, however, the writers of both texts are not through, but go on to invent reasons for and suggest implications of their findings.

In Ball's article, the place for explanations is in the final section, "Discussion." Here he offers plausible reasons for the nonsignificant relationships (as determined by the multivariate analyses) between black women's life satisfaction and their marital status or their family/household structure. To explain why having a husband appears to have minimal impact on life satisfaction, he must draw on the work of three other researchers, because the finding of nonsignificance alone does not suggest an explanation for itself. Ball's explanation is quite tentative, as the emphasized words indicate:

> As Liebow (1967) had indicated, black men *often* have difficulty competing in the labor market. Thus, their economic input *may be* minimal, and, as a result, their provision of other resources to the family *may be* lessened as well. . . . Staples (1981) explains that lower-class black men have been so handicapped by discrimination that their female counterparts have few suitable mate choices, and Higgenbotham (1981) points out that among the middle class, careers *often* take priority over marriage. Factors such as these . . . *may* lead black women to view their unmarried status as *not particularly* disadvantaged or dissatisfying. (p. 406; emphasis added)

Following this, in order to explain the nonsignificant relationship of family/household structure to life satisfaction, Ball similarly offers only suggestions. First, he hints that there may, after all, be a causal relationship between the two variables, because he points out that, in the bivariate analysis, the family/household structure variable "approaches statistical significance, p < .07" (p. 407). Then he focuses on the very slight difference in mean satisfaction levels for women living alone with a child and women living with a child plus another adult; he attempts to explain why such extension or augmentation of the family did not increase life satisfaction. His explanation relies in part on one of his own previous papers and in part on pure speculation. He surmises that there may be no "expressive" advantage to sharing a house, because of the crowding, noise, disarray, and stress. However, "one might suppose," he says, that living with friends or relatives would be "instrumentally advantageous," by which he appears to mean it would improve one's financial situation and therefore, possibly, one's life satisfaction. But he points out results from his 1981 paper showing that living in extended or augmented households adds very little to the "welfare ratio." Still, a footnote to this explanation adds another possibility: "Those who reside in extended or augmented households might have far lower welfare ratios if they did not share housing. In addition, their expenses would often be higher" (p. 407).

The positivist method does not appear to serve invention quite as well at the end of the report of a quantitative study as it does in the middle two sections. In the "Discussion" section, Ball is compelled to extrapolate reasons from numbers that do not in themselves suggest the reasons for why they are what they are; he must call on what he knows from others in his field, his other research, or his own speculations. It is paradoxical, as Brummett (1976) notes, that such a reconstruction must follow from a method that reduces and isolates in order to gain sufficient control over variables to study them objectively and to make predictions and state general laws. What the method seems to have yielded, in this case, is mainly more hypotheses to test, and only a few "bits and pieces of new knowledge" to add to the sociological jigsaw puzzle. Nevertheless, insofar as Ball has complied with his discipline's socially determined ways of seeking and confirming knowledge about reality, his text must be considered rhetorically sound for his audience. Since it was published in *Social Problems*, it apparently presents an acceptable argument in survey sociology, and it shows some of what a survey sociologist must know about his discipline's rhetoric.

Stack's discussion of the implications of her findings is much less tentative than Ball's. She does not limit the drawing of inferences from her observations to the final chapter, although Chapter 8, "Conclusions" (which was co-authored by John R. Lombardi), is clearly the part analogous to Ball's "Discussion." Since her conclusion also comments on marital status and household structure, I will use it to illustrate her more definitive stance on what her research ultimately implies. Stack's main point has been that domestic networks, not single dwellings and nuclear families, are the important unit to focus on if one wants to explain the culture of black ghetto dwellers. She asserts that these highly adaptive networks "comprise a resilient response to the social-economic conditions of poverty, the inexorable unemployment of black women and men, and the access to scarce economic resources of a mother and her children as AFDC recipients." She explains further,

> Attempted social mobility away from the kin network of exchanges and obligations, by means of marriage or employment, involves a precarious risk in contrast to the asylum gained through generosity and exchange. Thus, survival demands the sacrifice of upward mobility and geographic movement, and discourages marriage. (pp. 124–125)

With this conclusion, Stack is able to give a more direct explanation than Ball, who required the help of other research to suggest reasons why black women may not see marriage as particularly advantageous. What Ball only hinted at in his discussion of "instrumental" advantages to an extended or augmented household and in his footnote acknowledging the possible economic necessity of sharing a home, Stack also explains directly: Extension and augmentation of the family definitely contribute to one's economic survival.

In general, all of Stack's conclusions are more authoritatively stated than the cautious explanations of Ball's "Discussion." The differences in their audience and modes of publication help explain this: Ball's article is aimed at a more restricted, more homogenous audience and is printed in a journal that basically has as its goal, not earning money, but disseminating scholarly information. Stack's book is aimed at a wider audience and is printed by a publishing company that aims to make a profit through the widest possible sale of the book. An inexpensive paperback, *All Our Kin* has a provocative cover showing two partially lighted hands cupped around the title, which is in all-white letters on a black background. Inside the cover is another photo suggestive of a ghetto—a brick wall on which graffitti have been spray painted, including the title of the book. These illustrations obviously attempt to dramatize the contents and pique a reader's interest, and are very likely there at the instigation of the publishing company, not the author. Another publisher's gambit, praises of the book from two prominent scholars, Ward Goodenough and Joyce Ladner, are reproduced on the back cover. In contrast to all of this, Ball's article is not distinguished in any special way from the articles before or after it in the journal, except by a few features that create his special ethos, as I will explain later.

How might these differences in readership and mode of publication influence the relative authority of the concluding statements offered by each author? Fahnestock (1986) has used stasis theory, "a neglected component of classical rhetorical invention," to explain the differences in conclusions of scientific reports and journalistic accommodations of those reports. Traditionally, the four stases are referred to as *conjecture, definition, quality,* and *procedure.* According to Fahnestock, an original research report such as Ball's "engages an issue in the first or conjectural stasis: 'Does a thing exist? Did an event or effect really occur?'" (p. 291). In Fahnestock's use of it, the second stasis asks, "What is the reason for the effect?" Ball's article does, in the "Discussion" section, move cautiously into the second stasis; but as a rule, Fahnestock says, articles in professional journals do not move into the third and fourth stases. Such articles are, she says, a type of forensic discourse, concerned with establishing the validity of the observations they report; they are intended only to put forward claims that can be debated. Hence, Fahnestock explains, there is a preponderance of "hedges, qualifications, or 'modalities' that suggest that the information conveyed is not indisputable" (p. 288). We see many such hedges and qualifications in Ball's report.

Newspaper and magazine reports of scientific findings, however, change forensic discourse into epideictic; they celebrate science by focusing on the wonders and the applications of research. Journalistic accommodations attempt to sensationalize the findings, Fahnestock says, by using artwork, by giving dramatic titles to the accounts, by omitting most of the qualifications and hedges, by arranging material differently, and by focusing much more attention on the questions asked by the second, third, and fourth stases. Despite its cover, anyone who reads Stack's book will quickly realize that it is not sensationalized science; nevertheless, in its conclusions it clearly addresses the questions in Fahnestock's adaptations of the third and fourth stases: What value should be placed on these findings? What, if anything, should be done about them? Stack claims that black ghetto dwellers live the way they do because present "welfare policy encourages the maintenance of non-coresidential cooperative networks" and it "conspires against the ability of the poor to build up an equity" (p. 127). She charges the American economic system with maintaining a large "docile impoverished class" of unemployed and unskilled workers as a way of "holding down wages throughout the lower economic strata in our society" (p. 128). She does not directly put forward new proposals, but she does claim that "mere reform of existing programs" will not eliminate the problem.

Since the conclusion represents an addition to the original work that Stack wrote for her dissertation, it is possible that the publishing company urged her and co-author Lombardi to go beyond the conventional scholarly conclusions and attempt to answer the questions of the third and fourth stases, believing that such answers would broaden the appeal of the book. The back-cover endorsement from Joyce Ladner, a sociologist, praises the book for taking "the mighty jump from traditional anthropology to social criticism and public policy." Obviously, other readers might question whether Stack's findings justify the politically potent inferences she makes. But the interesting question here is this: Do her assumptions about what is knowable, how one knows it, and how certainly one can know it somehow lead more inevitably to a statement of stronger, more confident conclusions than do positivist epistemological assumptions? Since the positivist social scientist usually focuses the knowledge-gathering enterprise on a few controllable variables, such research seems inevitably to lead to very limited, cautious statements about what has been learned. These statements have to be put together with all related, but also limited, statements in order to get a big picture from which value judgments and policy statements might be drawn. A social scientist working from hermeneutic assumptions, using participant observer methods, however, experiences all the variables of a social phenomenon in situ and attempts to understand what they mean to insiders in the culture. If the observations are rigorous and extended enough, it seems to follow that the observer would feel more justified and more comfortable in making stronger claims. Hence, I doubt that the conclusion to Stack's book is there primarily at the publisher's instigation; more likely, it represents her own (and John Lombardi's) convictions about what her research ultimately means. I think that Ball's method does not engender the same level of confidence or conviction about knowledge claims, simply because the knowledge gained thereby is so limited and particularized.

Style

The numerous excerpts I have already cited from the two texts show contrasts in the style of the two authors. Style cannot help but reflect epistemological assumptions of the two researchers. In Ball's text, as noted, agency is frequently assigned to things, because Ball's role as knower and investigator is subordinated to what is to be known. He represents himself (by not representing himself) as the impersonal, dispassionate medium by which knowledge comes into being, as if to say that facts are objective and external to the knower. In his introduction, he does not depict himself as the interpreter of previous literature and the formulator of hypotheses; rather, he selects and organizes previous findings in such a way that the questions for his own study seem to arise naturally out of the existing body of literature. There is only one use of "I" in his entire report, in the fourth sentence of the abstract, where he claims his findings: "I found that married, widowed, and divorced women had the highest life satisfaction" (p. 400). Everywhere else, Ball uses impersonal subjects of verbs and passive voice in order to give the impression that knowledge is objective and independent of the methods of observation. He writes that such things as *research, this paper, the comparison, a table, a category, findings, a study, this variable*, and so on, all act—they *indicate, explore, examine, show, reflect, focus, find, reinforce, address*, and *bring to bear*.

In the "Method" section, particularly, there is no indication that people carried out the action of collecting and quantifying data; every action that isn't assigned to a thing or an abstraction is expressed in the passive voice, with no human agents included even in prepositional phrases. For example, he writes that "data were collected," "the dependent variable of life satisfaction was measured," "a six-catgory typology was developed," "no differentiation was made," and "social participation was determined by a composite score."

One hazard of using the passive voice is the dangling modifier, and Ball has two such modifiers; still, the overall style is clear and readable. One reason for this may be that Ball uses mainly simple and compound sentences. He avoids long, complicated sentences, and he does not subordinate a great deal. One notable use of subordination, however, illustrates the lengths a writer must go to in order to keep the discourse impersonal. In the "Discussion" section Ball writes, "That extension or augmentation did not increase life satisfaction may be explained in terms of both instrumental and expressive factors" (p. 407). He disguises his own role as the explainer, using a long, introductory subordinate clause as subject of the passive verb. Similarly, he inverts the order of another sentence in the "Discussion" section to draw the reader's attention to a result that he apparently finds worth noting: "Of greatest interest is the difference between the satisfaction levels of mothers who resided in attenuated families and those who resided with relatives or friends" (p. 407). One might well ask, "Of greatest interest to whom?" The answer is "To Ball," but he carefully subdues his own interest and enthusiasm by using such impersonal constructions.

Similarly, Ball is careful to subdue appropriately his explanations for the outcome of the statistical analyses, so that they don't claim too much. The verb "may" is conspicuous in 14 sentences of the "Discussion" section, along with other qualifiers: "generally," "probably," "appears," "approaches significance," "lends support." Ironically, for a method that is supposed to produce highly probable, hence reliable, results, there is a lot of softening when it comes time to discuss the implications of those results. But this is a common strategy for a writer addressing an audience of peers from the pages of a professional journal, as Fahnestock has shown. The cautious style also implies what I have suggested earlier about the jigsaw-puzzle-piece nature of very specific findings like Ball's: one doesn't claim to have put the whole picture together, merely to have contributed a few more pieces that *may* fit.

Ball's style also includes some jargon, but his writing is not rendered opaque by it. Except for the jargon of statistics, which he rightfully assumes his primary audience would know, he defines or contextualizes specialized terminology so that his style is quite clear. Jargon actually helps him to present his research more compactly; it has been argued that jargon may be a virtue of style in some scholarly fields (see Raywid, 1978, and Tudge, 1983).

In general, Ball's style may be described as relatively clear, impersonal, cautious, and uninspiring. Stack's style, on the other hand, is not so easily captured in a few words. She combines the style of a novelist or journalist with that of a scientist and a polemicist. Her style is easier to illustrate than to describe, so I will give a number of examples. The first example comes from Chapter 1. Here she begins with a journalistic description of The Flats, told from an omniscient point of view. Although it incorporates data about geography, population, income, and housing (without the cumbersome machinery of scholarly references), it becomes apparent that this is no mere enumeration of facts. The selection and presentation of facts gives the reader the distinct impression that the writer cares about her subject. For example, in chapter one she writes,

> In the last three years, in widely publicized cases, two Blacks in the community were murdered by white policemen. Both victims were about to be arrested for charges no more severe than speeding, and neither was armed. Each policeman faced a hearing but no punishment was decreed. No Black in The Flats was surprised. (p. 4)

Stack uses passive voice to great effect here. The passive focuses attention on the blacks and the actions done to them: Stack says bluntly that they were murdered. And though she does name the agents, "white policemen," in a prepositional phrase, they become faceless functionaries in an anonymous but powerful system. For she says that when they faced a hearing, "no punishment was decreed." Those who might have decreed the punishment are left unnamed, suggesting the impersonal and perhaps unfeeling nature of those who ought to see justice done.

Stack shifts from this point of view and more controlled style to a first-person point of view and more casual, self-revealing style with ease, especially when she uses an anecdote to make a point. For example, when she describes how her close friendship with Ruby Banks helped her form social relationships with Flats residents, she writes:

> At one large family gathering, relatives came from out of town to see Ruby's stepfather, who was sick. Ruby sensed their hostility and insecurity toward me. She

turned to me and said, "What is your white ass doing sitting down when there is so much cooking and work to be done in my kitchen?" I responded, "My white ass can sit here as long as your black ass can." With that, we both got up, went into the kitchen and got to work. (p. 16)

Stack is able to combine very skillfully this sort of telling anecdote, complete with the Flats dialect, into the same paragraph with the formal language of scholarly analysis and citation, as this paragraph illustrates:

An individual's reputation as a potential partner in exchange is created by the opinions others have about him (Bailey 1971). Individuals who fail to reciprocate in swapping relationships are judged harshly. Julia Rose, a twenty-five year old mother of three, critically evaluated her cousin Mae's reputation, "If someone who takes things from me ain't giving me anything in return, she can't get nothing else. When someone like that, like my cousin Mae, comes to my house and says, 'Ooo, you should give me that chair, honey. I can use it in my living room, and my old man would just love to sit on it,' well, if she's like my cousin, you don't care what her old man wants, you satisfied with what yours wants. Some people like my cousin don't mind borrowing from anybody, but she don't loan you no money, her clothes, nothing. Well, she ain't shit. She don't believe in helping nobody and lots of folks gossip about her. (pp. 34–35)

Since Stack did not tape record conversations, this sort of dialogue was reconstructed from notes and compared with someone else's observations. Stack's approximation of the dialect adds a great deal of realism, hence authority, to her writing. It also engages the reader, lay or professional.

When Stack does use professional jargon, it is usually in a context where it can be understood by a nonprofessional, although occasionally one gets the impression that a paragraph or two were meant for insiders only. For example:

In some loosely and complexly structured cognatic systems, kin-structured local networks (not groups) emerge. Localized coalitions of persons drawn from personal kindreds can be organized as networks of kinsmen. Goodenough (1970, p. 49) correctly points out that anthropologists frequently describe "localized kin groups," but rarely describe kin-structured local groups. (p. 94)

A nonprofessional reader could sort this out, given the text that follows and enough time, but it makes a distinction that only other anthropologists are likely to care about. Such passages are few.

In the final chapter, as I have described, Stack changes her voice and role from scientist to advocate of social reform. She boldly claims,

Welfare programs merely act as flexible mechanisms to alleviate the more obvious symptoms of poverty while inching forward just enough to purchase acquiescence and silence on the part of the members of this class and their liberal supporters. As we have seen, these programs are not merely passive victims of underfunding and conservative obstructionism. In fact they are active purveyors of the status quo, staunch defenders of the economic imperative that demands maintenance of a sizable but docile impoverished class. (pp. 128–29)

This passage is interesting for its animation of welfare programs: they are curious "flexible mechanisms" that "inch forward" to "purchase" and "silence" at the same time they are "passive victims" yet "active purveyors" and "staunch defenders." Here is clearly some indiscreet mixing of metaphors; however, the words do suggest sinister horror-film kinds of creatures that are able to appear passive and well-meaning at the same time they unobtrusively carry out the conspiratorial designs of their creators. At any rate, the tone and imagery here clearly show Stack's scorn for present welfare programs that, in effect, insure that the poor are likely to remain so.

In contrast to Ball's style, which reveals only guardedly his own intellectual excitement with his research, Stack's style frequently bespeaks her personal involvement with her subject. It seems logical that Ball is just as interested in the kind of research he does, since he has chosen to write a dissertation and at least three other papers on the subject. Yet the nature of his discipline's epistemology is such that the knower is not to be represented in the rhetoric, except as the disinterested medium for constructing and testing hypotheses, then reporting and explaining results. In contrast, the evolving epistemology of Stack's discipline, as it is represented in the new generation of ethnographies to which her own belongs, emphasizes the knower-knowledge interaction. Anthropology has not rigidified and codified *the* way to write an ethnography, so Stack is free to adapt the style of other kinds of writers in her attempt to present a holistic description and interpretation of life in The Flats. She shows her audience from a number of stylistic perspectives what it means to play the game of life by the rules of black urban ghetto dwellers.

Appeals

From the foregoing section it should be clear that the style of each text is meant to enhance the appeal of the argument each researcher presents. In fact, Kinneavy (1980) includes stylistic techniques with the three kinds of persuasive appeals identified by Aristotle (see *Rhetoric*): the appeal from character (ethos), the appeal to emotion (pathos), and the appeal to reason (logos). In this section I examine the extent to which both authors use the three traditional appeals to persuade an audience to accept their claims of new knowledge. However, I am borrowing from Aristotle only the three general headings and not necessarily the particular list of devices he assigns to each. Also, I will supplement the discussion of appeal to logic with Stephen Toulmin's analysis of practical argumentation.

The ethical appeal.   As Kinneavy points out, the ethical argument includes the following: "The speaker [writer] must appear to have a practical knowledge about the *reality* at issue, he must seem to have the good of the *audience* at heart, and he must portray *himself* as a person who would not deceive the audience in the matter at hand" (p. 238). How do Ball and Stack present themselves as persons of good sense, good will, and good character? Since Ball does not intrude directly into his text, he makes the ethical argument in more subtle ways. He is presented as a competent researcher by inclusion of the name of the college he is affiliated with directly under his name. This says that he has successfully passed through the graduate school apprenticeship and become a professor. An asterisk at the end of the title draws the reader's attention to a note at the bottom of page one, explaining that "this research was funded in part by grants from the National Institute of Mental Health 1012740 and Ferris State College" (p. 400), implying that he is a man to be trusted with public funds because he has a research agenda that will ultimately result in some public good. In this note Ball also names other persons he is grateful to, thus associating himself with people whose professional reputations are established. Granted, these features of a scholarly text are also either obligatory or conventional; yet they do subtly say things about the author that combine with other arguments to influence a reader's reception of the whole. His list of references includes 41 citations of other research, implying he is a competent scholar. The appearance of the four tables of statistical data also lends an air of learning and authority to the article. All of these things combine to make readers believe that Ball is a man of learning and good character who would not intentionally deceive them.

Stack employs many of the same types of devices that help to create an ethos. She has eight pages of bibliography, and citations, tables, and graphs scattered throughout the book as evidence of her learning. A publisher's note called "About the Author" on the last page of the book gives her educational and professional history, but also this more humanizing detail: "She . . . is now engaged in comparative research in urban white ethnic communities in the United States, where once again she and her co-workers, her son Kevin, and John Lombardi, also an anthropologist, will participate as a family in the daily life of the community" (p. 176). Her introductory explanation of how she got into The Flats shows her good sense, and her ability to win the trust of Flats residents implies her good will and good character. Her argument derives much strength from the fact that she practically lived in The Flats for 3 years. It lends tremendous credibility to her claims, because every claim is silently warranted by "I've been there; I know." The ethical argument is considerably stronger and much more direct in Stack's text than in Ball's.

The pathetic appeal.   It may seem strange even to think that academic discourse might use the pathetic appeal as a means of arguing for a claim of knowledge. We tend to think that such appeals are limited to advertising and politics, and that they are beneath the dignity of science. Even so, there is something of an emotional appeal in the way Ball begins his article:

> Black families in the United States continue to suffer disadvantages. The median income for black families in 1979 was $11,650, or 57 percent of that of white families, which was $20,520 (U.S. Bureau of the Census, 1980). In 1978, 42.7 percent of black families were headed by women, and 82 percent of those families contained children under 18. Forty-two percent of all black children resided in families headed by their mothers. In addition, the median income for households headed by black women was only 53 percent of those headed by black men. (p. 400)

It could be said that this is a mere recitation of facts, but it must also be pointed out that income of black families was not one of the main variables of Ball's study. He used it only as a control variable, and, in two of the three statistical analyses, it turned out not to be significantly related to life satisfaction. Why then, does he start with these facts, if not to awaken his readers to the plight of many black Americans? Aristotle points out that appeals to pity are aimed at producing action in the audience. Though Ball closes with no call for action except the traditional one for more research, he may seek to awaken the sympathy of fellow sociologists, hoping that they will be moved to do research on the same problem. He might also harbor the expectation that his research will be reviewed by those who make public policy, especially since his research was partially supported by a national grant. Perhaps he hopes his research will be instrumental in the developing of policies that will enhance the life satisfaction of black people. At any rate, this opening passage does appeal to the sympathy of the readers and to their sense of fairness.

Stack's ethnography clearly contains appeals to emotion, appeals that are calculated to make her audience act, or at least react. Several passages already cited show that she is appealing to her reader's sense of fairness, anger, pity, humor, and other feelings. Stack wants her readers to see that The Flats residents are caught in a web of prejudice, exploitation, unemployment, and welfare regulations that gives them little chance to escape their poverty, but she portrays them also as people motivated by loyalty and compassion towards kin and near-kin. It is precisely their loyalty and compassion that helps them survive. One story she recounts, entitled "Generosity and Poverty," illustrates my point. She relates that Magnolia and Calvin Waters once inherited $1500 from their uncle, who sold his small, run-down farm in Mississippi shortly before he died. At first they hoped to use the money, their first cash surplus ever, as a down payment on a house. But when news of the windfall spread through their domestic network, different kinsmen asked for assistance with unpaid rent, other bills, sickness, and funeral expenses. Magnolia and Calvin could not turn them down. When the welfare agency heard news of the inheritance, all benefits were cut off. "Within a month and a half," Stack writes, "all of the money was gone." She explains,

> random fluctuations in the meager flow of available cash and goods tend to be of considerable importance to the poor. A late welfare check, sudden sickness, robbery, and other unexpected losses cannot be overcome with a cash reserve like more well-to-do families hold for emergencies. Increases in cash are either taken quickly from the poor by the welfare agencies or dissipated through the kin network. (p. 107)

Obviously, readers of differing political and/or religious leanings will react differently to this story, some saying "How charitable the Waterses are!" and others saying, "It's their own fault for being such suckers." But no one will fail to react. Stack makes a strong pathetic appeal, risking that it may backfire, in hopes that it will move at least some to act in the way she intends them to, by believing her explanation for the persistence of poverty and by pressing for welfare reform that will let the poor build up an equity.

The logical appeal. For years logicians have asserted that scientists do not persuade, but rather demonstrate by a system of logical deduction or formal entailments that a certain conclusion must follow from particular axioms. Furthermore, these logicians claim, such a logical demonstration is the only *rational* ground for accepting a conclusion. This equation of formal logicality with rationality has been called into question, notably by Perelman and Olbrechts-Tyteca in *The New Rhetoric* (1969) and by Toulmin in *Human Understanding* (1972). They assert that the kinds of reasoning used in all practical affairs (including academic disciplines) have equally as good a claim on rationality as formal logic or mathematical proofs. Toulmin argues convincingly that history and cross-cultural comparisons will not support Cartesian claims of one universally valid, intuitively self-evident, impartial way of knowing which alone can be considered rational. Rationality, he says, has parallel "jurisdictions," each with its own methods and principles, and its historically evolved ways of introducing, criticizing, and developing concepts (p. 85). Two of Toulmin's other books, *The Uses of Argument* (1969) and *An Introduction to Reasoning* (1984) (with co-authors Rieke and Janik), present a concise method of analyzing the reasoning in arguments from various fields, a method I wish to explain here before proceeding to compare appeals to logic in the two texts.

Toulmin emphasizes that arguments are never free-standing, but always occur in a social context where the ideas can be evaluated by shared standards for testing their validity, relevance, and strength or weakness. These standards amount to "field-dependent" rules appropriate within an intellectual enterprise. But there are also "universal ('field-invariant') rules of procedure that apply to rational criticism in all fields and forums" (1984, p. 17). Among these invariants are four elements that can be found in "any wholly explicit argument": *claims, grounds*, *warrants* and *backings* (1984, p. 25). The *claim* is the assertion the arguer wishes the audience to accept. The *grounds* are the particular facts in the situation that make good the claim; grounds may be such things as experimental observations, statistical data, common knowledge, personal testimony, and so on. *Warrants* are those previously agreed upon facts, rules, laws, principles, statutes, formulas, and so forth, that authorize or license the movement from grounds to claim. *Backing* is the body of generalizations relied on to establish the soundness and relevance of the warrants.

In addition to these four invariant elements of argument construction, Toulmin, Rieke, and Janik posit two others that deal with the relative strength of an argument. In all practical realms of argumentation—and that includes all disciplines not concerned with purely formal methods of deduction or proof—warrants do not authorize absolutely the movement from particular grounds to particular claims. Accordingly, there are very likely to be *modal* terms that qualify the conclusion. Some examples of modal terms are words and phrases such as "necessarily," "certainly," "in all probability," "so far as the evidence goes," and so forth. These terms intervene between grounds and claim so that the grounds support the claim in a qualified way. Also, conditions and exceptions may be allowed for in a part of the argument that Toulmin calls the *rebuttal*. The rebuttal specifies extraordinary or exceptional circumstances that might undermine the force of the argument. According to Toulmin, modal terms reflect the relative strength of the argument, whereas rebuttals indicate its sometimes conditional character. These two parts of an argument, along with claim, grounds, warrant, and backing, are field-invariant; how each part is instantiated in a given argument, however, is field-dependent. Members of any discipline learn to reason using the kinds of grounds, warrants, and backing their colleagues require to judge the acceptability of claims. Not every argument explicitly includes warrants and backing or rebuttals, but these may usually be inferred, as I will show in the following examination of two claims from the two texts.

One claim Ball makes is that, among the black women he studied, widows showed the highest level of life satisfaction. The grounds for this claim are that, on a scale of a possible 10, widows recorded a mean life satisfaction level of 6.84, as compared to mean levels of 6.75 for divorced women, 6.28 for married women, 5.30 for separated women, and 4.98 for single women. The warrant that authorizes the movement from grounds to claim is that the differences between mean levels of life satisfaction were significant at the .001 level of probability. In other words, the statistical procedure for determining levels of probability warrants the claim that the observed differences in levels of life satisfaction are almost surely not random, and that what is true of the sample Ball studied is almost surely true of the larger population the sample represents. "Almost surely" would be the modal qualifier for this claim. The backing for this warrant is the whole of probability theory in statistics. No rebuttal is explicitly included in

Ball's argument, but one might be inferred from his earlier care in showing that his sample of women was representative of the larger population. Unless he made a sampling error, he implicitly argues, his claim should be accepted because it is grounded, warranted, and backed in the way that the members of his field require.

A claim from Stack's book, however, is grounded, warranted, and backed in quite a different way. One of her claims is that "the residence patterns and cooperative organization of people linked in domestic networks demonstrate the stability and collective power of family life in The Flats" (p. 90). This claim is contrary to that of others who have argued that urban black families are disorganized, deviant, and pathological. Stack's grounds for making her claim have already been given in detail earlier, in the description of the Waters domestic network together with the two charts and outline diaries showing the composition and relationships of the members of the network. The warrant that justifies moving from these grounds to the claim above is quite simply that Stack observed and recorded the data that support her claim and checked her understanding with native informants. A warrant, recall, answers the question, "What authorizes the movement from these grounds to that claim?" Stack's warrant answers, "Because I saw it and I know; moreover, the people I studied have verified that my understanding is correct." The backing for this warrant is the body of anthropological research, which honors the making of claims from such grounds by this means. The modal qualifier in Stack's claim might well be "in the Flats." She does not explicitly make this claim for other ghettos but stands by it for this one. Earlier in the book she notes that she observed intensely 15 "unrelated coalitions of kinsmen" (p. 11). The rebuttal in her argument might be something like this: "Insofar as the Waters network and the other 14 are typical of kin networks in The Flats, the claim is good."

Quantitative empiricists might well brand Stack's claim as too subjective and based on too few data; social anthropologists might well call Ball's claim trivial. Yet each researcher has constructed an argument that meets the field-specific standards of their respective disciplines for judging relevance and relative strength or weakness. Therefore, according to Toulmin, each argument is rational; each writer makes a sound appeal to the logic of his or her discipline.

SUMMARY AND CONCLUSIONS

Through this comparison of two social science texts, I have argued that social science writing presents arguments about the nature of reality, as each discipline views it from its own perspective. These arguments deserve to come under the heading of rhetoric just as surely as political speeches or newspaper editorials do, for, although they are concerned with quite different topics and aimed at rather specialized audiences, they present claims and evidence calculated to gain their audience's adherence to those claims, and they also make use of traditional kinds of argumentative appeals. I have argued that the way these texts were invented and arranged is due to the way their authors perceive reality, and that the authors' perceptions are due in turn to their membership in academic communities that have objectified in language and methodological approaches certain ways of experiencing and talking about social phenomena. These methodological approaches are based on assumptions about what can be known, how it can be known, and how certainly it can be known; and these assumptions dictate rhetorical choices about invention, arrangement, and even style.

At the beginning of this chapter I asked, "Is teaching a future or present social scientist to write well merely a matter of teaching a clear prose style? Is a required freshman course in composition sufficient training?" By now I hope it is clear that, in order to write quantitative sociology reports or ethnographies, a writer needs needs primarily to *think* like a quantitative sociologist or social anthropologist. Learning to think in this way may come in the course of the apprenticeship that students spend being enculturated into the knowledge, assumptions, techniques, and so forth, that define a discipline. But often the masters of the discipline do not raise to a level of articulate instruction how to write for the discipline, counting instead on simple association and imitation to do the job. And if students have not been in the discipline long enough to simply absorb these ways of thinking and writing, they will likely flounder around until more experience or some kind of tutelage provides what they need. The usual freshman course in composition is not likely to have given them the kind of specialized training they lack. What can be done for such students?

My answer to that question is, "More of the kind of analysis I have tried to do here." Thinking and writing in the sanctioned ways, as I have attempted to show, are so intertwined that to learn about one is to learn about the other. Analysis of a discipline's writing, since it presents some tangible traces of thought, offers perhaps the best approach to solving the problem of how to think/write for that discipline. Using traditional tools of rhetorical analysis and practical schemes of argument analysis, such as Toulmin's, the rhetorician can help articulate the epistemology that informs any piece of disciplinary discourse and show how it is manifest in rhetorical conventions. As Lester Faigley and I have argued elsewhere (Faigley & Hansen, 1985), it's not possible for teachers of writing to master the content of every discipline and to read and evaluate disciplinary arguments in the way insiders do. But teachers of writing can learn such basic things as which disciplines proceed from positivistic assumptions in their attempts to claim knowledge about reality and which ones proceed from hermeneutic assumptions. Without understanding the whole body of statistics, teachers can understand that statistical tests and probability levels are, like examples and reasons, kinds of evidence and ways of supporting claims. They can turn their skills of close reading of texts to analyzing the whys and wherefores of invention, arrangement and style in disciplinary discourse. By articulating their findings, they can give both masters and apprentices in the social science disciplines explicit declarative and procedural knowledge that will, I think, be welcomed, both for the practical ways it gives of talking about writing in that discipline and for the occasion it gives a discipline to examine its assumptions about knowledge and writing.[2]

REFERENCES

Ball, R. E. (1983). Marital status, household structure, and life satisfaction of black women. *Social Problems*, *30*, 400–409.

Bazerman, C. (1983). Scientific writing as a social act: A review of the literature of the sociology of science. In P. V. Anderson, R. J. Brockmann, & C. Miller (Eds.), *New essays in technical writing and communication: Research, theory, and practice* (pp. 156–184). Farmingdale, NY: Baywood.

Berger, P. L., & Luckmann, T. (1966). *The social construction of reality*. New York: Doubleday.

Bitzer, L. (1968). The rhetorical situation. *Philosophy and Rhetoric, 1*, 1–15.

Brown, R. H. (1977). The emergence of existential thought: Philosophical perspectives on positivist and humanist forms of social theory. In J. D. Douglas & J. M. Johnson (Eds.), *Existential sociology* (pp. 77–100). Cambridge, England: Cambridge University Press.

Brown, R. H. (1983). Theories of rhetoric and the rhetorics of theory. *Social Research*, *50*, 126–157.

Brummett, B. (1976). Some implications of "process" or "inter-subjectivity": Postmodern rhetoric. *Philosophy and Rhetoric*, *9*, 21–51.

Fahnestock, J. (1986). Accommodating science: The rhetorical life of scientific facts. *Written Communication*, *3*, 275–296.

Faigley, L., & Hansen, K. (1985). Learning to write in the social sciences. *College Composition and Communication*, *36*, 140–149.

Gilbert, G. N., & Mulkay, M. (1984). *Opening Pandora's box: A sociological account of scientists' discourse*. Cambridge, England: Cambridge University Press.

Gusfield, J. (1976). The literary rhetoric of science: Comedy and pathos in drinking driver research. *American Sociological Review, 41*, 16–34.

Hansen, K. (1987). *Rhetoric and epistemology in texts from the social sciences: An analysis of three disciplines' discourse about contemporary American blacks.* Unpublished doctoral dissertation, University of Texas at Austin.

Harley, J. K. (1983). The smell of the lamp: Bad writing in the behavioural sciences. *Canadian Journal of Education, 8*, 245–262.

Kinneavy, J. L. (1980). *A theory of discourse*. New York: W. W. Norton & Co.

---

[2] I would like to thank the following people who read early versions of this chapter and made many helpful suggestions: Lester Faigley, David Jolliffe, Beth Daniell, Mara Holt, Leon Anderson, and Jose Limon. This chapter presents only some of the research and conclusions of my dissertation (Hansen, 1987); I invite interested readers to consult it for a fuller discussion.

Lally, A. J. (1976). Positivism and its critics. In D. C. Thorns (Ed.), *New directions in sociology* (pp. 55–75). Totowa, NJ: Rowman and Littlefield.

Lynd, R. S. (1940). *Knowledge for what?* Princeton, NJ: Princeton University Press.

MacIver, R. (1930). Is sociology a natural science? *Publications of the American Sociological Society, 25,* 25–35.

Marcus, G. E., & Cushman, D. (1982). Ethnographies as texts. In B. J. Siegel, A. R. Beals, & S. R. Tyler (Eds.), *Annual review of anthropology, 11* (pp. 25–69). Palo Alto, CA: Annual Reviews, Inc.

McCloskey, D. (1984). The literary character of economics. *Daedelus, 113,* 97–119.

Morrison, D. E., & Henkel, R. E. (1969). Significance tests reconsidered. *American Sociologist, 4,* 131–140.

Myers, G. (1985). The social construction of two biologists' proposals. *Written Communication, 2,* 219–245.

Nelson, J. S. (1983). Political theory as political rhetoric. In J. S. Nelson (Ed.), *What should political theory be now?* (pp. 169–240). Albany, NY: SUNY Press.

Northrop, F. S. C. (1948). *The logic of the sciences and the humanities.* New York: Macmillan.

Oberschall, A. (1972). The institutionalization of American sociology. In A. Oberschall (Ed.), *The establishment of empirical sociology* (pp. 187–251). New York: Harper & Row.

Perelman, C., & Olbrechts-Tyteca, L. (1969). *The new rhetoric: A treatise on argumentation* (J. Wilkinson & P. Weaver, trans.). Notre Dame, IN: University of Notre Dame Press.

Raywid, M. A. (1978). Power to jargon, for jargon is power. *Journal of Teacher Education, 24,* 95.

Sanday, P. R. (1979). The ethnographic paradigm(s). *Administrative Science Quarterly, 24,* 527–538.

Selvin, H. C., & Wilson, E. K. (1984a). Cases in point: A limited glossary of stumblebum usage. *The Sociological Quarterly, 25,* 417–427.

Selvin, H. C., & Wilson, E. K. (1984b). On sharpening sociologists' prose. *The Sociological Quarterly, 25,* 205–222.

Simons, H. W. (1985). Chronicle and critique of a conference. *Quarterly Journal of Speech, 71,* 52–64.

Stack, C. B. (1975). *All our kin: Strategies for survival in a black community.* New York: Harper Torchbooks.

Thorns, D. C. (1976). The growth of the sociological method. In D. C. Thorns (Ed.), *New directions in sociology,* (pp. 9–22). Totowa, NJ: Rowman and Littlefield.

Toulmin, S. E. (1969). *The uses of argument.* Cambridge, England: Cambridge University Press.

Toulmin, S. E. (1972). *Human understanding: The collective use and evolution of concepts.* Princeton, NJ: Princeton University Press.

Toulmin, S. E., & Leary, D. E. (1985). The cult of empiricism in psychology and beyond. In S. Koch & D. E. Leary (Eds.), *A century of psychology as science* (pp. 594–617). New York: McGraw-Hill.

Toulmin, S. E., Rieke, R., & Janik, A. (1984). *An introduction to reasoning* (2nd ed.). New York: Macmillan.

Tudge, C. (1983). A time and a place for jargon. *New Scientist, 97,* 674–675.

Weaver, R. M. (1970). Language is sermonic. In R. L. Johannesen, R. Strickland, & R. T. Eubanks (Eds.), *Language is sermonic* (pp. 201–225). Baton Rouge, LA: Louisiana State University Press. (Original essay published 1963)

Weaver, R. M. (1985). *The ethics of rhetoric*. Davis, CA: Hermagoras Press. (Original work published 1953)

Weimer, W. B. (1977). Science as a rhetorical transaction: Toward a nonjustificational conception of rhetoric. *Philosophy and Rhetoric, 10,* 1–29.

Williamson, S. T. (1947). How to write like a social scientist. *The Saturday Review of Literature, 30,* 17–27.

Ziman, John (1968). *Public knowledge.* Cambridge: Cambridge University Press.

6 Scientific Composing Processes: How Eminent Scientists Write Journal Articles*

Jone Rymer

Wayne State University

What do experienced scientists actually do when they compose research papers for publication? How do leading scientists prepare, write, and revise the results of their laboratory experiments for scientific journals? The project reported in this chapter sheds new light on these questions through interviews with nine eminent researchers in the natural sciences about their composing practices, and through a case study of one of these scientists composing an article which was subsequently published in a principal academic journal. The scientists' views about their writing form the basis for analyzing the composing aloud protocols derived from the case study.

Following a review of the current knowledge about composing scientific discourse, the chapter explains the composing strategies of the nine scientists, characterizes the case study subject in light of the data about the panel members, and describes major results of the protocol analysis. The study concludes that some traditional attitudes toward scientific writing are questionable. Specifically, it suggests that scientists' composing processes:

- exhibit a full range of approaches from linear procedures focused on planning, to full scale impressionistic drafting focused on revision; and
- typically involve the discovery of new ideas and information about the research and its meaning.

Overall, therefore, this study of eminent scientists indicates that scientific composing practices may not differ radically from those of other kinds of professionals.

* I want to thank the scientists who participated in this research, especially the one who is the subject of the case study.

SCIENTISTS AS WRITERS: CURRENT KNOWLEDGE ABOUT
COMPOSING SCIENTIFIC DISCOURSE

Most scholars interested in scientists' production of experimental papers do not accept the conventional notion that the writing task is one in which scientists simply record what they did in the laboratory to produce their results. Among rhetoricians, sociologists, and philosophers of science—most of whom have been influenced by Popper (1959, 1962), Polanyi (1962), Kuhn (1970), Toulmin (1972), and others—the scientists' perspective is assumed to be a preconceived frame of reference which determines the observations they make about the natural world. Accordingly, the experimental paper is regarded both as the vehicle for giving meaning to those observations and for persuading the scientific community that those observations are truths.

The assumption that science is a rhetorical enterprise places great importance on scientists as creators of scientific meaning in texts. Sociologists of science have long proclaimed that experimental articles are fictions that hide and misrepresent researchers' actions according to certain conventions (Medawar, 1964). Recently, a new breed of sociologists has begun to study scientific texts as products of social activity (Bazerman, 1983; Myers, 1986). Rather than attempting to use scientific discourse as a window on the laboratory and pronouncing it to be *fraudulent* (Medawar's term), they have investigated the relationship of the discourse to its context and "convincingly refute[d] the traditional view that scientific texts simply and unproblematically report on nature as revealed through empirical investigation" (Bazerman, 1984, p. 39).

These new sociological studies have focused on scientific writing as the focal point, not the resource, for learning about scientific activities in the laboratory (Gilbert & Mulkay, 1984, p. 15). Using microscopic observations of routine laboratory practices, some scholars have shown how scientists' writing imposes a logical structure, after the fact, on the mass of confusion in the lab and decontextualizes these activities. Thus, the texts establish the scientists' credibility and persuade the community that their claims should be accepted as facts (Latour & Woolgar, 1979). Others have demonstrated how the discourse itself contributes to what they call the *construction* of scientific knowledge by contrasting the everyday life in the lab ("where the making of selections dominates the scene") with the conventionalized representation in the scientific paper ("[which] offers a curiously purged residual description, constituted more by what is not at stake in the research . . . than by what is"; Knorr-Cetina, 1981, p. 115). Still others have shown that there is infinite variety in the ways that scientists choose to represent their actions and beliefs in discourse and that the depersonalized, objective scientific style of experimental papers plays a significant role in the creation of what is accepted as scientific knowledge (Gilbert & Mulkay, 1984).

Not surprisingly, rhetoricians have explored various aspects of "the rhetoric of science" (for example, Campbell, 1975; Miller, 1985; Overington, 1977; Weimer, 1977; Zappen, 1983) and one topic they have illuminated is how the conventions of scientific texts operate. Gross (1985), for example, has demonstrated how the genre dictates certain choices of form and content while serving to justify the writer's belief that the scientific enterprise leads to reliable, valuable knowledge about the natural world. According to Halloran (1984, p. 70), however, "while a number of scholars have been arguing theoretically that science is rhetorical, very little attention has been paid to particular cases of scientific rhetoric."

Some studies now are based on particular cases; studying the conventions of the genre, for example, Bernhardt (1985) uses a selection of articles in the natural sciences to conclude that seven rhetorical acts bring the writer or the reader to the surface of the text. Other scholars have demonstrated through analyses of individual publications that a scientist may use rhetorical decision-making even in the selection of experiments (Bazerman, 1984), and that an individual scientist can create markedly different representations of scientific ethos (Halloran, 1984).

Studies of Professionals Composing At Work

But despite all of this scholarly interest in the rhetorical functions of scientific reporting, little research has been conducted on scientists' actual writing of the experimental article. In fact, very little research has been done on the workplace composing processes of any professionals (but see Broadhead & Freed, 1986; Odell, Goswami, Herrington, & Quick 1983; Selzer, 1983). Moreover, surveys of the composing processes of technical/scientific workers have only minimal relevance to scientists writing scientific discourse because survey results differentiate neither the profession nor the genre (Roundy & Mair, 1982; Paradis, Dobrin, & Miller, cited in Anderson, 1986). In reviewing knowledge of composing at work, therefore, scholars frequently have called for research on various professionals engaged in producing their naturalistic writing, their typical tasks on the job instead of assignments imposed by the investigator (for example, Faigley, Cherry, Jolliffe, & Skinner 1985, p. 58).

Closest to answering this call on scientists' writing is Myers's illuminating case study (1985) of researchers in the natural sciences writing grant proposals. Interviewing the writers and analyzing texts of proposal drafts, Myers describes the composing processes of scientists establishing relationships with the scientific community and building consensus among their colleagues. During composing, his two subjects come to new and quite different strategies for presenting the self in their proposals (neither too meek nor too assertive) and for making claims about their work—balancing its originality while confirming current wisdom. Myers's descriptions of the use of ethos and pathos in the construction of scientific arguments is pertinent to an understanding of the scientific composing process, but his investigation has two limitations: his methods are confined to interviews and text analyses (which rely heavily on what the subjects know and are willing to reveal, as well as on the investigator's interpretations); and the scope of his study is restricted to grant proposals, an ancillary genre to the experimental results paper.

Myers's claims—that the proposal is the most persuasive document scientists write, and that it is critical to maintaining the scientific enterprise, disseminating knowledge, and forming scientific beliefs—are true, but they ignore the centrality of the journal paper. The proposal certainly plays a significant role in science, but the primary document—according to scientists themselves and to scholars in the various disciplines that study science—is the journal paper, a genre that is, in fact, also very persuasive, but is the more so when it seems not to be. Authorities in science studies such as Ziman (1967, 1976, p. 99) describe "the primary paper in a learned journal" as an argument that is "the most important medium of scientific communication." Traditional sociologists such as Price (1963, p. 68) define the paper as the record of the scientists' claim to the work. Sociologists taking an anthropological approach, such as Latour and Woolgar (1979, p. 71), assert that "the production of papers is acknowledged by participants as the main objective of their activity." Philosophers of science, such as Ludwik Fleck depict journal publications as texts of the vanguard of research, where the scientist asks that his claims be accepted by the collective community as part of scientific truth (1979, pp. 118–124). In short, scientists' composing practices are most relevant in producing documents in the genre that they describe as original research results published in the primary literature (Day, 1979, pp. 1–3) but simply call *papers*.

Composing Aloud as a Technique with Professionals At Work

Focusing on primary results papers that scientists publish in academic journals, this study uses, not only interviews and text analyses, but features protocol analysis of transcribed audio tapes of the scientist thinking aloud while in the act of writing. Developed by cognitive psychologists of the human processing school (Newell & Simon, 1972), the think-aloud technique and process tracing analysis have been adapted to composing (Hayes & Flower, 1980, 1983; Swarts, Flower, & Hayes, 1984) and proven to be very productive in studying children's and students' writing (for example, Emig, 1977; Flower & Hayes, 1977, 1980a, b, 1981a, b; Graves, 1975; Perl, 1979).

While popular for studying students' writing, composing aloud has not been applied extensively to writers engaged in their naturalistic tasks at work (Humes, 1983, pp. 202–203; Faigley et al., 1985, p. 58). In practical terms, the intrusive nature of composing aloud makes it difficult to get professionals to apply it to their writing on the job. Moreover, Flower and Hayes set an example of experimental conditions for compose-aloud research, including artificial assignments that would elicit articulation of writers' strategies—rather than allowing them to rely on stored habits. The notion that only experimental assignments would produce rich protocols carried over to studying writers at work. Scholars tended to assume that composing aloud was impossible for professionals because familiarity with their tasks would prevent them from articulating anything meaningful (a view seemingly confirmed by Cooper and Odell's early study, 1978).

Although composing aloud has limitations as a research technique (Cooper & Holzman, 1983; Dobrin, 1986; Nisbett & Wilson, 1977; Steinberg, 1986), cognitive psychologists consider that verbal reports produced by think-aloud procedures can be reliable and valid data about cognitive processes in adults (Ericsson & Simon, 1980, 1984). Certainly, professionals' familiarity with their naturalistic tasks would not necessarily prevent them from articulating much of what they know while composing aloud. Since the technique has provided much information about writers' processes unavailable by other methods—particularly because people don't remember, never realized, or won't admit everything that they, in fact, do when they write (Flower & Hayes, 1981a, p. 368; Tomlinson, 1984)—composing aloud should be applied as one of the methods to investigate scientists' processes in writing scientific discourse.

THE PANEL OF SCIENTISTS: SELECTION AND METHODS OF INVESTIGATION

The purpose of this project was to define the writing practices of expert scientists whose documents unquestionably meet or exceed the expectations and standards of the scientific community. Such experts publish frequently in the best journals, have their work read and used by many other scientists, and influence the writing of others—both by example and by their roles as trainers. Clearly, scientists meeting these standards would be experts as defined by the communities in their specialities, not by the investigator with particular ideas about what constitutes good scientific writing.

Criteria for Defining Expert Scientists

To represent this concept of the expert as defined by the scientific community, three major criteria were used in selecting the scientists for this study: prestigious publication records, high citation indexes, and extensive experience training graduate students. All nine panelists met the three criteria.

Authors frequently published in the closely refereed journals of academic societies were selected because they are experienced writers whose texts are considered competent by members of their discipline. Having numerous publications in the most prestigious scientific journals is a clear indication that the scientists' work is regularly judged and found acceptable by their peers. As

Eugene Garfield, the chief editor at the Institute for Scientific Information, says, "The world of science is very large. Over one million scientists publish from time to time. Of these, however, a small percentage publish a large percentage of all papers. That is one kind of productivity measure" (Garfield, 1981, p. 13).

Authors highly cited in the publications of their colleagues were selected because their writing is influential in the scientific community. Whereas frequency of publication indicates acceptance by the scientific community, the citation counts in Science Citation Index show how often these authors' work is used by their fellows. As Garfield continues, after discussing numbers of publications, "there is an even smaller number [of scientists] who have a significant impact, which is largely reflected in citations" (Garfield, 1981, p. 13). Sociological studies of citation indexes have established that citation counts do reflect the reputation and influence scientists have on their particular scientific communities (Cole & Cole, 1973, p. 27; Price, 1963, p. 77, 1970; Small, 1977, p. 158). High publication and citation rates together warrant that scientists' communities judge their journal papers to be credible, if not authoritative, within a discipline.

Established mentors for graduate students were selected because they manage the apprenticeship system and train novices in writing scientific discourse. Much of science is "a kind of craft, or embodied expertise, which is not incorporated into the . . . reporting that is characteristic of scientific literature" (Lynch, Livingston, & Garfinkel, 1983, p. 209). Not only do the leaders of university research laboratories impart this tacit knowledge to their graduate student-apprentices, they also teach them the publishing game in their discipline, including the actual writing of research papers. These principal investigators are the composition teachers for the next generation of scientists.

In addition to these essential criteria, all subjects were sought in a single field. Specialists in the natural sciences were selected because these disciplines do the largest amount of publishing (Garfield, 1981) and because the most is known about their production of documents. It is, after all, to the life sciences that sociologists turned their attention, calling them "the most authoritative and esoteric system of knowledge in modern societies" (Knorr-Cetina & Mulkay, 1983). All panelists were chosen from one discipline, to eliminate any differences in practice caused by variation in specialities (Garfield, 1981; Meadows, 1974, pp. 201–203).

Composition of the Panel of Scientists

The nine scientists selected according to these criteria are natural scientists affiliated with units in biochemistry; they call themselves biochemists, enzymologists, or molecular biologists. All hold university professorships and head large research groups comprising many postdoctoral fellows, research associates, graduate students, and technical support personnel. All act as research directors and instructors, imparting all the knowledge and skills necessary to become a scientist, including learning how to write scientific papers.

Most significantly, each panel member is highly successful, both by publication counts in the journals of the academic societies and by the citation indexes. Most of the panelists have published over 100 articles, many in primary journals, with the range of their bibliographies extending from 70 papers to well over 200. Of greater significance, all are highly cited in the Institute for Scientific Information's "Science Citation Index," three of the nine ranking among the top 1,000 most cited scientists in the world—meaning that they represent about 0.1 % of the regularly publishing scientists worldwide (Garfield, 1981, p. 14).

All scientists on the panel were interested in the topic of writing journal papers—particularly in learning how other scientists' procedures differed from their own, or in learning techniques to make themselves more efficient or more effective. The panel may, therefore, be biased due to self-selectivity; scientists with little interest in writing would probably not have participated. Despite their high productivity, however, several of the members did not believe they were proficient writers. Some felt their procedures were very inefficient, becoming effective only with great effort; in fact, they seemed embarrassed to reveal their composing practices until they were promised absolute anonymity. So while the panel is composed of expert scientists, it is not necessarily composed of expert writers—despite their prodigious bibliographies.

Methods

This investigation of scientists' production of primary scientific discourse used two research methods: (a) interviews of several scientists to build a framework to conduct and interpret in-depth case studies, while identifying subjects for composing aloud; and (b) case studies of some scientists from the panel writing journal articles while composing aloud.

The first major purpose for interviewing was to gain data from retrospective analysis of scientists about their composing processes, so that results from any case study could be interpreted in the light of this group's practices. Although the panel cannot be considered representative of all senior scientists, it does allow a broader perspective from which to view case studies. The secondary and more practical purpose for interviewing was to engage potential subjects in the project's topic and convince some of them to participate in a time-consuming, extensive case study.

The scientists were interviewed for 1 to 3 hours using an audiotaped open-questionnaire method. The conversations were guided by a set of questions focusing on attitudes toward writing, individual composing procedures, and criteria for writing scientific papers, but also dealing with contextual influences, collaborative authorship arrangements, and training graduate students to write. Each scientist discussed his work (all the subjects are male) by showing drafts and finished products of journal articles in progress or recently completed. All the scientists were asked to participate in a case study using the method of composing aloud.

Of the nine scientists, five expressed willingness to try composing aloud while writing a scientific paper. Of these five, two were unable to participate at the present time; one tried to write while thinking aloud but gave up because he felt that his normal processes were intruded upon. One tried for several sessions but bowed out (with the full agreement of the investigator); his composing aloud was mainly verbalization of his drafted words, with long silences while he thought, sometimes accompanied by vague, embarrassed explanations like "I'm having a problem with this sentence." One of the three scientists who attempted to compose aloud was able to master the technique so as to accomplish his own ends (that is, write his paper to his own satisfaction) while thinking aloud in enough detail to warrant carrying out the full investigation. Because of the complexity involved in composing a whole journal paper, he is the sole subject of this stage of the research.

Some researchers have expressed dissatisfaction that because composing aloud requires subjects who can do adequate oral reporting while writing, it does not allow a random sample (Humes, 1983, p. 213). This is a matter of concern, but case studies typically are based on nonprobability samplings which restrict drawing inferences about the general population anyway. Although this case study is considered within the perspective gained through the panel of scientists, the results are exploratory; they cannot be generalized. Conclusions from this research can, however, form hypotheses for future studies of multiple subjects.

SUBJECT OF THE CASE STUDY: COMPARISON OF INDIVIDUAL COMPOSING PRACTICES WITH THE PANEL SCIENTISTS

Subject J, a biochemist, is a full professor in one of the leading biochemistry departments in the country, heads a research lab of about 10 people, serves on the editorial board of an academic journal, and has served as a National Institutes of Health grant reviewer. The author of over 150 papers, the majority in academic society journals, he had a citation index of over 3,000 references to over 90 papers during 1965–1978 (the period covered by the only ISI citation study ranking the most cited scientists; Garfield, 1982). He is one of the three panel members who rank among the most frequently cited scientists in the world.

Within his particular scientific community, therefore, Subject J is an expert, one whose written products have high visibility and are regularly used by others to do their own science. The prospect of studying J's writing raises several questions: What composing procedures does this very experienced scientist use to turn out these successful products? How do contextual factors such as the research team itself influence these procedures? What composing strategies is he handing down to his apprentices, the graduate students and postdoctoral fellows in his laboratory?

Viewing Subject J in the context of the panel of scientists provides a framework for understanding his writing an article for the *Journal of Biological Chemistry*. Although the practices and attitudes of the panelists cannot be assumed to be representative of all senior biochemists, the data from their interviews at least allows outside observers to judge whether Subject J's case study is markedly unusual. Considering a range of his peers' practices can shed light on Subject J's composing practices, his attitudes toward writing and publishing science, and his control of the task situation.

Composing Processes in Comparison with Panelists

On the basis of the case study and the panel survey, Subject J's writing practices are not atypical for eminent scientists. In fact, all of J's major characteristics as a writer fall within the peer scientists' range of behaviors. For example, in his outlining techniques, his methods of drafting, his use of graphics, and his reliance on his own previous work, Subject J's composing procedures are quite typical of the panelists.

Among various planning techniques, outlining is one that most of the panel scientists report that they never use, though a few typically construct real outlines and use them. In interviews, Subject J claimed he never outlines; but in writing the paper for this study, he frequently made rudimentary lists of key words or items to cover, either just prior to drafting or during a composing session. Whether such grocery lists are outlines is debatable. They certainly show little resemblance to those constructed by Subject S, who builds successively more elaborate outlines which gradually grow into the paper itself. Probably it is fair to classify subject J's outlining technique as rudimentary and occasional.

On drafting habits, the panelists range all the way from "spew and revise" writers to one "perfect first drafter" (Gould, 1980, p. 100). Like several of his peers who follow the former routine, J simply plunges in, trying to get something down on paper. Similarly, Subject D reports:

> "I just try to put something down that makes sense, fits in, and not spend a long time on it. It's much better if I can just get something down. . . . Lots of barriers to get that first couple sentences, first paragraph."

At the other end of the spectrum is Subject Y, whose first drafts are nearly identical with his published articles:

> "what I tend to do in writing up a paper is to do a fair amount of thinking about it before I actually start writing . . . and I prepare graphs before I start writing, so I will have an idea what I want to have in my paper . . . and then I will start writing around the graphs . . . then I find generally that writing goes very quickly, and I just sit down and write, and I don't look back in general, as to what I've written, until I've reached the end of the paper."

Some invention procedures—using graphs, tables of data, and the author's own previous papers as planning devices—characterize all the panelists' practices. Typically, figures and tables of the data (and sometimes fragments of the materials and methods section) function as visual aids to invention and as organizing points during both planning and drafting. Most of the scientists also use their own previous papers to aid their invention. Much like the rhetoricians and sociologists who describe each new paper as a building block in a research team's overall plan (Gross, 1985; Latour & Woolgar, 1979), Subject D explains his own procedure in words that well represent most of his fellows, including Subject J:

> "I usually take a most recent paper . . . so I'm making a start . . . the next chapter of the story . . . you might as well say that we're telling this project and previously we had this, and now we have such and such available method."

Attitudes Toward Writing in Comparison with Panelists

Subject J's attitudes toward the process of composing and publishing scientific papers are not atypical of the panelists' views. A majority of the scientists on the panel are dissatisfied with their writing procedures, believing they expend more time and energy than is necessary and even suffer acutely while writing papers. Subject J expresses strong dissatisfaction with the inefficiency of his methods, a view echoed by another panel member: "I'm dissatisfied with the fact that it is such a slow, long process. I'm pretty sure that I take more time than others. . . . I think that I probably spend twice the time that the average person does."

Although a few panelists express confidence in their writing skills (notably including Subject Y, the scientist who has a reputation as a good writer among his peers), most of these highly published scientists do not see themselves as expert writers with a repertoire of strategies for completing their tasks effectively and efficiently. Quite the opposite is true for several on the panel: They lack confidence in their skills and are actually embarrassed about their composing methods.

Despite doubts about their procedures, all of the scientists feel generally confident about their products and most are very much involved—some even truly excited—about publishing their results. Here is Subject Y:

> "I'm pretty interested in [publishing my data], pretty excited about it because there's no point in publishing it unless you find it interesting and uh, so I want to try and get it across and express some of that same excitement that I feel about it to the rest of the world. . . . science is my life, clearly. . . . I am spending . . . all of my waking hours in some way or other thinking about the paper. And then at times I'm really excited about it."

The confidence and excitement seem to be well grounded in realistic assessments of how readers will judge each of the papers they write. Subject M, for example, says: "I think I'll get a good response out of it, but it is not as complete and strong a set of data as I would like." Most of the panelists seem well aware of the significance of their projects. Much of their work they see as mundane science, filling in the pieces of the puzzle, but some of it they forecast to be breakthrough, revolutionary science. In fact, some of them speak in almost revolutionary terms echoing Kuhn, describing their normal, mundane papers in comparison with their exciting breakthroughs, the ones that represent a big leap forward. Subject S, for example, one of the three panelists with the high citation counts, comments:

"When people talk about excitement and breakthroughs and all that, that's 5 or 10 percent of our life. When you talk about writing papers, there'll be one out of 10 that has a large percent of discovery in it. The rest is fitting, matching, testing . . . and when you get through, everyone says, yah, I thought that would probably work."

In an early interview prior to writing the paper, Subject J clearly defines which type of article he believes he is about to draft: "It's very high quality and therefore we will publish in the *Journal of Biological Chemistry* . . . the most prestigious journal in our discipline." In his opinion this paper will be one of those small number of exciting breakthroughs:

"This one is very special to me, and it's not just because I want to add another paper to my bibliography, but I think it's very, very significant, and I'm pleased with the way it came out. . . . I think it's going to be a classic study, and so I'm excited about writing it. . . . I have thought about it. I sort of held it, oh like a little jewel in the back of my head, uh, it . . . gives me a lot of pleasure just to think about it, and the time is right. . . . It's a beautiful story."

Since the completed paper was accepted immediately by a major journal with only minor changes (deleting one procedure, adding one bit of information, and correcting a couple of mechanical errors), the scientific community initially corroborated the author's judgment.

This particular article should call forth his best efforts as a writer, and because, it is "special science," it might make his procedures readily available to the investigator. In writing a "normal science" paper, the scientist might rely on automatic choices and thus have little decision-making to articulate while composing aloud.

Management of the Task in Comparison with Panelists

In managing the writing of journal papers, Subject J is also typical of the scientists on the panel. In carrying out his tasks, he typifies the behavior of his colleagues (for example, writing longhand on legal pads, submitting drafts for typing section by section), but he conducts the overall effort in a manner representative of most of the panelists. Subject J's integration of his own efforts with those of his collaborators well represents the panel's scientists in both the division of labor and in the sequential preparation of the paper's sections.

Almost all research in the life sciences, including the reporting of results, has been a team effort for some time (Meadows, 1974, pp. 199–201; Price, 1963, p. 89). Although details of these collaborative arrangements vary from laboratory to laboratory, two principal modes of collaborative composing prevail among the panel scientists. Either a junior member or the principal investigator himself assumes major authorship; under both plans, other collaborators also participate in the writing.

For ordinary science, representing the great majority of total output, someone *other* than the principal investigator does the actual writing. One of the group members drafts most of the paper; then the head of the group revises and edits it to ensure that it meets his standards and that this new "chapter" fits into his overall publication plan for reporting from his lab. Frequently, graduate students are the major writers of these papers. Sometimes their mentors provide overall guidance and do some revision; at other times, senior scientists treat graduate students' manuscripts with benign neglect; at still others, they simply use novices' efforts as rough drafts. Thus, the graduate students of these panel members learn to write scientific discourse by a variety of apprenticeship methods.

Those panel scientists who do not take papers drafted by others so seriously edit only what they find intolerable to sign their names to. Such papers bear the senior author's name, but they certainly are *not* his compositions, as the panelists readily admit. Other scientists, however, expect the manuscripts drafted by their subordinates to be equal to their own documents, meeting not only the same scientific standards they impose on their own writing but their stylistic ideas as well. In fact, some of these professors do not teach their juniors to write; they simply treat such drafts as raw materials to create their own papers in their own style.

In the other, less common type of collaboration, the laboratory head is actually the writer. This arrangement, which may sound conventional to an outsider, is relatively *unusual*. It prevails in projects in which the senior scientist is intimately involved (perhaps even doing some of the bench work himself) or those reporting what he believes to be highly significant results. In these projects, the head scientist considers himself the author and typically writes the introduction, the discussion, and the abstract. Other team members still do some of the drafting, however, usually preparing an initial manuscript of the sections on materials/methods and results, as well as the figures.

This collaborative arrangement, in which the principal investigator acts as the major author, was adopted by Subject J in writing the *JBC* article. The paper, with pieces prepared by five team members and some contribution by a outside collaborator, was produced with the following division of labor: Subject J, by his own account, did the creating and the managing—the hypothesizing, thinking, planning, organizing, and the guiding of other team members in preparing their portions. More significant, he himself wrote three key sections: the introduction, the discussion, and the abstract. Although two postdoctoral fellows each wrote certain parts of the materials/methods and results sections, Subject J did all the revising and editing himself. (The research fellows and two graduate students did the laboratory work, with a senior scientist at a research institute doing one set of critical experiments.)

Like this division of labor, Subject J's method for sequencing the composing tasks represents a typical collaborative practice among the panelists. While they do not all follow precisely the same sequence to produce the sections of a paper, their practices represent variations on a single pattern which can be characterized as follows:

- The figures (charts, graphs) are roughed out by those who have collected the data.
- The materials/methods and results sections are written by one or more of those who have collected the data.
- The title and introduction are written by the main writer (a team member who usually is not the laboratory director).
- The discussion section (whether independent or incorporated into the results) is written by the main writer. (An alternative sequence reverses the introduction and the discussion sections so that the latter is drafted with the results section.)
- The abstract is prepared by the main writer.

This general arrangement of functional tasks—a plan that diverges radically from the sequence suggested by the standard textbook authors (Day, 1979)—characterizes the panelists' typical behavior and certainly describes accurately the procedures followed by Subject J in writing the case study paper. (See the Appendix for a detailed history of writing the *JBC* paper.) Some aspects of these arrangements seem to be merely conventional, but others are clearly functional; for example, most of these sequences capitalize on certain formal components of one section to aid the invention for later sections (such as the figures and the introduction helping the writer plan the discussion).

Subject J's case study, therefore, features a paper produced according to a conventional sequence and by a typical collaborative composing process in which the head scientist himself authors most of the manuscript. The document produced by Subject J meets the criteria of effectiveness established by his expert community: it was published by the leading journal in the discipline. This paper is the focus of this case study.

CASE STUDY METHODS

Subject J composed aloud an entire scientific paper reporting the results of his research team's experimental work. According to his typical practices for a paper he values highly, this means that he supervised the entire writing project; drafted the introduction, the discussion, and the abstract; and revised the materials/methods and results sections which were drafted by his subordinates. The composing aloud followed the general scheme of the think-aloud procedure, in which the subject is asked to articulate his thoughts while in the act of writing. One marked difference from the standard procedures was that the subject was not asked to confine his remarks to the writing task. Instead an instruction sheet advised: "Try to articulate your thoughts as much as you possibly can . . . [even if] much of what you think may seem irrelevant to you." The purpose of this modification was to expand the data collected to include contextual matters relating to both the community of scientific workers and the environment of the laboratory. All 17 composing sessions (spanning 3 1/2 months) were audiotaped, and the tapes were transcribed and analyzed. To supplement this protocol analysis, the investigator observed the author in several of the sessions, silently taking notes about his activities in the act of writing.

Subject J was interviewed before the composing began, frequently after writing sessions, and periodically throughout the subsequent months of preparation for publication. The interviews permitted the scientist to report on the composing he did between the writing sessions—the extensive thinking and planning he did on the paper while away from his desk. In addition, the interviews allowed J to explain some of his procedures, to describe some of the contextual influences on his writing and thinking, and to articulate some of his thoughts that he was unable to describe while writing. (A subject may be cognizant of many more thoughts than he can articulate while composing; an immediate debriefing can capture some of these.)

The data from the case study include the protocols; the observer's notes for seven of the composing sessions; the interview transcripts; all of the drafts, revisions, notes, and typed copies of revisions the author produced for the paper; referees' comments and the subsequent changes made by the author; together with all correspondence about the paper—particularly an argument between Subject J and a collaborator from another institution.

The history of producing this paper, a naturalistic writing task completed under quasi-experimental conditions in the usual working environment, is very long and complex (as shown in Appendix A.) Each activity took several sessions, with no clear demarcation into stages; for example, J begins to revise almost simultaneously with beginning to draft. These two stages are arbitrarily divided here at the point he announces that he has finished the rough draft. On the third session of March 24, he suddenly interrupts his review of text, saying:

"I have had it! I am done. . . . I have essentially the structure . . . I may modify, but I feel as if I have all my thoughts down. . . . this needs some polishing, but essentially at this moment, I think it is finished. I have to put some references and things of that sort, but I think it is finished." [M24C3])[1]

Using J's own demarcation, then, drafting and revising can be differentiated. Completing the drafts of the introduction and the discussion required 7 hours (spread over several sessions); revising these two sections took an additional 6 hours.

The case study of Subject J yielded meaningful, rich protocols. In early compose-aloud sessions, J frequently fell silent or merely verbalized the words he was drafting, but after several sessions he began articulating many of his thoughts while writing, eventually becoming quite proficient at doing both verbal activities simultaneously. Nevertheless, he did not find composing aloud easy: "The process of writing, speaking aloud, and thinking . . . one appears to inhibit the other. I've adapted to it, but I find it extremely difficult" (M20/1). And it caused him to be more inefficient than usual: "I'm sure that my verbalizing things . . . slowed me down, but I don't know if they had a qualitative difference in the way I do things or not" (M25B2).

The compose-aloud experiment corroborated some of J's reports about his writing procedures in the interviews, but also brought to light matters about which he was mistaken or had no recollection. For example, one of Subject J's frequent strategies for choosing words while drafting is to sound out several alternatives before putting anything on paper; not only is this strategy irrecoverable through review of his manuscripts, but since he was only dimly aware of it prior to the study, he did not report it when interviewed. On quite a different level, Subject J did not realize how much his writing typically engages him when he is not drafting until he tried—for purposes of the investigation—"to defer most of my thinking processes for these composing periods . . . and I think this is a little unnatural . . . and so I feel agitated, frustrated, and anxious" (M20/1). Provoked by this conflict, he became aware of his subconscious mental activities away from the desk: "sentences or expressions that bother me, they stick in my mind. I work them out while I'm shaving or while I'm driving, or in the middle of the night. . . . I guess I'm not even aware that they're being worked out" (M20/2).

The compose-aloud technique, in short, made J more aware of himself in the act of writing, and this perception encouraged him to articulate self-reflective thoughts during the writing sessions. As he says, "I have a feeling that the whole process of verbalization, saying it aloud, may have served as a catalyst for my

---

[1] Quotations from the protocols are designated as follows: single quotation marks for the author reading text; double quotation marks for verbalizing unwritten text (rehearsing it or trying it out) and for articulating a thought that has not been written down; and diagonal lines for articulating text as it is being drafted. Quotations are identified to the composing session by the following key: month, day, session in the day, page in the session. Hence, M24C3 is March 24, the third (C) session of that day, on the third page of the protocol. (Days with single sessions have no letter in the code.)

reflection about the process" (M20/12). Although Subject J was advised to ignore the tape recorder and the investigator, this struck him as a highly naive notion, as he notes: "Composing aloud is like giving a speech. I'm self conscious about my language. I have an audience. . . . I am aware of your [the investigator's] presence whether you're here or not"—an issue that Dobrin (1986) has discussed.

During the composing sessions, J frequently digresses to watch and comment—often with surprise—about his typical behavior as a writer:

> "It suddenly occurs to me that seeing my offering in print gives me an entirely different view of the work. . . . I never realized it before, but I interact differently with a typed copy than I do with a written copy . . . I get an overall, a much better general view of the work. . . . I can see the whole landscape." (M20/12)

Occasionally, he becomes quite self critical:

> "Attested, assessed. Those two words. . . .I guess I got my key words—for every word I have a synonym and I say it out loud and find the one that best fits the situation, and sometimes it's a hair-line decision. I go back and forth. It's very queer. I waste a lot of time with it, and either one could do, but I've got this tremendous sensibility about words." (M30A4)

Some of his analyses are very sophisticated and accurate, as here describing his recursive activity:

> "The pieces all fit together, and they . . . were fragments at the beginning, and what's interesting is that each section is almost an independent unit in itself. And it's like in biology, uh, ontogeny. . . . And so each section is almost like a microcosm of the entire piece. So within each section I . . . [am] looking for order, fitting it together, and then I'm really not sure how the various pieces are going to fit together, so I work on the pieces . . . and then I'm going to put it together." (M22B4)

And sometimes he elaborates fairly detailed self analyses of the shortcomings of his methods:

> "I wrote it over, my goodness, how many times. One, two, three, four, five, six, seven times. . . . I have a whole section written. I try to join them together. One thing doesn't follow from another, so first I have to modify the sentence immediately following the previous section and then as I go along I have to modify one sentence after another, and that's what's happening here. . . . That's really interesting . . . it's a struggle and maybe this shows that it's a very inefficient style and maybe I ought to really try to write in a straight linear pathway instead of, even if it hurts . . . it's so painful this way." (M25A9)

He even sets goals for himself to improve:

> "There really is a competition because there are two ways of saying something, and
> when it's written down, it can push out of your mind what is not written down. . . .
> I should have written it down immediately. These things are sometimes so fleeting.
> You have 'em, and before you have a chance. . . . That's something I ought to
> remember. If I get an idea, I should write it down without looking, because when
> you look, you see how you have done it previously." (M30A3)

These comments do not represent what the scientist claims he normally would have thought about while writing. Thus, if this study had aimed to construct a cognitive model, his concerns about his writing procedures could be viewed as a distortion of the data. However, in this exploratory study, J's growing self awareness under the aegis of composing aloud is a source of insight into his regular writing practices and, therefore, simply one more avenue to understanding scientists' writing.

OVERALL RESULTS OF THE PROTOCOL ANALYSIS

Analysis of Subject J's composing process suggests numerous important issues, many lying beyond the scope of this paper. Two points are of central interest and will form the subjects of the next two sections in this report: the scientist's reliance on revision as a functional strategy, and his active discovery procedures.

Subject J's composing is highly recursive and relies heavily on revising. Throughout his writing process, he constantly repeats planning, generating, ordering, translating, reviewing, revising/editing; in fact, almost the whole of his writing procedures could well be called revision. Such recursiveness challenges some common conclusions about the procedures of professionals who write on the job: that true experts in a genre do little revising, and that the writing procedures of scientific and technical professionals is typically logical and linear—characterized by substantial planning prior to drafting and minimal use of revising.

Subject J actively discovers new knowledge while drafting and while revising his journal articles—both for the paper itself and for his research. This discovery process challenges the conventional positivist view that reporting experimental results means presenting a predetermined set of facts in a mechanical fashion. Instead, the discovery process here corroborates the rhetorical view of the scientist-writer as a maker of meaning who learns what he knows partly through the act of writing.

The protocols in this case study are long and highly detailed, furnishing evidence about many issues related to writing and publishing scientific texts. Although J's self-reflective thoughts as a writer do expand his protocols, the major causes of the detailed protocols are to be found in his typical writing practices, particularly in his revising and discovery procedures. On the one hand, despite the author's experience in producing journal articles, he is an inefficient writer who constantly revises. Whereas some scientists on the panel write a whole experimental paper in a few days, J's papers typically stretch out over weeks or—like this one—over months, and require numerous revisions. On the other hand, J's writing is a focal point for thinking about the research and making sense of the results, of determining what the science all means. Both of these matters, which tend to elongate the protocols, characterize J's typical procedures for writing papers.

This scientist's writing process also serves other functions for him; for example, while composing, he manages some of the activities of the research laboratory. As head of the research team, Subject J uses the occasion to train scientists on his staff and to direct their collaborative activities. Subject J evaluates his lab personnel in the midst of writing his papers—perhaps because composing demands that he simultaneously review both his junior colleagues' lab work and their writing.

While preparing this paper, J spent considerable time analyzing the capabilities of several members of the team. For example, one of J's new postdoctoral fellows had drafted part of the methods and results sections. While reviewing this material, the senior scientist proceeds to develop his opinion of the new worker. Early he notes: "What he wrote was not quite correct . . . not precise." Next he observes an omission: "He doesn't say a damn thing about it—holy cow. Boy, he just left it out." But this initial surprise gives way to a more critical perspective: "what he had written here just ain't true. . . . Damn it, I remember when I told him he had to do this and he didn't see any reason why . . . he's very enthusiastic but just doesn't think it through." Next he suggests that "he pinched this from a previous paper," which finally develops into an overall job evaluation: "_____ is a good technical guy if someone sits on him, but he is not a first-class scientist. He lacks critical acumen" (M30A3,5; M30B1–2).

These activities related to running the team contribute indirectly to composing the document, and represent a conventional part of this scientist's team-centered writing process. Moreover, in some wider sense managing the team is a requirement for producing experimental papers in the natural sciences. The fact that such issues characterize J's protocols suggests that a scientist may be accomplishing quite diverse objectives while composing, and that the text may not be the only product by which to judge the efficiency or effectiveness of his procedures.

THE ROLE OF REVISION IN EXPERIENCED SCIENTISTS' COMPOSING PROCESSES

Among the composing strategies available to writers, revision has probably provoked the most scholarly attention (Flower, Hayes, Carey, Schriver, & Stratman, 1986; Witte, 1985). Certainly, a critical question about experienced scientists' writing procedures is: Do they revise their journal articles? Furthermore, do the conclusions from studies on other groups of writers' revision habits apply to scientists, and if so, which ones?

Do scientists, for example, like the "experienced writers" studied by Sommers (1980) or the "advanced student writers" studied by Faigley and Witte (1981), revise globally and extensively—reviewing their texts, "reseeing" them, and altering meaning to reflect their new perspectives? Or do they, like the technical and scientific writers studied by such investigators as Selzer (1983), Roundy and Mair (1982), Ewing (1984), and Broadhead and Freed (1986) follow a logical, linear, scientific model of composing—one with discrete stages, an emphasis on planning prior to drafting, and minimal revision? Or do they, like the "expert" professionals described and *represented* by Donald Murray, revise little because "as we become familiar with a genre we can solve more writing problems in advance of a completed text" (Berkenkotter & Murray, 1983, p. 171)? In short, do experienced scientists follow the standard advice of most textbook authors (for example, Monroe, Meredith, & Fisher, 1977) who say that scientists should plan everything prior to beginning to draft, or do they side with those (such as Murray himself [1968], Edmond Weiss [1982], and the Council of Biology Editors [1972]) who insist that all professional writers, including scientists, must revise?

A Range of Strategies

This study demonstrates that experienced scientists use a wide range of composing strategies, and that many revise extensively because they are seeking excellence. All the panel scientists regard journal articles as their most significant writing, and all but one do whatever they can to produce the best quality product of which they are capable, no matter what the cost. As Scientist M says:

> "I struggle with the way I want to say it and organize it from the first draft to the last draft. . . . I can't believe that other people are that deliberate . . . in thinking about what word they're using, and how they're saying it."

Although this scientist can't believe that his peers struggle so much, most of them expressed very similar views, all but one insisting that journal papers get their very best efforts. In fact, most of them would undoubtedly be shocked by Subject Y's opinion, the most highly cited scientist on the panel:

> "I don't think it's worth the time to polish a paper infinitely. . . . Many people spend an agonizing amount of time when they're getting their paper ready . . . go through one draft after another. I feel it's not worthwhile because I figure that, um, the average paper that I write is probably going to get read by no more than ten people. . . . I really don't think it is worth the effort to make it a literary masterpiece."

Although his comment seems cynical, Subject Y's views may be as much the result of pride in his own facility as a writer as they are a devaluation of journal papers. Since he prepares an article in a single draft with very few changes and is known among his colleagues for writing excellent papers effortlessly, his disdain for others' revising tends to corroborate the notion that many scientists, if not most, typically do revise their journal papers, many endlessly so.

For unlike Subject Y, most of the panelists do seem to aim for a masterpiece. Comparing journal articles with other documents, Subject P says, "I . . . write them [letters, memos, reports] off once and never look at them again. I don't feel as if I have to take pains." With journal papers, however, he and most of his fellows on the panel work extremely hard at their writing, despite their years of experience successfully publishing in this genre. And for several this means revising extensively. Journal papers are clearly valued documents in which quality matters more to the scientist than the time he must spend doing the job. Since revising their special writing is typical of professionals in many fields (Couture & Rymer, 1987), it could be expected that even many highly experienced scientists might revise.

On the one hand, several do plan extensively and carefully, and do some revising; on the other hand, several members of this panel—including Subject J—do not plan much prior to drafting, but instead emphasize revising as their major composing operation. Here is Subject S, for example:

> "I evolve a paper out of the mist. It comes in pieces, each piece being smoothed a bit as it comes along. And so it isn't a linear thing starting at the beginning and going to the end, but rather clusters. . . . [I] may work on one part ignoring all the other parts. . . . Sometimes you start putting them together and you find that they just don't fit. . . . [I] loop back a lot. I used to refer to it as 'blanket stitching.' You create a new context, and then you go back and bring the old information into the next context, and that creates a whole new perception."

Subjects C and P are also recursive writers who plan, generate, draft, and review all at once. Subject C works from the sentence level up, building his paper in one huge draft, whereas P finds out what he wants to say through innumerable separate drafts which he revises sequentially. Subject P says that his procedure requires:

> "Writing it several times until I see how the ideas I'm going to convey crystallize, and then sort of letting the paper flow. . . . I write the paper and let it come as it comes. . . . My first draft is an enormous, lengthy, amorphous mass. . . . I find myself crossing out . . . I do a tremendous amount of pruning."

Whatever strategy each scientist uses, he obviously believes it to be the best way he can achieve quality journal articles. Based on the practices of the panelists, expert scientists' best methods seem to exhibit a wide range of composing strategies, from a linear model focused on planning to a highly recursive model focused on revising—with most all of them revising their papers in their search for excellence.

Visions and Revisions

Subject J's composing process is heavily dominated by revision, both during the drafting stage and after its completion. Like Subject P, he interacts with the text, and his procedures are highly recursive—constantly looping back and planning, setting goals, generating text, reviewing, and revising, even editing—all on very small pieces of text, and all to be repeated again and again on new sections of the manuscript.

Distinct points do mark J's progress through to the completion of the article, stages characterized by different activities and different levels of involvement (but hardly stages in the traditional linear conception of composing). However, this overall movement toward finishing the product is subsumed by the overarching composing strategy: to get something down on paper so that it can be revised. The discernible stages of this process are (a) incubating, (b) drafting/revising, and (c) revising overall.

Incubating, rather than explicit preplanning, prepares J for writing the paper.   J thought about this particular journal article for several months, anticipating the writing of it with great relish. As the moment for beginning the writing approached, he became excited about the project, turning over ideas and meditating on them, feeling great satisfaction about the results. All of the planning during this stage was mental, most of it occurring while the author was engaged in other activities like driving to work or attending a "boring" seminar. The evidence of the protocols supports Subject J's own analysis that most of this planning was quite impressionistic, much of it pleasurable contemplation of audience reaction. At its most organized, he describes his planning as putting together a story:

> "I guess I had outlined in my mind prior to drafting five or six fundamental points I

knew I was going to hit. And this [current issue he is drafting] was one of them. . . .
I did not know the relationship; I didn't know the order or the sequence. I'm still
not certain of the sequence. . . . It's a starting point. There's a logic to the
development of the story, and this just has to be in the middle or the end." (M22d2)

J's preparation for writing does not appear to be an explicit planning stage for
his drafting. Rather, he prepares himself for writing by immersing himself in his
story; what guides his writing, then, are his strong feelings and mental images
about this story he wants to tell. Finally sitting down to draft, he does prepare
himself in a more explicit way, referring to the data and figures, as well as to his
own previous papers bearing on the topic. But he never outlines or maps out the
paper before he starts to write. To conclude that he doesn't plan his writing
before drafting is true in some conventional sense, but it does not convey the
reality of his preparation for composing.

Drafting/Revising is a fused function, the focal point of J's writing procedures.   Subject J demonstrates that, in a naturalistic writing task, drafting and
revising often cannot be separated, and that revising begins on mental plans,
even before there is any extant text (Witte, 1985). The scientist mentally plays
with ideas, changing them frequently before committing anything to paper, and
rehearses orally, trying out and rejecting some alternatives before writing down
possibilities to review and revise. When drafting, he writes sentences in pieces
by a process of trial and error, pausing often to review what he has just written or
what precedes it, and making changes, big and small, from the moment anything
is written down.

Essentially, his approach is based on generating, and later manipulating,
inspirations which occur to him either prior to or during drafting—what Flower
and Hayes call "the generate and test strategy" (1981b, p. 40). Often, he is
seized by one idea or key word about some aspect of the material; then consults
the data to verify the facts, and immediately tries to get something down on
paper—a phrase, a sentence, perhaps a paragraph. Then he begins to revise it—
planning, forming, shaping, and polishing all at once. Although incubation
continues to occur between sessions, now the author also does some specific
planning—both while drafting and while incubating—occasionally even jotting
down phrases, key words, or points to cover. However, most of the real planning, goal setting, arranging, seems to take place during the drafting—after J has
gotten something on paper. Here he comments after drafting one small section:

"I'm glad I have something written down. . . . When it's written down you have
something to work with . . . I'm not at sea. . . . It's gotta be written down, and then
you can play with it; it's like a puzzle. You gotta have something down on paper.
. . . I really wasn't sure exactly how it was going to come out. I guess sometimes
one thing leads to another . . . my writing may not be linear, but may involve
jumping over a chasm, from one island to another." (M22A2)

This metaphor quite accurately describes J's process of working from the germ of an idea or from a key word or phrase which he thinks of while incubating between sessions. After musing over this idea—which can be a point for any place in the paper, not necessarily the section subsequent to the one which he was drafting—the author frequently reviews the data, and then simply makes a stab at drafting, trying to create some text that will express his notion about the idea. Immediately, then, he stops to review what he has written to see whether it translates his inner feeling into language, giving his mental images and vague plans some shape and form for himself (Perl, 1979; Vygotsky, 1962). Because the text rarely suits his inner idea, he begins to revise, a process which can mean as much as 12 different versions of a single sentence. Eventually, he achieves a sense of closure on a particular section, or more typically, he simply decides to move on, adding it to his pile of drafted pieces—each in rather stark isolation because he does not think much about the role the section will play in the whole, nor how it will relate to the surrounding materials:

> "So what I want to do now is look over the data, and I know that I want to deal with these . . . reactions. And to be perfectly honest, again this is sort of in the middle of the paper. I don't know where it's going to fit in the paper, so what I've done is I'm going back. I started out dealing with the precipitation data, and then I got one of the key points that I wanted to make and so I concentrated on it, and I sorta know where that's going. It's like a stone, and the stone is well formed, and I know it's typography and geography. And now I'm going back, and I'm going to deal with another stone which is unknown, so to speak. I'm feeling around it. . . . I have the data in front of me, a chart. I sort of have a feeling of what I want to say, but now I have to decide how I'm going to say it. And I guess I'll start out by making a generalization, see what happens, where it goes." (M22A1)

Working from the inside out characterizes J's drafting process. J typically focuses on particular words buried somewhere in the middle of a section and then works outward in a recursive, nonlinear fashion. His word play—with numerous oral and written trials over the choice of common words more than scientific terms—seems to represent part of his invention process; he must find the exact word in order to begin the flow of text. It is a way he plans—or perhaps taps into his vague impression of a plan—and creates the discourse by matching text with his internal sense of what he wants to say.

> "We have defined binding characteristics" [oral trial]
> "Nah. That's not what I want to say."
> "Because we have defined . . . "
> "Let's try."
> /In this study we have characterized the binding/
> "Nah."
> /We have defined/

"investigated. discovered."
"No."
'We have defined'
/the binding characteristics/
"Established is the word."
/We have established/
"Because that's it. That's the word."
'In this study we have established the binding characteristics.' (M11/10)

The choice of the word established here does not seem very significant, but because it matches the notion of what J feels about the work, the stance he wishes to take toward it, he can now go forward. In a way, he can respond to the rightness of this one sentence, and then build on it, constructing the text from the bottom up, sentence by sentence, but not necessarily in order. For example, he says, "Got an idea in the lunch line. Wrote down on a scrap of paper. . . . That expression, 'It is possible to conceive' turned out to be the key to the sentence and to the whole thought. . . . Now [I can write] the front end of it" (M22D1). It is clear that in such cases he is tapping some inner impression about the shape and expression of his writing. In other situations, the emphasis is less on matching the inner template and more on building from a first, quite general statement, and interacting with it to go forward. In fact, J has a very strong belief in the power of the first words in any section of text ("It's that first sentence that will lead me" (M22A6]), seeing them as catalysts to his composing even more than as potential pieces of the product:

> "So that's a general sentence, and I guess that's a good way to start thoughts. General sentences and then you can get into the specifics, and then, maybe sometimes you'll cut off the general sentence. . . . But I feel comfortable, and that sort of gets me started." (M22A1)

If he cannot generate a good starting sentence, he sometimes takes a phrase or sentence from one of his own publications, or even from someone else's:

> "I have before me a paper by _____ and I'm going to snitch some of the phraseology. . . . So I used his sentence structure, but I put my own, put it into my own words and rearranged it some. . . . I've got my start." (M22A3)

Once a sentence that is more than a catalyst for composing has been generated, the author goes back to retest it against his inner notion of what he wanted to say, but also against other criteria for excellence, most particularly sound; as he frequently asks himself, "Does it ring right?" After listening to his words by reading them over and over, as well as testing for other personal standards such as conciseness, he typically recopies the sentence(s) to provide himself with a sense of closure ("And now I'm going to copy it, and I realize as I copy it, I get that really good feeling" (M24C1). Only then does he begin to fit the piece into a paragraph, a task that means he must frequently revise—yet again.

J's problem solving throughout the paper can be characterized as this double movement of generating text that will represent his inner idea and text that will meet his specific set of criteria (e.g., sounds right). In meeting these goals, the author typically "satisfices," settling—at least momentarily— for a less than perfect answer so that he can move ahead: "I'll just leave that for awhile. . . . That's a terrible scientific word, but I'll write it anyway" (M20A9). In this overall strategy of satisficing, global problems interrupt drafting, and small revisions interrupt higher order activities. The strategy reduces complexity by defining problems narrowly and dealing with them one at a time, and seems to reduce anxiety by allowing the writer to work for perfection in stages.

Typically, J states a problem ("Well, I guess the first thing that I have to do is think of the title"), stabs at a solution, reviews it according to some criterion ("Let's see what I called my last paper"), and then begins to reconsider, either by offering a new solution that will meet the criticism he leveled at the first ("It's too much like the other one"), or by setting up a new goal ("No, I think I want to give it a title that's catchy, that's very informative"), attempting to find a solution to meet it, and immediately critiquing his effort ("Just isn't catchy. Gotta sell the stuff. Doesn't mean that you gotta be dishonest. But it's gotta be something that really catches people's eyes, so they stand up and pay attention"). Most usually, however, at this point he satisfices, so that he can drop the issue and move ahead: "Oh, screw it. You know, I can come back. The title will probably be involved. There's a lot of different ways I can do it" (M6B1).

Although J satisfices temporarily, he strives for perfection, continually coming back to join one small section—say a paragraph or two—with another small section, and then to revise the whole:

> "I've joined a couple pieces together, the writing is poor, but the ideas and continuity seem to be here, I think. So now I think I'll go back, because I see this whole thing fitting together. And seeing whether or not I can put it together a little better. So I'm going to start rewriting." (M22A4)

However, this revising is the same kind of interaction with the text that has been going on throughout the drafting session, and the author himself says that at this point he has not completed the first draft. In sum, drafting, for Subject J, is revising.

Overall revision after drafting is a significant function in J's process. Although Subject J revises constantly while drafting, much revision remains to be done when he finally pronounces the draft completed. Now for the first time he pulls the whole manuscript together, including the sections written by his collaborators, and sees it whole. Now he must review pieces of text in light of the whole and graft the sections one to the next. Here is a typical comment he makes in the midst of reviewing the draft:

> "Gonna have to change the whole damn thing [a paragraph]. I can use what I've written, but I have to modify it. I guess it makes me angry because I worked each of these parts out, and then because they are all separate they don't fit together and I have to generate a transition [and] watch carefully what came before, and it just doesn't match." (M25A4)

Also left over from drafting are some of his many partially solved problems. Although by this point he has revised every section numerous times, some of the difficult choices in the draft are now relived. Typically, he recapitulates his former thinking and reconfirms the solution, but occasionally he creates a new answer, particularly on some of his conflicted word choices. Sometimes he composes totally new sentences, and he even drafts anew the whole conclusion to the discussion.

As part of creating a unified whole out of all the separate pieces, the scientist also revises the collaborators' manuscripts to mesh with his major sections, as well as to suit his style and standards for scientific papers. This point in the writing process is actually a reading process: Subject J reads and rereads the entire paper several times, attending to a different set of criteria during each pass. First, he verifies all parts of the manuscript against the data, checks the accuracy of the collaborators' work, and looks for repetitions and omissions among the various sections. Then he reads for wordiness, his own major writing fault as diagnosed by numerous referees: "One wants to be really sharp and precise if it's possible and decide what you want to say. And I tend to be kinda wordy, and I want to get away from that" (M22A1). He also watches for many other matters such as variety of diction ("I use that word various too much") and accuracy of reporting ("I like 'were selected' because that is exactly operationally what happened"). He also attends to editing, particularly parallelism and punctuation, though he often leaves small mechanical issues up to the editor ("Almost [seems] as if there should be a colon here; not sure about the use of the colon"). Most especially, he shows great concern for the reader ("I just have a feeling that starting out the sentence with a word like that would not help the reader").

Much of the writing at this point reflects the demands of the genre. Subject J reviews the figures prepared by his subordinates and revises several better to support his message. He drafts the abstract, treating it in a comparatively offhanded way, and integrates the figures and legends into the manuscript.

The final issues he confronts are the conventional requirements of the experimental paper ("Where were the tubes made?") and the format requirements for the target journal ("Do we abbreviate milliliters?").

Expert Scientists as Revisers

Quite clearly, Subject J is a highly recursive writer, relying mainly on revising to achieve the product he desires. His case study, considered together with the evidence from those other panelists who also "plan little and revise endlessly," challenges the assumption that highly experienced professionals, even those expert in a genre, tend to make most of their decisions in advance of drafting and revise minimally. More significant, it challenges the assumption that *scientists* tend to have essentially linear composing processes with discrete stages focused on careful planning prior to drafting. Instead it suggests that senior scientists—like other expert professionals—may be either logical planners/builders of documents that they envision closely prior to drafting, or impressionistic holists who spew and then revise to find out what they mean (Wason, 1980, p. 134)—or anything in between these two extremes.

Although his composing style may be typical of many experienced scientists, Subject J seems to be highly inefficient, practicing many strategies that are not assumed to characterize expert writers. J's habit of looking for exactly the right word (trying out some orally and some by jotting down possibilities) consumes much time, as does his tooling and retooling of sentences—particularly because he typically recopies by hand so that he can review the new version immediately. Most pernicious, however, is his lack of overall planning. Because he devises individual segments with little attention to their relationship with contiguous sections, revision is mandatory when he incorporates any one piece into the whole. This habit of focusing exclusively on the text at hand becomes a real impediment when J cannot see how to string together the various parts (M18/1–2) or when he likes an ill-fitting passage so much that he attempts to rework the surrounding framework rather than discard it (M20/2–3). It is a fact that Subject J rewrites almost every word he drafts several times; lack of planning necessitates many of these revisions.

Whether J's overall strategy is effective for him is a much more complex question. Certainly many of his time-consuming writing habits (for example, his word play) do not particularly improve the document—lending support to the research that shows that extensive revisers don't necessarily produce better papers (Bridwell, 1980). Still, whether or not J's methods are inefficient, they *do* work for him—not only to produce scientific papers that readily get accepted by journal reviewers and used by other researchers, but to facilitate other objectives, such as managing the project team and other even more important goals. As many researchers have pointed out, composing is meaningful only in context, and, for this scientist, writing up his results has numerous contextual ramifications and influences not apparent if his discourse is narrowly viewed as the sole product of his efforts. The most significant of these factors, one that is an essential component of J's composing itself and directly related to his revision strategies, is interpreting the scientific results, to be discussed in the next section.

DISCOVERY OF NEW MEANING IN THE EXPERIENCED
SCIENTISTS' COMPOSING PROCESSES

Traditionally, scientists have assumed that their task was to present their research results as simply and clearly as possible so that others could replicate them (Day, 1979; Council, 1972). As David Hamilton (1978, p. 36) notes, scientific writing has usually been perceived "as separable from the main work of science, not the means by which science comes into being, but a task appended to what science really does."

Foreign to this positivist perspective is a prevalent rhetorical view of writing as a discovery process in which the writer learns what he means in the act of developing and articulating his text (for example, see Berthoff, 1981; Emig, 1977; Knoblauch & Brannon, 1983; Murray, 1978, 1980; Odell, 1980). But does "writing as a mode of learning" apply to scientists? Some rhetoricians believe that "writing is the way by which the scientist comes to know his work most fully; it is his most thorough way of understanding what he does" (Hamilton, 1978, p. 32). Others believe that scientists do create their texts but that, unlike creative writers, they know what it all *means* after the research is completed and before the writing begins. As Steinberg says: "A report writer may discover a better way to say something or to organize something, but that isn't the same thing [as discovering new ideas]" (1980, p. 162). Nevertheless, researchers have found that some professionals do discover new ideas and learn something of what their facts mean while writing technical documents (Berkenkotter, 1981; Paradis, Dobrin, & Miller, cited in Anderson, 1986; Roundy & Mair, 1982). Yet little empirical evidence exists to support the assumption that scientists use writing as discovery.

This study suggests that many scientists do learn much about their scientific results in the act of writing. Of the nine scientists on the panel, Subject J was one of two who during the interviews claimed that discovery played no part in his process for writing journal articles. The compose-aloud protocols, however, demonstrated that discovery is a significant component in J's writing, and participation in the compose-aloud sessions enabled him to perceive this fact. The single scientist (Subject M) who initially claimed that he learned nothing while writing up his results was simply defining writing as drafting, as his comments show: "Surprises come earlier, before we even start the writing . . . in the process of the writing, I do very little thinking there." Subject M's discovery process lies in "outlining the paper. . . . I love that part of it. . . . The creativity is pretty much over . . . by the time that the outline is done." The other seven scientists readily acknowledged that they discover new aspects about the scientific information while writing their papers. At times their discoveries radically change their interpretations of the data, in some cases even sending them back to the lab to validate their new claims.

Discovery and the Research Process

Since research and writing are coextensive processes (Bazerman, 1983), the role discovery plays in the scientist's writing depends on the way he relates the two. At one extreme are scientists who do their research with only vague notions about ensuing publication. The most radical among them may work without clear hypotheses—so that their fellows sometimes disparage them as "the data collectors." While engaged in experiments, these researchers consider the potential meanings of the results, but by the time they sit down to write, they typically have much left to interpret and explain; often they must begin by stating—for the first time—the hypotheses they supposedly set out to prove. For some of these writers, composing the journal article is messy and inefficient because they have no hypotheses to guide them during drafting. They discover the meaning of the research in the process of writing itself, typically by developing their ideas through several revisions of the text. Here is Subject P, who writes "innumerable drafts":

> "Once one has started to write a paper, it often looks very different from what the raw data suggested to you. Sometimes . . . you suddenly find that you are, in fact, espousing quite a different doctrine to what you did when you started writing the paper. . . . As I write, suddenly I find the kaleidoscope effect flicks over, and I see something in an entirely new light. I think that the act of writing is almost the important thing about the analysis of the data . . . this is where you do analyze your data."

At the other extreme, are researchers who thoroughly integrate the science and the writing, using the planned document to govern the experimental work. Subject S's initial composing stage includes outlining the future paper, so that its major points can guide the research: "the planning of the paper is really part of the process of structuring the research. . . . The research is being done to reach a purpose. . . . Therefore, the intent to publish the paper is there before the research begins." For these scientists, the writing process coincides with the beginning of the project; experiments are undertaken to substantiate claims the researcher intends to assert in the paper. As Subject Y says, "I will plan experiments along the way with how they would look in the publication." Subject D notes the benefits of this closely integrated approach:

> "I think that if it's [the paper] planned that way, then actually it makes the research more efficient. You find out that by doing that you're only doing a minimum number of experiments to prove a point. . . . I think that the paper, for my own benefit, serves a very important direction in the research itself."

Managing a project in such an integrated fashion, a scientist establishes a feedback relationship between the research and the writing, with the writing guiding and clarifying the investigation—even serving as a design check. For a few panelists, this is a radical manifestation of the "incremental" method advocated by some textbooks (Monroe et al., 1977, pp. 4–8), in which the two processes (research and writing) proceed in stages so the paper develops in sections along with the research: "Since we're always writing and always doing work," according to Subject D, "it's a little hard to say, well, where it initiated." Subject S is even more explicit: "Sometimes the outline isn't anything like it really ends up. . . . Sometimes you start putting them [the results] together and you find that they just don't fit. . . . And then you have to go back to the lab and fill in."

Even prestigious scientists may select experiments to support a rhetorical purpose (Bazerman, 1985), but some scientists on the panel disparage the experiment-to-prove-the paper approach, charging that such researchers are merely adding pieces to a jig-saw puzzle. Subject K, for example, is blunt in his criticism of scientists who design their research to fit their publication plans: "In my opinion, logic doesn't play near the role in science that we like to think. . . . The people who have definite preconceptions don't see, and they never make the big discoveries." Admitting that mere "filling-in-the-blanks" is frequent, Subject S says "that's the ninety percent of ordinary science," but in "some of them [my papers] . . . it takes shape as you write it." Perhaps planning scientific work with an eye on publication operates appropriately for normal science but less effectively for revolutionary research. Still, the choice of planning in detail or learning in the act of writing may be more a matter of the scientist's personality than of whether the work is paradigm-shattering (Jensen & DiTiberio, 1984); after all, most of these scientists did not follow Subject S's claim to use different procedures for routine and special journal articles (though such a differentiation is clearly a possibility [Couture and Rymer, 1987]).

Although there are essential differences among these perspectives on the role of writing in the scientific research process, all panel members believe that they use some aspect of composing to help make meaning out of their scientific results. Even the perfect first drafter (Subject Y) admits to learning new things about his data during composing: "We have a number of times when we are actually putting a paper together . . . made something clear that we didn't understand." Whether they emphasize planning or revising, writing is part of all these scientists' overall discovery processes—though, admittedly, those who emphasize revising do learn much more in the act of writing, particularly because drafting itself is associated with discovery.

Discovery in Subject J's Composing

In an interview before the composing sessions began, J contended that he did *not* learn anything new about the scientific information while writing a paper. In fact he held strongly to the notion that he knew the results and had interpreted them, so that sitting down to write was simply representing the known in language. During the compose-aloud sessions, he became more and more aware of himself as a writer, and gradually realized what the protocols clearly manifested: discovery—in the largest sense of reinterpreting the results and of opening up new research ideas while writing—was a regular part of his composing of journal papers:

> "Although in previous discussions I tried to indicate that this [discovering new ideas] was not so, maybe it is so. By that I mean that writing forces one to consider and reconsider and ponder, and I guess I have to admit that during the writing one does think more pointedly about what one has done . . . and I think it is entirely possible, in fact, I remember . . . incidences where I'm writing and suddenly run into the laboratory and say, hey [name] . . . have you thought about this possibility? . . . So although I thought everything was in my mind, I guess when you are writing per se, certain relationships or thoughts do emerge which are not there prior, and it is a way of concentrating your attention and your thought on the problem. And I guess that I have to admit, although I wasn't even aware of it, now that I'm thinking deeply about it, that yes, one can get ideas, one can think of different ways of interpreting the data, in fact, that is exactly what is happening now. . . . And during this process we do talk about alternate explanations, and is this the only way, the only idea? . . . And the whole problem is that I was previously trying to act in a vacuum [answer questions in interview] and now I can recall, you know, scores of times when I got up from my writing and ran into the laboratory and said, hey, have you thought of this possibility?" (M17/7–8)

In light of the panelists' claims that they make discoveries during the writing process, Subject J's belated recognition that he did acquire new knowledge through composing is striking confirmation that some scientists reject the traditional view that writing up the results is a mechanical act. Scientists in general may seem to conceive of themselves as transmitters of the truth, reporters whose language is simply a window through which their readers can see the facts. In believing that the inductive logic of their account reports faithfully what happened in the lab, such scientists justify their actions to themselves in their papers (Gross, 1985). Subject K, echoing the rhetoricians, social scientists, and philosophers of science, describes such other scientists like this:

> "In writing papers, scientists go back and rewrite the history of the experiment. . . . Eventually many of these scientists believe their own rewriting and think that is the way they behaved, what they did. They don't recognize the accidents, the intuitions, the leaps of faith, the sudden connections."

Although this characterization of scientists in general may still have some validity, the evidence from this study suggests that many scientists recognize that their perspective is critical to making scientific meaning and acknowledge that writing is a way of knowing and learning about science.

Levels of Discovery

Subject J's protocols show several levels of discovery of new meanings and new knowledge, both during and after the draft/revise process. As discussed above, one of J's major strategies is to work out the meaning by making a stab and then reflecting on what he sees. Sometimes he describes this in quite mystical terms of tapping into his creativity so that the meaning will form in the act of articulation: "I don't really know what's going to come out, and I start talking (or writing) and then the ideas sort of form around what I start to say" (M22B6). Or as he says in another session, "Ah, I just don't know exactly where I'm going. The words are sort of just pouring out of me" (M18/9).

If there were any doubt that J finds out what he means about the content of the paper and its organization by drafting, he confirms the fact quite directly in the midst of one session: "It suddenly occurs to me that when I first sat down to write this paper I didn't know exactly where I was going, and I had a lot of trouble. . . . But I know where I'm going now" (M12/2–3). This type of recursive process in which writing and reviewing the text facilitate new goals has been described by several scholars describing general writers (Berkenkotter, 1981; Flower & Hayes, 1981a, b).

On a higher level, J interprets the results differently than he had anticipated prior to drafting:

"all at once I got a further insight. . . . I was talking about the problem of heterogeneity . . . and then it suddenly occurred to me that the proteins were not present in equivalent amounts due to variation in their content . . . I hadn't thought about that before, and it just strengthened the drama of the study and so I wrote it in. This is the first time since I've been writing this that something new appeared which I had not thought . . . I had thought that most of the stuff was already in my head." (M18/1)

On a still higher plane, the composing itself assists the scientist in working out the article's overall meaning, the broad significance of the results, in actually learning what he knows. In one sense this is using writing as a way of testing the design; by writing about the research, the scientist can see what is missing and what needs to be done. J uses composing in this way several times, to go back into the lab and check out something that doesn't seem quite right. More significantly, his composing facilitates the research process by enabling him to synthesize information and actually develop an hypothesis which he has never stated before, as in the act of discovery described below:

"And what's so unusual about it. There's a more unifying hypothesis, and that is the fact of the uniqueness of the system in that."

/A subunit has/

"I guess I really don't know how I want to present it."

"And in fact, I'm putting things together, maybe, I don't know if it's for the first time, but this is the point I want to make, in the precipitation studies, it's coming to me, in the precipitation studies."

/The Type A substance/

"That's it."

'The Type A substance'

"Tremendously important."

"Nah. I don't want to say that. . . . But the way I want to say it is coming to me."

"I guess I feel peaceful now because I know exactly what the job is and I just have to phrase it right." (M20/9-10).

Finally, at the highest level, Subject J is provoked by the text he perceives in front of him to create new research ideas and plan future projects. Composing then is a grid for anticipating the next investigation:

"And I guess my mind is wandering to what else we could do with that . . . . I wonder if it pays to try it with some other kind of cells to see whether or not. . . . It's a common feature. Now it never occurred to me, but maybe we ought to look at the sequence studies. Maybe there is a clue. . . . This is something that could be very interesting. The sequence studies. . . . Never thought of this before. . . . We don't have a great deal of sequence information . . . And I wonder whether or not there is some unifying hypothesis. . . . This is really absolutely new. . . . How about subunit structure? Nobody has ever thought about that. . . . Oh, oh, I think maybe I'm on to something. . . . Anyway, gotta review that data. . . . In fact, now I got a great idea. Fantastic idea. . . . And I guess I've opened up a whole box here." (M20/11-12)

Quite clearly, the composing itself has triggered the ideas for a new investigation. Because J had claimed in his interviews that he did not discover anything new while writing, the evidence from his protocols seems strong confirmation of the message from the panel: Many scientists do discover some of what they know about their scientific results while they are actually drafting. For them, the very *act* of composing can be instrumental, not only in giving form and shape to their presentation, but in finding out what their results mean, in developing what they know scientifically, and even in determining the direction of their future research.

Obviously, since these scientists who discover actively while writing are also those who revise extensively, the whole discovery model of composing and the extensive revision it typically demands can be denigrated as simply inefficient, the result of inadequate planning (Witte, 1985, p. 269). But the endless revisers among these scientists are working to impose meaningful order (perhaps in a fashion that appears disorderly) on the mass of laboratory chaos. Rather than simply reporting experiments whose results tidily fit clear hypotheses, they must now create scientific truths out of what they can envision in their data. Making scientific meaning in this way is not necessarily a rational, scientific process, though it may result in very significant scientific papers. In short, the kind of scientist one is may imply the kind of writer one must be, or perhaps being a writer comes first and helps form the kind of scientist one becomes.

CONCLUSIONS

This study challenges some of the conventional wisdom about scientific composing. The evidence presented here suggests that eminent scientists use multiple approaches in writing experimental papers, not only a linear model focused on detailed planning, but a full range of strategies, including highly recursive models focused on revision. Because they value the quality of their publications, however, scientists typically revise and polish the drafts of their experimental papers, regardless of their overall approach to composing. This study also suggests that scientists frequently discover new ideas about their experimental results and what the science means while composing their journal papers. All of these hypotheses should be tested on a random sample of experienced natural scientists.

This study also uncovers potentially fruitful areas for further exploratory investigation. Do eminent scientists follow quite different composing practices for breakthrough research papers than they do for routine publications? Aside from managing the project team, what other job-related tasks do scientists typically accomplish while composing their experimental papers? How does the research team function in preparing the scientific paper; for example, do members collaboratively compose the various sections of the paper (the results as opposed to the discussion) in radically different ways?

Finally, this study uncovers several interesting pedagogical issues. For one, it challenges the validity of teaching student scientists the rational, scientific way to write up their research results. Because some eminent scientists find that highly planned research and composing methods may inhibit significant science, the very notion of a scientific model of composing becomes supect. Perhaps students should be exposed to a variety of models, including one that might promote discovery.

This study of nine eminent scientists is only a beginning toward understanding scientific composing processes. But this beginning shows that scientists are tellers of tales, creative writers who make meaning and who choose the ways they go about doing so. As Subject J muses, looking over his data and thinking about what it means to him: "I guess the question I'm asking now is: How do you tell it? Do you tell it like it is, or do you tell it like you predicted it, or the story it makes, or what?" (M22A5).

APPENDIX
HISTORY OF SCIENTIST WRITING THE JBC PAPER

Pre-Drafting (approximately 3 years)

1. Research planned and directed by chief scientist and carried out by two postdoctoral fellows and two graduate students (almost 3 years).
2. Figures and tables roughed out by postdoctoral fellows.
3. "Materials and Methods" and "Results" sections drafted by post-doctoral fellows.
4. Paper incubated by chief scientist (almost 6 months).

Drafting/Revising (approximately 3 weeks)

1. Drafted/revised "Introduction" section (three sessions over a 4-day period). Drafted in first session, revised a typed copy in second session, and revised the final typed manuscript in a third.
2. Reviewed "Materials and Methods" and "Results" to plan writing of the Discussion, and reviewed the figures and tables (one session).
3. Drafted/revised "Discussion" (six sessions over a 2-week period).
4. Revised typed copy of "Discussion" and integrated sections for retyping (two sessions over a 2-day period). (Pronounced: "Now the paper is done.")

Revising/Editing (approximately 2 months)

1. Revised "Materials and Methods" and "Results" sections written by collaborators (three sessions over a 3-day period).
One month later:
2. Reviewed and revised "Discussion," and wrote "Abstract" and title (one session).
Three weeks later:
3. Assembled all manuscript parts together in sequence. Revised and inserted legends (written by collaborators), revised the abstract, inserted references, numbered figures (one session).
4. Submitted the manuscript to three colleagues for review, including the outside collaborator.

Submitting for Publication

Four months later:
5. Incorporated minor changes from collaborators, adjusted authorship, and submitted the paper.
Six months later (that is, 1 year after drafting began):
6. Published the paper in the *Journal of Biological Chemistry*.

REFERENCES

Anderson, P.V. (1985). What survey research tells us about writing at work. In L. Odell & D. Goswami (Eds.), *Writing in nonacademic settings* (pp. 3–83). New York: Guilford.

Bazerman, C. (1983). Scientific writing as a social act: A review of the literature of the sociology of science. In P.V. Anderson, R.J. Brockmann, & C. Miller (Eds.), *New essays in technical and scientific communication: Research, theory, practice* (pp. 156–184). Farmingdale, NY: Baywood.

Bazerman, C. (1984). The writing of scientific non-fiction: Contexts, choices, constraints. *Pre/Text. 5,* 39–74.

Berkenkotter, C. (1981). Understanding a writer's awareness of audience. *College Composition and Communication, 32,* 388–399.

Berkenkotter, C., & Murray, D. (1983). Decisions and revisions: The planning strategies of a publishing writer, and response of a laboratory rat—or, being protocoled. *College Composition and Communication, 34,* 156–172.

Bernhardt, S.A. (1985). The writer, the reader, and the scientific text. *Journal of Technical Writing and Communication, 15,* 163–174.

Berthoff, A.E. (1981). *The making of meaning.* Montclair, NJ: Boynton/Cook.

Bridwell, L.S. (1980). Revising strategies in twelfth grade students' transactional writing. *Research in the Teaching of English, 14,* 197–222.

Broadhead, G.J., & Freed, R.C. (1986). *The variables of composition: process and product in a business setting.* Carbondale, IL: Southern Illinois University Press.

Campbell, P.N. (1975). The *personae* of scientific discourse. *Quarterly Journal of Speech, 61,* 391–405.

Cole, J.R., & Cole, S. (1973). *Social stratification in science.* Chicago, IL: University of Chicago Press.

Cooper, C.R., & Odell, L. (Eds.). (1978). *Research on composing: Points of departure.* Urbana, IL: NCTE.

Cooper, M., & Holzman, M. (1983). Talking about protocols. *College Composition and Communication, 34,* 284–293.

Council of Biology Editors. (1972). *CBE style manual* (3rd ed.). Washington, DC: American Institute of Biological Sciences.

Couture, B., & Rymer, J. (1987). *Toward a profile of writing on the job: Results from the writers' survey.* Manuscript submitted for publication.

Day, R.A. (1979). *How to write and publish a scientific paper.* Philadelphia, PA: ISI Press.

Dobrin, D.N. (1986). Protocols once more. *College English, 48,* 713–725.

Emig, J. (1971). *The composing processes of twelfth graders.* Urbana, IL: NCTE.

Emig, J. (1977). Writing as a mode of learning. *College Composition and Communication, 28,* 122–128.

Ericsson, K.A., & Simon, H.A. (1980). Verbal reports as data. *Psychological Review, 87,* 215–251.

Ericsson, K.A., & Simon, H.A. (1984). *Protocol analysis: Verbal reports as data.* Cambridge, MA: MIT Press.

Ewing, D.P. (1984, March). *Invention and planning processes of upper-level managers.*

Paper presented at the meeting of the Conference on College Composition and Communication, New York.

Faigley, L., Cherry, R.D., Jolliffe, D.A., & Skinner, A.M. (1985). *Assessing writers' knowledge and processes of composing.* Norwood, NJ: Ablex Publishing Corp.

Faigley, L., & Witte, S. (1981). Analyzing revision. *College Composition and Communication, 32,* 400–414.

Fleck, L. (1979). *Genesis and development of a scientific fact.* (F. Bradley & T.J. Trenn, Trans.). Chicago, IL: University of Chicago Press. (Original work published 1935.)

Flower, L. (1981). *Problem-solving strategies for writing.* New York: Harcourt Brace Jovanovich.

Flower, L., & Hayes, J.R. (1977). Problem-solving strategies and the writing process. *College English, 39,* 449–461.

Flower, L., & Hayes, J.R. (1980a). The cognition of discovery: Defining a rhetorical problem. *College Composition and Communication, 31,* 21–32.

Flower, L.S., & Hayes, J.R. (1980b). The dynamics of composing: Making plans and juggling constraints. In L.W. Gregg & E.R. Steinberg (Eds.), *Cognitive processes in writing* (pp. 31–50). Hillsdale, NJ: Erlbaum.

Flower, L., & Hayes, J.R. (1981a). A cognitive process theory of writing. *College Composition and Communication, 32,* 365–387.

Flower, L., & Hayes, J.R. (1981b). Plans that guide the composing process. In C.H. Frederiksen & J.F. Dominic (Eds.), *Writing: The nature, development, and teaching of written communication* (pp. 39–58). Hillsdale, NJ: Erlbaum.

Flower, L., Hayes, J.R., Carey, L., Schriver, K., & Stratman, J. (1986). Detection, diagnosis, and the strategies of revision. *College Composition and Communication, 37,* 16–55.

Garfield, E. (1981, October 12). The 1,000 contemporary scientists most-cited 1965–1978. Part 1. The basic list and introduction. *Current Contents,* (41), 5–14.

Garfield, E. (1982, May 24). The 1,000 most-cited contemporary authors. Part 2B. Details on authors in biochemistry, biophysics, cell biology, enzymology, genetics, molecular biology, and plant sciences. *Current Contents,* (21), 5–13.

Gilbert, G.N. & Mulkay, M. (1984). *Opening Pandora's box: A sociological analysis of scientists' discourse.* Cambridge, England: Cambridge University Press.

Gould, J.D. (1980). Experiments on composing letters: Some facts, some myths, and some observations. In L.W. Gregg & E.R. Steinberg (Eds.), *Cognitive processes in writing* (pp. 97–127). Hillsdale, NJ: Erlbaum.

Graves, D.H. (1975). An examination of the writing processes of seven year old children. *Research in the Teaching of English, 9,* 227–241.

Gross, A.G. (1985). The form of the experimental paper: A realization of the myth of induction. *Journal of Technical Writing and Communication, 15,* 15–26.

Halloran, S.M. (1984). The birth of molecular biology: An essay in the rhetorical criticism of scientific discourse. *Rhetoric Review, 3,* 70–83.

Hamilton, D. (1978). Writing science. *College English, 40,* 32–40.

Hayes, J.R., & Flower, L.S. (1980). Identifying the organization of writing processes. In L.W. Gregg & E.R. Steinberg (Eds.), *Cognitive processes in writing* (pp. 3–30). Hillsdale, NJ: Erlbaum.

Hayes, J.R., & Flower, L.S. (1983). Uncovering cognitive processes in writing: An introduction to protocol analysis. In P. Mosenthal, L. Tamor, & S.A. Walmsley, (Eds.), *Research on writing: Principles and methods* (pp. 207–220). London: Longman.

Humes, A. (1983). Research on the composing process. *Review of Educational Research, 53,* 201–216.

Jensen, G.H., & DiTiberio, J.K. (1984). Personality and individual writing processes. *College Composition and Communication, 35,* 285–300.

Knoblauch, C.H., & Brannon, L. (1983). Writing as learning through the curriculum. *College English, 45,* 465–474.

Knorr-Cetina, K.D. (1981). *The manufacture of knowledge: An essay on the constructivist and contextual nature of science.* Oxford, England: Pergamon.

Knorr-Cetina, K.D., & Mulkay, M. (Eds.). (1983). *Science observed: Perspectives on the social study of science.* London: Sage.

Kuhn, T.S.(1970). *The structure of scientific revolutions* (2nd ed.), *International Encyclopedia of Unified Science, 2* (2). Chicago, IL: University of Chicago Press.

Latour, B., & Woolgar, S. (1979). *Laboratory life: The social construction of scientific facts.* Beverly Hills, CA: Sage.

Lynch, M., Livingston, E., & Garfinkel, H. (1983). Temporal order in laboratory work. In K.D. Knorr-Cetina & M. Mulkay (Eds.), *Science observed: Perspectives on the social study of science.* London: Sage.

Meadows, A.J. (1974). *Communication in science.* London: Butterworths.

Medawar, P.B. (1964, August 1). Is the scientific paper fraudulent? *Saturday Review,* pp. 42–43.

Miller, C.R. (1985). Invention in technical and scientific discourse: A prospective survey. In M.G. Moran & D. Journet (Eds.), *Research in technical communication: A bibliographic sourcebook* (pp. 117–162). Westport, CT: Greenwood.

Monroe, J., Meredith, C., & Fisher, K. (1977). *The science of scientific writing.* Dubuque, IA: Kendall/Hunt.

Murray, D.M. (1968). *A writer teaches writing: A practical method of teaching composition.* Boston: Houghton Mifflin.

Murray, D.M. (1978). Internal revision: A process of discovery. In Cooper, C.R., & Odell, L. (Eds.), *Research on composing: Points of departure* (pp. 85–103). Urbana, IL: NCTE.

Murray, D.M. (1980). Writing as process: How writing finds its own meaning. In T.R. Donovan & B.W. McClelland (Eds.), *Eight approaches to teaching composition* (pp. 3–20). Urbana: NCTE.

Myers, G. (1985). The social construction of two biologists' proposals. *Written Communication, 2,* 219–245.

Myers, G. (1986). Writing research and the sociology of scientific knowledge: A review of three new books. *College English, 48,* 595–610.

Newell, A., & Simon, H.A. (1972). *Human problem solving.* Englewood Cliffs, NJ: Prentice-Hall.

Nisbett, R.E., & Wilson, T.D. (1977). Telling more than we can know: Verbal reports on mental processes. *Psychological Review, 84,* 231–58.

Odell, L. (1980). Teaching writing by teaching the process of discovery: An interdisciplinary enterprise. In L.W. Gregg & E.R. Steinberg (Eds.), *Cognitive processes in writing* (pp. 139–154). Hillsdale, NJ: Erlbaum.

Odell, L., Goswami, D., Herrington, A., & Quick, D. (1983). Studying writing in non-academic settings. In P.V. Anderson, R.J. Brockmann, & C.R. Miller (Eds.), *New essays in technical and and scientific communication: Research, theory, practice* (pp. 17–40). Farmingdale, NY: Baywood.

Overington, M.A. (1977). The scientific community as audience: Toward a rhetorical analysis of science. *Philosophy and Rhetoric, 10,* 143–64.

Perl, S. (1979). The composing processes of unskilled college writers. *Research in the Teaching of English, 13,* 317–336.

Polanyi, M. (1962). *Personal knowledge: Towards a post-critical philosophy.* Chicago, IL: University of Chicago Press.

Popper, K. (1959). *The logic of scientific discovery.* New York: Basic.

Popper, K. (1962). *Conjectures and refutations: The growth of scientific knowledge.* New York: Harper & Row.

Price, D.J. de Solla. (1970). Citation measures of hard science, soft science, technology, and nonscience. In C.E. Nelson & D.K. Pollock (Eds.), *Communication among scientists and engineers* (pp. 3–22). Lexington, MA: Heath.

Price, D.J. de Solla. (1963). *Little science, big science.* New York: Columbia University Press.

Roundy, N., & Mair, D. (1982). The composing process of technical writers. *Journal of Advanced Composition, 3,* 89–101.

Selzer, J. (1983). The composing processes of an engineer. *College Composition and Communication, 34,* 178–187.

Small, Henry G. (1977). A co-citation model of a scientific speciality: A longitudinal study of collagen research. *Social Studies of Science, 7,* 139-166.

Sommers, N.I. (1980). Revision strategies of student writers and experienced adult writers. *College Composition and Communication, 31,* 378–388.

Steinberg, E.R. (1980). A garden of opportunities and a thicket of dangers. In L.W. Gregg & E.R. Steinberg (Eds.), *Cognitive processes in writing* (pp. 155–167). Hillsdale, NJ: Erlbaum.

Steinberg, E.R. (1986). Protocols, retrospective reports, and the stream of consciousness. *College English, 48,* 697–712.

Swarts, H., Flower, L.S., & Hayes, J.R. (1984). Designing protocol studies of the writing process: An introduction. In R. Beach & L.S. Bridwell (Eds.), *New directions in composition research* (pp. 53–71). New York: Guilford.

Tomlinson, B. (1984). Talking about the composing process: The limitations of retrospective accounts. *Written Communication, 1,* 429–445.

Toulmin, S. (1972). *Human understanding: The collective use and evolution of concepts.* Princeton, NJ: Princeton University Press.

Vygotsky, L. (1962). *Thought and language.* (E. Hanfmann & G. Vakar, Trans. & Eds.). Cambridge, MA: MIT Press.

Wason, P.C. (1980). Specific thoughts on the writing process. In L.W. Gregg & E.R. Steinberg (Eds.), *Cognitive processes in writing* (pp. 129–137). Hillsdale, NJ: Erlbaum.

Weimer, W.B. (1977). Science as a rhetorical transaction: Toward a nonjustificational conception of rhetoric. *Philosophy and Rhetoric, 10,* 1–29.

Weiss, E.H. (1982). *The writing system for engineers and scientists.* Englewood Cliffs, NJ: Prentice-Hall.

Witte, S.P. (1985). Revising, composing theory, and research design. In S.W. Freedman (Ed.), *The acquisition of written language: Response and revision* (pp. 250–284). Norwood, NJ: Ablex Publishing Corp.

Zappen, J.P. (1983). A rhetoric for research in sciences and technologies. In P.V. Anderson, R.J. Brockmann, & C. R. Miller (Eds.), *New essays in technical and scientific communication: Research, theory, practice* (pp. 123–138). Farmingdale, NY: Baywood.

Ziman, J. (1967). *Public knowledge.* Cambridge, England: Cambridge University Press.

Ziman, J. (1976). *Force of knowledge.* Cambridge, England: Cambridge University Press.

Author Index

Subject Index

257

Style, 197–201
Surveys, 12–13

T
Teaching and writing, 127–128, 141–145
Topoi, 41–43, 67

W
Ways of speaking, 50–52
Writing across the curriculum, 2, 4, 19, 89
Writing and learning, 19–24, 126–127, 155–163
Writing curricula, 17
Writers' knowledge, 35–38, 53, 66–67